EFFECTIVE INTERVENTIONS
FOR SOCIAL–EMOTIONAL LEARNING

Effective Interventions for Social–Emotional Learning

FRANK M. GRESHAM

THE GUILFORD PRESS
New York   London

Copyright © 2018 The Guilford Press
A Division of Guilford Publications, Inc.
370 Seventh Avenue, Suite 1200, New York, NY 10001
www.guilford.com

Printed in the United States of America

This book is printed on acid-free paper.

Last digit is print number: 9 8 7 6 5 4 3 2 1

The author has checked with sources believed to be reliable in his efforts to provide information that is complete and generally in accord with the standards of practice that are accepted at the time of publication. However, in view of the possibility of human error or changes in behavioral, mental health, or medical sciences, neither the author, nor the editor and publisher, nor any other party who has been involved in the preparation or publication of this work warrants that the information contained herein is in every respect accurate or complete, and they are not responsible for any errors or omissions or the results obtained from the use of such information. Readers are encouraged to confirm the information contained in this book with other sources.

Library of Congress Cataloging-in-Publication Data is available from the publisher.

ISBN 978-1-4625-3199-8 (paperback)
ISBN 978-1-4625-3200-1 (hardcover)

To my past, present, and future students,
who continuously provide me with the motivation
and dedication to provide evidence-based
assessment and intervention practices
for children and youth with emotional
and behavioral challenges

About the Author

Frank M. Gresham, PhD, is Professor in the Department of Psychology at Louisiana State University. He is a Fellow of the American Psychological Association (APA) and of APA Divisions 16 (School Psychology), 5 (Quantitative and Qualitative Methods), and 53 (Society of Clinical Child and Adolescent Psychology). He is a recipient of the Lightner Witmer Award and the Senior Scientist Award from APA Division 16. Dr. Gresham is one of the few psychologists to be awarded Fellow status in the American Association for the Advancement of Science. His research and more than 260 publications address topics including social skills assessment and intervention, response to intervention, and assessment and interventions for students with emotional and behavioral disorders. He is codeveloper of the Social Skills Improvement System Rating Scales.

Preface

Landmark longitudinal studies have documented the fact that poor peer relations in childhood predict serious adjustment difficulties during adolescence and early adulthood. These difficulties in social–behavioral competence and peer relations lead to short-term, intermediate, and long-term complications in the educational, psychosocial, and vocational domains of functioning. This body of research prompted an intense interest in the development of preventive interventions among researchers studying peer relations. The logic behind this interest was that timely interventions focusing on improving childhood peer relations could significantly reduce exposure to the risks associated with peer rejection and isolation, promote healthy socialization, and foster positive long-term outcomes.

A great deal of attention has focused on the assessment of skills that contribute to the development of children's social–emotional competencies. More recently, there has been a push by educators, policymakers, and researchers to focus on developing these competencies within the school context.

In 1994, the phrase "social–emotional learning"(SEL) was first used by the Collaborative for Academic, Social, and Emotional Learning (CASEL). CASEL, a multidisciplinary organization, identified five core domains: (1) self-awareness, (2) self-management, (3) social awareness, (4) responsible decision making, and (5) relationship skills. Many of the social skills described in this volume can be organized into these five domains.

This book is based on the premise that effective SEL programs explicitly and directly teach social skills. Characteristics of these effective interventions can be conceptualized by the acronym *SAFE*. That is, interventions should be *sequenced, active, focused,* and *explicit.* Readers will note that all recommended SEL interventions described in this book are based on the SAFE conceptualization.

The purpose of this book is to provide professionals with evidence-based social–emotional assessment and intervention strategies for children and adolescents. The book covers typically developing children and adolescents with difficulties in social relationships; individuals with specific mental health diagnoses such as autism spectrum disorders, intellectual disability, and social (pragmatic) communication disorder; and the deaf/ hard-of-hearing population. The major themes of this book will be definitional and conceptual issues in social skills assessment and intervention, standards for determining evidence-based practices, social–emotional assessment strategies, multi-tiered social–emotional interventions (universal, selected, and intensive), and social–emotional assessment and intervention strategies for specific populations. The book concludes with a series of illustrative case studies highlighting evidence-based social–emotional assessment and intervention strategies.

Intended audiences for this book are clinical child and adolescent psychologists, school psychologists, counseling psychologists, clinical social workers, school counselors, and behavioral support personnel in schools. Graduate courses appropriate for this book are courses in school-based and clinic-based interventions for children and youth, assessment of social–emotional functioning in children and youth, social–emotional interventions, and consultation strategies for teachers and parents.

Contents

CHAPTER ONE

Definitional and Conceptual Issues in Social–Emotional Learning

Comprehensive longitudinal studies, meta-analyses, and literature reviews have documented that poor peer relations in childhood are predictive of serious adjustment difficulties in adolescence and early adulthood (Cowen, Pedersen, Babigian, Izzo, & Trost, 1973; Newcomb, Bukowski, & Pattee, 1993a; Parker & Asher, 1987; Prinstein, Rancourt, Guerry, & Browne, 2009). These difficulties in social–behavioral competence and peer relations lead to short-term, intermediate, and long-term challenges in the educational, psychosocial, and vocational domains of functioning (Dodge, Dishion, & Lansford, 2006; Kupersmidt, Coie, & Dodge, 1990; Newcomb et al., 1993a). This line of research accumulated over the past 35 years has prompted an intense interest in the development of preventive interventions among researchers studying the deleterious effects of peer relationship difficulties. This logic was based on the notion that timely interventions focusing on improving childhood peer relations could reduce exposure to the risks associated with peer rejection and social isolation, promote healthy socialization, and foster long-term positive outcomes (Bierman, 2004; La Greca, 1993; Rubin, Bukowski, & Laursen, 2009).

A great deal of attention over the last 10 years has focused on children's social–emotional competence and includes assessment and intervention with social skills that contribute to the development of these social–emotional competencies. More recently, there has been a push by educators, policymakers, and researchers to focus on promoting the development of

1

children's social–emotional competencies within the school context. This is evidenced by the recent inclusion of social–emotional learning (SEL) as distinct state learning standards in school districts across the country because these competencies are linked to positive academic and psychological outcomes (Weissberg, Durlak, Domitrovich, & Gullotta, 2015). A large corpus of research involving over 500 evaluations from preschool to higher education has demonstrated the effectiveness of universal school-based SEL interventions (Collaborative for Academic, Social, and Emotional Learning, 2012).

CONCEPTUALIZATION OF SOCIAL COMPETENCE

The construct of social competence has been conceptualized and operationalized from many different perspectives and theoretical orientations across the various specialties within psychology, special education, and applied behavior analysis. An adequate conceptualization of social competence is important because it guides evidence-based assessment and intervention strategies. At least three general conceptualizations of the construct of social competence have been discussed in the research literature.

Sociometric Conceptualization

One conceptualization is termed the *sociometric conceptualization* of social competence. This approach primarily uses indices of sociometric status to operationalize social competence. As such, individuals who are rejected or neglected by peers are considered to be socially incompetent and individuals who are accepted or popular with peers are considered to be socially competent. An individual's sociometric status refers to how a person perceives others in terms of likes and dislikes and how other persons perceive the individual (Hartup, 2009). Sociometric status is based on a large amount of information including who wants to associate with whom, who wants to engage is certain social activities with others, and who likes or dislikes someone within a social network. Comprehensive sociometric assessments are typically based on indices of *social preference* and *social impact* (Peery, 1979) and derivations of these constructs have been used to classify individuals as rejected, neglected, controversial, and popular (Coie, Dodge, & Coppotelli, 1982).

Despite its relative objectivity, the major drawback of a sociometric conceptualization of social competence is that it often cannot identify the specific behaviors within specific situations that lead to peer acceptance or rejection. Some research does suggest that the behavioral correlates of various sociometric statuses are topographically different. For example, the behavioral correlates of *peer rejection* typically include behaviors such as aggressive behavior, impulsivity, and negative social interactions with peers (Coie, Dodge, & Kupersmidt, 1990). In contrast, the behavioral correlates of *neglected sociometric status* include behaviors such as anxiety, social withdrawal, depression, and low rates of positive social interaction (Newcomb et al., 1993a). These behavioral correlates, however, are relatively low in magnitude and most certainly do not entirely explain or account for an individual's particular sociometric status.

In addition, positive or negative sociometric status can occur for reasons that have nothing to do with social skills strengths or weaknesses. For example, it has been shown that physical, attractiveness/unattractiveness, positive/negative reputational biases, critical negative behavioral events, race/ethnicity, and cross-sex nominations are related to positive or negative sociometric status (Rubin et al., 2009).

Social Learning Theory

Other researchers and theorists have used a *social learning conceptualization* of the social skill construct (Elliott & Gresham, 2008; Gresham & Elliott, 2008). In this view, numerous variables account for an individual's deficiencies in prosocial behavior and excesses in competing problem behaviors. Figure 1.1 depicts a model that identifies five major reasons for deficient social skills functioning: (1) lack of knowledge, (2) lack of practice and/or feedback, (3) absence or inattention to social cues, (4) lack of reinforcement, and (5) presence of competing problem behaviors. This particular model uses three distinct theoretical learning theories to explain social skill deficiencies and excessive competing problem behaviors.

Social learning theory, based on the early work of Bandura (1977, 1986), utilizes the concept of vicarious learning and the role of cognitive–mediational processes to explain which environmental events are attended to, retained, and subsequently performed when a person is exposed to modeling stimuli. The concept of reciprocal determinism is a central feature of social learning theory, which describes the role an individual's behavior has on changing the environment and vice versa (Bandura, 1986).

Cognitive-behavioral theory is a second learning theory used to explain deficient social skills functioning. This approach is based on the assumption that an individual's behavior in response to environmental events is mediated by cognitions or thoughts (Mayer, Van Acker, Lochman, & Gresham, 2009). Interventions based on cognitive-behavioral theory present individuals with social situations in which a variety of internal and external social cues are present. These cues are made more or less salient to a person based on past learning history and current environmental circumstances.

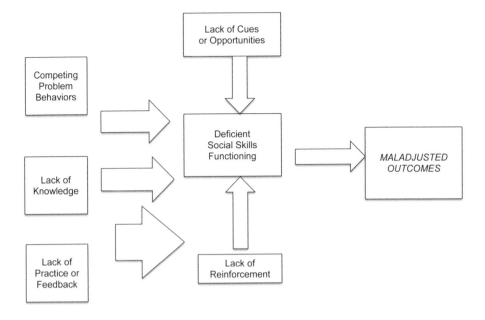

FIGURE 1.1. Five major reasons for social skills deficiencies.

The goal of cognitive-behavioral interventions is to change maladaptive self-statements, attributions, and perceptions to increase overt prosocial behavior and to decrease maladaptive social perceptions and attributions that lead to competing problem behaviors. Strategies such as self-monitoring, self-instruction, self-evaluation, and social problem solving are typically used in cognitive-behavioral approaches (Lochman & Gresham, 2009).

Applied behavior analysis is a third learning theory used to explain social skills deficits and competing problem behavior excesses. Applied behavior analysis is based on the work of Skinner (1953) in operant conditioning and is grounded in the concept of the three-term contingency that describes the relationships among antecedent events, behavior, and consequent events.

Applied behavior analysts identify the conditions that reinforce (positively or negatively) the occurrence of specific problem behaviors that need to be modified. Functional behavioral assessment is central to the identification of environmental conditions that are functionally related to the occurrence of problem behaviors (Gresham, Watson, & Skinner, 2001). In this approach to SEL intervention, applied behavior analysis is used to replace competing problem behaviors with prosocial behaviors that serve the same behavioral function. This process is known as positive replacement behavior training (Maag, 2005).

Social Validity Conceptualization

A final approach to conceptualizing social skills is based on the notion of social validity (Wolf, 1978). According to this conceptualization, social skills are those behaviors that, within a given situation, predict important social outcomes for children and youth. These important social outcomes might include peer acceptance, friendships, academic achievement, significant others' (teachers' and parents') judgments of social competence, consistent school attendance, and absence of school disciplinary referrals. This conceptualization has the advantage of being able not only to specify behaviors in which an individual is deficient, but also to directly relate these social behaviors to socially important outcomes that society values.

The issues of *social significance* and *social importance* are most relevant to a social validity conceptualization of the social skills construct. The social significance of the goals specified by an SEL intervention is an important consideration. For example, a practitioner may want to increase the number of "thank you" verbalizations exhibited by a child. Although this would appear to be a socially significant goal, significant others (teachers and parents) may not consider it a socially significant goal. A broader goal, such as increases in all positive verbalizations, might be considered more socially significant, and hence more socially valid by significant others in the child's environment.

It is important to recognize that the social significance of behavioral goals in SEL interventions is based on subjective evaluation (Kazdin, 1977; Wolf, 1978). Subjective evaluations are judgments made by persons who interact with or who are in a special position to judge behavior. Parents, teachers, counselors, social workers, and other significant persons in an individual's environment are likely candidates for subjectively evaluating the goals of SEL interventions.

Evaluating the social importance of the effects produced by social–emotional interventions is crucial. The question here is: Does the quantity and quality of behavior change make a difference in terms of an individual's functioning in particular settings? In other words, do changes in targeted social skills predict an individual's standing on important social outcomes? In this conceptualization, the effects of SEL interventions can be classified based on a social validity criterion. In this classification system, these measures represent socially valid treatment goals because social systems (e.g., schools, mental health agencies) and significant others (teachers and parents) refer children and youth on the basis of these treatment goals. These measures are socially valid in the sense that they predict long-term outcomes that are important to society including events such as school dropout, delinquency, adult mental health difficulties, and arrest rates (Kupersmidt et al., 1990; Parker & Asher, 1987; Walker, Ramsay, & Gresham, 2004). More details on how one might quantify the social importance of the effects of social–emotional interventions are discussed in Chapter 3.

THE IMPORTANCE OF SOCIAL COMPETENCE

An important distinction in the theoretical conceptualization of social behavior is the distinction among the concepts of social skills, social tasks, and social competence. *Social–emotional skills* can be conceptualized as a specific class of behaviors that an individual exhibits in order to successfully complete a social task. Social skills are best thought of as a response class that is defined as an integrated group of behaviors that have varying topographies or forms of behavior that produce the same effect on the environment. *Social tasks* include such things as peer group entry, having a conversation, making friends, or playing a game with peers. Social tasks require different response classes to successfully complete that social task. Asher and McDonald (2009) suggest that a social-task perspective is based on the assumption that the various tasks have their own distinct challenges and require various social behaviors that are task-specific. Table 1.1 shows examples of various social tasks that might be required of children and youth.

Social competence, in contrast, is an evaluative term based on judgments (given certain criteria) that an individual has performed a social task adequately. Social agents make these judgments based on numerous social interactions with given individuals within natural environments (e.g., home, school, community). This conceptualization states that social skills are a specific class of behavior exhibited in specific situations that lead to judgments by significant others that these behaviors are competent or incompetent in accomplishing specific social tasks. It should be noted that

TABLE 1.1. Examples of Social Tasks

• Complimenting others	• Ignoring classmates who are distracting
• Asking for help	• Asking for help from adults
• Having a conversation	• Saying nice things about others
• Joining ongoing play activities	• Respecting the property of others
• Dealing with teasing or name calling	• Standing up for others who are being treated unfairly
• Negotiating with others	• Making friends easily
• Listening to others	• Participating in games or group activities
• Persuading others	
• Expressing feelings	• Resolving disagreements without getting angry
• Following teacher directions	• Making a compromise during a conflict
• Participating appropriately in class activities	

judgments of social competence or incompetence differ across social agents making these judgments. As such, social behaviors judged to be competent by classroom teachers might not be judged as competent by a child's peers. In fact, researchers have made a distinction between teacher-preferred and peer-preferred social skills (Gresham & Elliott, 2008; Walker, Irvin, Noell, & Singer, 1992).

Teacher-preferred social–emotional skills are behaviors that facilitate the process of children and youth meeting the behavioral demands and expectations that the majority of teachers require in order to successfully manage instructional environments. Behaviors such as compliance with teacher directives, following classroom rules, working independently, and listening carefully to the teacher are examples of these teacher-preferred social skills. *Peer-preferred* social–emotional skills are behaviors that facilitate the accomplishment of satisfactory peer relationships, that develop friendships, and that support and maintain social networks.

During middle school, a third form of social adjustment termed *self-related* social–emotional skills assume increased importance. Self-related social skills include behaviors such as managing one's emotions, being organized, regulating one's behavior, asserting oneself, coping with relational aggression, and protecting one's reputation. These types of social skills are most relevant to adolescent social development (Walker et al., 2004).

If children and youth fail to satisfactorily negotiate teacher-related, peer-related, and self-related social skills, they are at increased risk for later school failure and vocational adjustment in early adulthood. Figure 1.2 presents a conceptual model of teacher-related, peer-related, and self-related social skills with associated long-term positive and negative outcomes.

Social Skills as Academic Enablers

Researchers have documented meaningful predictive relationships between children's social behaviors and their long-term academic achievement (DiPerma & Elliott, 2002; Malecki & Elliott, 2002; Wentzel, 2009). It has been documented that children who have positive interactions and relationships with their peers are academically engaged and have higher levels of academic achievement (see Wentzel, 2009, for a review). The notion of *academic enablers* evolved from the work of researchers who explored the relationship between students' nonacademic behaviors (social skills and motivation) and their academic achievement (Gresham & Elliott, 1990; Wentzel, 2005, 2009; Wentzel & Watkins, 2002).

Researchers make a distinction between academic skills and academic enablers. Academic skills are the basic and complex skills that are the primary focus of academic instruction. In contrast, academic enablers are the attitudes and behaviors that allow students to participate in and ultimately

Teacher-Related Adjustment		Peer-Related Adjustment		Self-Related Adjustment	
Adaptive	*Maladaptive*	*Adaptive*	*Maladaptive*	*Adaptive*	*Maladaptive*
• Asks for help • Follows directions • Ignores distractions • Follows rules • Shows concern • Stays calm	• Tantrums • Disobeys rules • Talks back to adults • Is impulsive • Is inattentive • Gets distracted	• Cooperates • Supports peers • Leads peers • Shows empathy • Affiliates with peers • Stands up for peers	• Bullies others • Fights • Gossips about peers • Excludes peers • Withdraws • Acts lonely	• Controls emotions • Regulates behavior • Asserts self • Protects reputation • Takes criticism well • Compromises	• Has low energy • Is lethargic • Is depressed • Is anxious
OUTCOMES					
Positive	*Negative*	*Positive*	*Negative*	*Positive*	*Negative*
• Teacher acceptance • School achievement	• Teacher rejection • Referral for specialized services • School dropout and failure • Low performance expectations	• Peer acceptance • Positive peer relations • Friendships	• Rejection/neglect • Low social involvement	• School success • Respected by peers • Respected by adults	• Low self-esteem • Disciplinary referrals • School maladjustment

FIGURE 1.2. Social–behavioral competencies.

benefit from academic instruction in the classroom. Research using the Academic Competence Evaluation Scales (ACES; DiPerma & Elliott, 2000) showed that academic enablers were moderately correlated with students' academic achievement as measured by standardized achievement tests (median r = .50). In a major longitudinal study, Caprara, Barbaranelli, Pastorelli, Bandura, and Zimbardo (2000) found that teacher ratings of prosocial behaviors in third grade were better predictors of eighth grade academic achievement than academic achievement in third grade.

Work by Wentzel (2005) has shown that various aspects of peer relationships are predictive of children's motivational and academic functioning at school. This line of research shows that children's level of peer acceptance are positively related to motivation, school satisfaction, goal-directed learning, interest in school, and self-perceived academic competence. Additionally, having friendships is related to school grades and achievement test scores in both elementary- and middle school-age children. Wentzel (2005) suggests that positive relationships with peers provide a context that supports the development of positive motivational orientations toward academic achievement.

Most researchers have concluded that positive peer interactions promote displays of competent forms of social behavior that in turn promote successful academic performance. Behaviors such as cooperation, following rules, and getting along with others create efficient classroom environments and allow students to benefit from academic instruction. Displays of prosocial behavior and restraint from disruptive and antisocial forms of behavior have been consistently and positively related to achievement motivation and academic success (Wentzel, 2009). Socially competent behavior provides the essential basis for learning that allows students to benefit from classroom instruction (DiPerma & Elliott, 2002).

Problem Behaviors as Academic Disablers

Although social skills function as academic enablers, it has been shown that problem behaviors, particularly externalizing behavior patterns, interfere with or compete with the performance of both social and academic skills (Gresham, 2010; Gresham & Elliott, 2008; Walker et al., 1992). In other words, these competing problem behaviors have been known to function as *academic disablers* in that they are associated with decreases in academic performance. Children and youth with externalizing behaviors such as aggression, noncompliance, and/or teacher defiance often have moderate to severe academic skill deficits that are reflected in below-average academic achievement (Coie & Jacobs, 1993; Hinshaw, 1992; Offord, Boyle, & Racine, 1989). It is unclear whether these academic problems are primarily correlates (moderators), causes (mediators), or consequences of problem behaviors; however, there is little doubt that the presence of these problem behaviors greatly exacerbates low academic performance. As these children progress through their school careers, their academic deficits and achievement problems become even more severe (Walker et al., 1992, 2004).

An important consideration in the conceptualization of social–emotional skills deficits is the influence of competing problem behaviors on an individual's level of social skill functioning (Gresham & Elliott, 2008). Competing problem behaviors effectively compete with, interfere with, or block the exhibition of a particular social skill. Competing problem behaviors can be broadly classified as *externalizing* behavior patterns (noncompliance, aggression, impulsive behaviors) or *internalizing* behavior patterns (social withdrawal, anxiety, depression). For example, a child with a history of noncompliant, oppositional, and impulsive behavior may never learn prosocial behavior alternatives such as sharing, cooperation, and self-control because of the absence of opportunities to learn these behaviors caused by the competing function of these externalizing behaviors (Eddy, Reid, & Curry, 2002). Similarly, a child with a history of social anxiety, social withdrawal, and shyness may never learn appropriate social behaviors because of avoidance of the peer group, thereby creating an absence of opportunities to learn peer-related social skills.

Some social–emotional skills deficits are due primarily to motivational variables rather than to a lack of exposure or knowledge concerning how to enact a given social skill. One of the most conceptually powerful learning principles that can be used to explain the relationship between social skills performance deficits and competing problem behaviors is the *matching law* (Herrnstein, 1961, 1970). The matching law states that the relative rate of a given behavior matches the relative rate of reinforcement for that behavior. In other words, response rate matches reinforcement rate. Matching is studied experimentally in an arrangement known as concurrent schedules of reinforcement, which refers to an experimental arrangement in which two or more behaviors are reinforced according to two or more simultaneous, but quantitatively different, schedules of reinforcement.

Matching deals with the issue of "choice behavior" in that behaviors having a higher rate of reinforcement will be "chosen" more frequently than behaviors reinforced at lower rates. Research in naturalistic classroom environments has consistently shown that behavior rates observed under concurrent schedules of reinforcement closely follow the matching law (Martens, 1992; Martens & Houk, 1989; Martens, Lochner, & Kelly, 1992; Snyder & Stoolmiller, 2002).

Maag (2005) suggested that one way to decrease competing problem behaviors is to teach *positive replacement behaviors*, or what he called replacement behavior training (RBT). RBT may help solve many of the problems described in the social–emotional skills training literature such as poor generalization and maintenance, modest effect sizes, and social invalidity of target behavior selection. The goal of RBT is to identify a prosocial behavior that will replace the competing problem behavior. Conceptually, RBT depends on identifying *functionally equivalent behaviors*. Behaviors are said to be functionally equivalent if they produce similar amounts of functionally relevant reinforcement from the environment.

IDENTIFICATION OF SOCIAL SKILLS STRENGTHS AND DEFICITS

An important consideration in conceptualizing social–emotional skills is to identify social skills strengths, acquisition deficits, performance deficits, and competing problem behaviors. Figure 1.3 provides a framework for conceptualizing social behavior. There are four steps in using the framework in Figure 1.3: (1) identifying social skills strengths, (2) identifying social skills performance deficits, (3) identifying social skills acquisition deficits, and (4) identifying excessive problem behaviors. Social–emotional skills strengths are represented by a child knowing and using a particular social skill consistently and appropriately. Social–emotional skills performance deficits are reflected in a child knowing how to use a social skill, but who does so inconsistently. A social–emotional skills acquisition deficit describes a situation in which the child does not sufficiently know the skill or how to use it appropriately. Finally, an excessive problem behavior interferes with a child's performance of a learned social skill. Specific procedural details regarding how to quantify social skills strengths, performance deficits, acquisition deficits, and excessive problem behaviors are presented in Chapter 3.

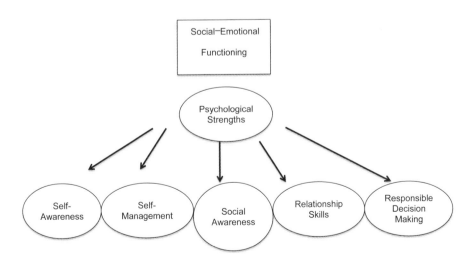

FIGURE 1.3. Framework for conceptualizing social behavior.

Acquisition versus Performance Deficits

The distinction between social skills acquisition and performance deficits is important because different intervention approaches are called for in remediating these differing social skills deficits. They also dictate different instructional contexts (e.g., general education classrooms vs. pullout groups).

Acquisition deficits result from a lack of knowledge about how to enact a given social skill, inability to fluently perform a sequence of social behaviors, or difficulty in knowing which social skills are appropriate in specific situations (Gresham & Elliott, 2014). Based on this conceptualization, acquisition deficits can result from deficits in social–cognitive abilities, difficulties in integrating fluent behavior patterns, and/or in appropriate discrimination of social situations. Acquisition deficits are perhaps best thought of as "can't do" problems because the child cannot perform the social skill under the most optimal conditions of motivation. Remediation of these types of deficits requires direct instruction of social skills in protected settings that will promote the acquisition of socially skilled behaviors.

Performance deficits can be conceptualized as the failure to perform a social skill at an acceptable level despite the child knowing how to perform it. These types of social skills deficits can best be thought of as "won't do" problems because the child knows what to do, but chooses not to perform a particular social skill in given situations. These types of social skills deficits can best be thought of as *motivational* or performance problems rather than learning or acquisition problems. As such, remediation of these types of deficits requires manipulating antecedents and consequences in naturalistic settings to increase the frequency of these behaviors.

THE IMPORTANCE OF SOCIAL–EMOTIONAL COMPETENCE

Many children and youth have deficits in social–emotional competencies that negatively impact their academic performance and social relationships. In a national survey of students in grades 6–12, less than half of these students reported that they had social competencies such as conflict resolution skills, decision-making skills, and empathy (Benson, 2006). Almost 30% of these students by the time they reach high school are involved in multiple high-risk behaviors such as substance abuse, sex, depression, and attempted suicide. There is a consensus among educators and mental health professionals that universal school-based efforts to facilitate students' social–emotional competence represent a promising approach to enhance school and life success (Zins & Elias, 2006).

The Collaborative for Academic, Social, and Emotional Learning

CASEL is an organization devoted to evidence-based SEL as a key component to assist in the establishment of SEL from preschool-age children to those in high school. The goals of CASEL are to promote the science of SEL, to expand SEL practices, and to inform state and federal policymakers about the importance of these programs. CASEL (2005) has targeted five interrelated sets of cognitive, affective, and behavioral competencies: (1) *self-awareness*, (2) *self-management*, (3) *social awareness*, (4) *relationship skills*, and (5) *responsible decision making*. These competencies are intended to promote better adjustment and social behaviors, fewer conduct problems, diminished emotional distress, and improved academic achievement. Table 1.2 provides specific behavioral examples of these five core areas of SEL identified by CASEL

What evidence is there that universal SEL programs implemented in schools produce the intended outcomes? Durlak and colleagues conducted a meta-analysis of 213 school-based universal SEL programs involving 270,034 students in kindergarten through high school across multiple outcome measures (Durlak, Weissberg, Dymnicki, Taylor, & Schellinger, 2011). These outcome measures included social/emotional skills, attitudes toward self and others, positive social behaviors, conduct problems, emotional distress, and academic performance. This meta-analysis sought to answer the following four questions:

1. What outcomes are achieved by interventions that attempt to enhance children's emotional and social skills?
2. Can SEL interventions promote positive outcomes and prevent future problems?
3. Can SEL programs be successfully conducted in the school setting by existing school personnel?
4. What variables moderate the impact of school-based SEL programs?

The six primary outcome measure categories used in this meta-analysis are described below. *Social and emotional skills* included evaluations of different types of cognitive, affective, and social skills related to areas such as identifying emotions from social cues, goal setting, perspective taking, problem solving, conflict resolution, and decision making. *Attitudes toward self and others* combined positive attitudes about oneself, school, and social topics. This category included self-perceptions (e.g., self-esteem, self-concept, and self-efficacy), school bonding, and prosocial beliefs about violence, helping others, social justice, and drug use. All of these outcomes were based on student self-reports. *Positive social behavior*

TABLE 1.2. CASEL Competencies and Behavioral Examples

CASEL competency	Behavioral examples
Self-management	• Resolves disagreements calmly. • Stays calm when teased. • Makes compromises in conflicts. • Responds appropriately when pushed/hit. • Takes criticism without becoming upset.
Social awareness	• Tries to understand others' feelings. • Tries to make others feel better. • Forgives others. • Tries to comfort others. • Shows concern for others.
Relationship skills	• Makes eye contact when talking. • Speaks in appropriate tone of voice. • Makes friends easily. • Interacts well with others. • Invites others to join activities.
Responsible decision making	• Takes care of others' things. • Is well behaved when unsupervised. • Respects the property of others. • Takes responsibility for his or her own actions. • Does what he or she promised. • Takes responsibility for his or her own mistakes.
Self-awareness	• Understands his or her emotions. • Has a positive mind-set. • Has a sense of self-efficacy. • Is optimistic. • Recognizes how thoughts, feelings, and actions are connected.

included outcomes such as getting along with others based on teacher, parent, or observer reports. These outcomes reflected daily or typical behavior rather than performance in hypothetical situations. *Conduct problems* included measures of various types of externalizing behavior problems such as classroom disruption, noncompliance, aggression, bullying, school suspensions, and delinquency. Measures of these behaviors were based on teacher reports, parent reports, observations, or school records. *Emotional distress* consisted of measures of internalizing behavior problems and included teacher and parent reports of depression, anxiety, stress, or social withdrawal. *Academic performance* included standardized reading or math achievement test scores and school grades in the form of overall grade point average. Compared to controls, SEL participants demonstrated significantly improved social and emotional skills, attitudes, behavior, and academic performance. More specific detail on these universal SEL programs is discussed extensively in Chapter 2.

CONCLUDING REMARKS

Clearly, the acquisition and performance of social skills, or what some call SEL, is an important aspect of a child's social development that also impacts academic performance and long-term life skills. The use of evidence-based approaches is an important topic in fields such as medicine, education, and applied psychology (clinical, counseling, and school). As expected, unfortunately a wide gap exists between research and practice in all fields, including the field of social skills and SEL.

Rogers (2003) presented a comprehensive *diffusion model* that helps us to conceptualize the various stages of diffusion of evidence-based practices. In the first stage, the concept of "dissemination" assumes priority. Dissemination refers to the communication of accurate and useful information to potential users about a given program. In the second stage, "adoption" becomes important; this occurs when other people decide to try out or adopt a particular program. The third stage of diffusion is "implementation," which refers to the implementation of a program in a high-quality manner to test a program's ability to produce changes. The fourth stage of diffusion is "evaluation," which describes a program's ability to achieve its intended goals. The final stage of "sustainability" describes a situation in which a particular program has become a routine feature or aspect of an organization's procedures. Weissberg and colleagues suggested several ways to make progress in the above different stages of program diffusion (see Weissberg et al., 2015). According to these authors the central feature of program diffusion is *collaboration* among relevant stakeholders interested in SEL programs. In short, relevant stakeholders should work together to in supporting broader implementation of evidence-based SEL programs. These stakeholders include educators, family members, researchers, policymakers, advocates, and funding agencies.

CHAPTER SUMMARY POINTS

- Meta-analyses and literature reviews have documented that poor peer relations in childhood predict serious social adjustment issues in adolescence and early adulthood.

- Research over the past 35 years prompted an intense interest in the development of preventive interventions among researchers studying the deleterious effects of peer relationship difficulties.

- Much attention over the past 10 years has focused on the assessment and intervention of children's social–emotional competence.

- There has been a recent push by educators, policymakers, and researchers focusing on the development of children's SEL competencies.

- A sociometric conceptualization of social competence emphasizes the degree to which children are accepted, rejected, or neglected by their peers.

- A major drawback of a sociometric conceptualization of social competence is its failure to consistently identify specific behaviors in specific situations that lead to peer acceptance or rejection.

- A social learning theory conceptualization of social competence identifies five major reasons for deficient social skills functioning: (1) lack of knowledge, (2) lack of practice or feedback, (3) absence of or inattention to social cues, (4) lack of reinforcement, and (5) presence of competing problem behaviors.

- Three distinct learning theories have been used to address and explain children's social skills deficits: (1) social learning theory, (2) cognitive-behavioral theory, and (3) applied behavior analysis.

- A social validity conceptualization of deficits in social competence deals with the social significance and social importance of social skills in predicting short-term, intermediate, and long-term outcomes.

- Important distinctions are made between the concepts of social skills, social tasks, and social competence.

- Social skills are a specific class of behaviors that an individual exhibits in order to successfully complete a social task.

- Social tasks require the integration of different response classes to successfully complete a social task.

- Social competence is an evaluative term based on judgments that an individual has performed a social task adequately.

- Distinctions are made among teacher-preferred, peer-preferred, and self-related social skills.

- Teacher-preferred social skills are behaviors that facilitate the meeting of the behavioral demands and expectations that teachers require to effectively manage instructional environments.

- Peer-preferred social skills are behaviors that facilitate the accomplishment of satisfactory peer relationships, promote friendships, and support and maintain social networks.

- Self-related social skills include behaviors such as managing one's emotions, being organized, regulating one's behavior, asserting oneself, and coping with relational aggression.

- Social skills function as academic enablers in that children with higher levels of social skills generally have higher levels of academic achievement.

- Problem behaviors function as academic disablers in that children with higher levels of externalizing problem behaviors have lowered academic achievement.

- The relationship between social skills and competing problem behaviors is perhaps best explained by the matching law.

- The matching law states that the relative rate of behavior will match the relative rate of reinforcement for that behavior (response rate matches reinforcement rate).

- The two fundamental types of social skills deficits are acquisition deficits and performance deficits.

- Acquisition deficits reflect "can't do" problems because the individual cannot perform a given social skill under optimal conditions of motivation.

- Performance deficits reflect "won't do" problems because the individual knows how to perform the skill, but does so infrequently.

- CASEL is an organization devoted to evidence-based SEL strategies.

- CASEL targets five broad areas of social–emotional functioning: (1) self-awareness, (2) self-management, (3) social awareness, (4) relationship skills, and (5) responsible decision making.

- A comprehensive meta-analysis of 213 studies concluded that compared to controls, SEL participants demonstrated significantly improved social and emotional skills, attitudes, behavior, and academic performance.

CHAPTER TWO

Evidence Base for Social–Emotional Learning Interventions

Clearly, a scientific field cannot progress without considering proper research methodologies to establish what is and what is not known about phenomena of interest. The primary goal of research methodology is to allow professionals to draw valid inferences from controlled research that are not confounded or otherwise disconfirmed by plausible rival hypotheses. All areas of applied psychology and other behavioral sciences that utilize interventions to deliver services have embraced the notion of *evidence-based practices* to bridge the research-to-practice gap in various areas (Gersten et al., 2005; Horner et al., 2005; Kazdin & Weisz, 2003).

The goal of this chapter is to present information that will assist professionals in making wise and strategic investments of time and energy regarding effective evidence-based practices for SEL interventions. These decisions occur in a series of three specific steps. Step 1 in this process is to identify a set of practices that have been shown to have an acceptable evidence base upon which they are supported. Step 2 is to select from among these identified practices in a way that matches to a problem and solves it better that what is currently being used. Step 3 is to implement these practices with high treatment integrity so that the chance of success is maximized. This chapter focuses on methodological procedures and practices that can be used to support evidence-based SEL interventions.

WHAT IS EVIDENCE?

Defining what qualifies as evidence and basing one's actions on the resulting definition is often a challenging task. Some professionals accept what they consider to be evidence only if it fits their preexisting belief systems or opinions, and they will reject any evidence that does not conform to these beliefs. In social psychology, the concept of *cognitive dissonance* can be used to explain this phenomenon. Cognitive dissonance is the tendency of individuals to strive for consistency among their beliefs, attitudes, and behaviors and any inconsistency among these beliefs, attitudes, and behaviors is rejected despite overwhelming disconfirming evidence. For instance, if you purchase an expensive new home and it turns out to have numerous construction problems, you will tend to maintain that it is a good house despite its numerous imperfections. Unfortunately, scientific evidence for or against phenomena functions in much the same way. Kauffman (2014) adeptly captured this idea as follows:

> Science is a cruel mistress. It demands doubt and brooks no choice to believe an alternative explanation when the evidence served up by fidelity to its method undermines faith in that alternative. This is a bitter pill for many to swallow, so it is not at all surprising that many politicians and educators—including many special educators, including those who study emotional and behavioral disorders (EBD)—find science unpalatable. (p. 1)

It is unfortunately the case that many professionals cherry-pick from science those concepts and practices that are consistent with their beliefs, attitudes, and past practices while ignoring scientific findings that are inconsistent with these beliefs. For example, some reading "experts" continue to believe in and practice the whole-word approach to reading instruction despite the overwhelming scientific evidence supporting phonic and phonemic-awareness approaches to reading instruction (National Reading Panel, 2000). It comes as no surprise then that many individuals have trouble accepting the verdict of scientific evidence because it requires them to reject their long-held cherished beliefs and values.

Different fields have different criteria and standards that they use to identify and establish what constitutes acceptable levels of scientific evidence. In law, different types of direct and indirect evidence are used to establish a person's innocence or guilt. Direct evidence includes physical evidence, eyewitness testimony, and confessions of guilt. Indirect, or circumstantial, evidence includes past behavior, character testimony, and expert witness testimony. Juries and judges weigh each of these types of evidence differently. In paleontology, different types of evidence are used to support the theory of evolution. These types of evidence might include fossil evidence, genetic evidence (DNA), or distributional evidence (species are not randomly distributed across different geographic regions). Charles Darwin's work on the origin of species was largely based on his ability to make discrete observations and recordings of natural events and synthesize them in a manner that supported his theory of evolution. To take a last example, in physics evidence about the laws of nature derives from one of two major theories: quantum theory or the theory of relativity. Quantum theory is concerned with the discrete rather than the continuous nature of phenomena at the atomic and subatomic level, whereas relatively focuses on the description of phenomena that takes place from the perspective of an observer. Each theory in physics uses somewhat different standards for what each considers admissible evidence (Issacson, 2007).

Some individuals and organizations falsely dichotomize interventions and practices into evidence-based and non-evidence-based categories. Research, however, does not fall neatly into these two somewhat arbitrary categories. Research evidence is best thought of as existing on a *continuum* anchored by evidence-based and non-evidence-based poles. This conceptualization requires that we think in terms of levels, or strata, of evidence demonstrating stronger or weaker forms of scientific support. Kazdin (2004) distinguishes between an absolute threshold versus a hierarchical approach in evaluating evidence. The threshold method is an absolute standard, whereas the hierarchical method is a relative standard that considers a range of evidence generated by different research methods. I subscribe strongly to the hierarchical approach for establishing an evidence base for certain practices and procedures. Determining whether a particular treatment or practice is evidence-based requires that we evaluate the research methodology used. We should evaluate the extent to which the research methodology controls for various threats to internal validity, external validity, construct validity, and statistical conclusion validity (Shadish, Cook, & Campbell, 2002).

EVIDENCE-BASED TREATMENTS VERSUS EVIDENCE-BASED PRACTICES

Evidence-based practice (EBP) is an approach to clinical practice that began in medicine around 1992 under the term "evidence-based medicine." Since that time, many other fields such as speech–language pathology, audiology, nursing, psychology, education, and social work have adopted EBP. EBP involves making decisions about how to promote desirable outcomes by utilizing and integrating the best available scientific evidence coupled with practitioner expertise and organizational resources. EBP sometimes comes into philosophical conflict with traditional practices. For example, a surgeon may utilize a procedure that has a 20% mortality rate because he or she prefers it over other procedures, he or she was trained in the procedure, and it is easier to perform the chosen procedure over other procedures having a 10% mortality rate. Clearly, this would be unacceptable practice that would not be tolerated by medical ethics boards.

EBP involves making clinical decisions for treatments based on a review of information from rigorous research instead of relying on rules, single observations, or tradition. This approach to treatment has been around for over 30 years in universities and has gradually made its way into everyday clinical practice. EBP moves away from the "old" medical model that is based on the logic of you have X disease, so you take Y pill. Key aspects of EBP include the development of questions using research-based evidence, examination of the level of type of evidence considered, and the evaluation of treatment outcomes using rigorous research-derived methods.

Researchers make a distinction between the terms *evidence-based treatments* and *evidence-based practices*. Evidence-based treatments are treatments that have been shown to be efficacious through rigorous research methods that have good internal validity. These treatments produce their effects under highly controlled experimental conditions. Evidence-based practices, in contrast, are treatment approaches rather than a specific intervention applied to an individual. Evidence-based treatments are used to make decisions about individuals such as being a responder or nonresponder to a treatment. Evidence-based practices are grounded in scientific research that supports implementation of intervention approaches across studies, groups, sites, investigators, and contexts. Evidence-based practices rely on studies that emphasize high external validity rather than high internal validity.

Researchers also distinguish between efficacy research and effectiveness research. *Efficacy research* focuses on measurable effects of specific interventions with the randomized controlled trial (RCT) being the prototypical example (Nathan, Stuart, & Dolan, 2000). Efficacy studies compare one or more experimental treatments with one or more control conditions (e.g., no-treatment controls, delayed-treatment controls, or placebo-treated controls). Again, efficacy studies have high internal validity, meaning that they have been conducted under stringent experimental conditions.

Effectiveness research seeks to determine whether treatments have measurable beneficial effects across broad populations in real-world settings (Nathan et al., 2000). Effectiveness research has high external validity and is concerned with the extent to which a causal relationship is established and persists in the face of variations in settings, individuals, treatments, and outcomes (Shadish et al., 2002). Effectiveness research uses broadly defined outcome measures rather than specific, narrowly construed outcome measures that are typically used in efficacy research. Usually, effect sizes are smaller in effectiveness studies than in efficacy studies because interventions are (1) implemented in real-world, sometimes chaotic environmental conditions and (2) they are implemented in the absence of the supports, technical assistance, and trouble-shooting typically provided by their developers in efficacy evaluations. As a general rule, practitioners prefer effectiveness studies because they have passed the difficult test of "real-world" application. Unfortunately, such interventions are not always available for solving particular problems, so less robust interventions may have to be considered.

TYPES OF RESEARCH EVIDENCE

Gathering and synthesizing the best research evidence is the foundation of EBPs. As I mentioned earlier, I advocate for the *hierarchical method* for interpreting research evidence because it allows for the presentation of a range of evidence generated by different research methods. Multiple types of research evidence varying in quality are used to support EBPs: they include (1) efficacy studies, (2) effectiveness studies, (3) cost-effectiveness studies, (4) longitudinal intervention outcome studies, and (5) epidemiological studies. Various types of research methodologies are better suited for answering certain questions than others. These methodologies include:

- Observation of individuals within target settings, including case studies, can be a valuable source of hypotheses generation concerning the social–behavioral challenges of children and youth.
- Qualitative and mixed methods research can be used to evaluate the subjective or real-world experiences of individuals undergoing an intervention. These methods use *grounded theory* that focuses on developing hypotheses to describe a process that is not well understood (Sabornie & Weiss, 2014).
- Single-case experimental designs are valuable in drawing causal inferences about the effectiveness of interventions for *individuals* in a controlled manner (Horner et al., 2005b).
- Epidemiological research is used to track the availability, utilization, and acceptance of various intervention procedures (Vidair et al., 2014).
- Moderator–mediator studies can be used to identify correlates and causes of intervention outcomes and to establish mechanisms of change for specific intervention procedures (Baron & Kenny, 1986).
- RCTs or efficacy studies can provide the strongest type of research evidence that protects against most threats to the internal validity of research studies (Shadish et al., 2002).

- Effectiveness studies can be used to assess the outcomes of interventions in less controlled, real-world settings and to determine whether causal relationships persist across individuals, treatment agents, and/or participants.
- Meta-analyses of research literature provide a quantitative metric or index concerning the effects of multiple studies on various target populations, age groups, genders, settings, and/or types of outcome measures.

INSTITUTE OF EDUCATION SCIENCES RESEARCH STANDARDS

The Institute of Education Sciences (IES) supports research over a diverse set of topics and for a range of purposes. Topics include school readiness, achievement in core academic content (reading, mathematics, writing), and behaviors that support learning in academic contexts. IES supports research ranging from translational research to the evaluation of the impact of interventions that are implemented at scale (effectiveness studies). IES has a specific topic area devoted to social and behavioral outcomes to support learning. Under this rubric, IES funds research on behavioral interventions designed to manage, control, and prevent a range of behavior and antisocial problems such as social skills, violence toward peers or adults, self-injury, noncompliance, bullying, and withdrawal. The long-term outcome of this funded research will be an array of tools and strategies that have been documented to be effective for preventing behavior problems and improving the behavioral skills, emotional skills, social skills, and academic performance of students with or at risk for disabilities from kindergarten through grade 12.

IES specifies five goals of research under the above topic: Goal 1: exploration, Goal 2: development and innovation, Goal 3: efficacy and replication (efficacy studies), Goal 4: scale-up evaluations (effectiveness studies), and Goal 5: measurement.

Goal 1: Exploration

IES funds projects that explore the relations between education outcomes and malleable factors, or those factors that can be changed, such as child behaviors or education programs, practices, and policies, as well as mediators and moderators of those relations. Research that explores the relations among malleable factors and educational outcomes is termed *translational research* because it is intended to inform the development of interventions, programs, practices, and policies that can improve education outcomes.

A Goal 1 exploration study in the area of social skills might explore the relationships among levels of social skills, gender, and age on standardized academic achievement tests in elementary school-age children.

Goals 2: Development and Innovation

Goal 2 projects focus on developing education interventions, programs, practices, products, and policies designed to improve existing education interventions. These funded projects require an iterative process of designing, testing, revising, and testing to produce a product or system that functions in a way the developer intends for it to function and that can be implemented in actual education delivery settings. A Goal 2 project in the area of social skills might be the development and implementation of universal, selected, and intensive SEL interventions in a limited number of schools without using randomized or quasi-experimental research methodologies. The focus of a Goal 2 study is *not* to conduct a highly controlled efficacy study but rather to develop and implement a procedure or practice to demonstrate it can work in authentic educational settings.

Goal 3: Efficacy and Replication

Goal 3 studies involve efficacy or replication studies using experimental and quasi-experimental research designs. These studies seek to evaluate the efficacy of newly developed or existing education programs, practices, and policies under tight experimental conditions. Efficacy projects provide an estimate of how potent the intervention is for producing the desired outcome. IES describes *potent* as the strength of the impact of the intervention that could be expressed by various effect size estimates. An example of a social skills Goal 3 study might be a RCT of Tier 2 or selected SEL intervention in which half of the participants are randomized to the SEL intervention and the other half randomized to a delayed-treatment control group.

Goal 4: Scale-Up Evaluations

Goal 4 research projects are designed to test interventions that have already demonstrated efficacy in Goal 3 projects on a much larger scale. Scale-up evaluations determine whether or not an intervention is effective when it is implemented under conditions that would be typical if the school district were to implement it on its own without special support from the developer or a research team across a variety of conditions. Scale-up evaluations provide an estimate of how robust the intervention is. That is, will it produce similar effects across different student populations, across different types of schools, and across different treatment implementers? An example of a Goal 4 intervention might be to test the effectiveness of a Tier 1 or universal social skills curriculum in which half of the schools in a district are randomized to the social skills curriculum and the other half are randomized to a no-treatment control condition.

Goal 5: Measurement

Goal 5 projects entail studies designed to develop and validate measurement instruments that are intended for use by practitioners for screening, progress monitoring, and outcome assessments. Measurement projects are intended to establish the reliability and validity of various measurement instruments. An example of a Goal 5 project might be to conduct a series of studies examining discrepancies among teacher, parent, and student ratings of social skills and problem behaviors using extant behavior rating scales. These studies would refine knowledge of informant discrepancies by examining variables that moderate informant discrepancies as well as investigating whether informant discrepancies predict relevant educational outcomes.

Summary

IES intends for its research programs to contribute to the generation of new knowledge and theories relevant to learning, instruction, and educational systems. The goal structure of IES's research programs divides the research process into stages. Goal 1 projects generate hypotheses about the components and processes involved in learning and instruction and in the operation of educational systems. Goal 2 projects build on prior theoretical and empirical work to propose a theory of change for a specific intervention. Goal 3 and 4 projects assess the impact of specific interventions and test the theory of change developed in Goal 2 projects in efficacy of scale-up evaluation studies. Finally, Goal 5 projects assess the technical quality of screening, progress monitoring, or outcome measurement instruments. Collectively, work across the various five goals should not only yield the practical benefits about the effects of specific interventions on education outcomes, but also contribute to the larger picture of scientific knowledge and theory on learning, instruction, and educational systems.

THREATS TO DRAWING VALID INFERENCES

Evaluation of evidence-based interventions depends on the validity of making inferences about the phenomenon being investigated. *Validity* can be defined as the truth of an inference or the degree to which evidence supports an inference being true or correct (Shadish et al., 2002). The philosophy of science uses correspondence theory that states a knowledge claim can only be true if it corresponds to what we know about the real world. What we think we know about the real world, however, may have various interpretations depending upon one's theoretical orientation. For example, in quantum physics, the *uncertainty principle* states that the very act of observing something affects the accuracy of that observation. The implication of the uncertainty principle is that no objective reality exists apart from our observations of this reality. The uncertainty principle contradicts what is assumed to be true in classical physics, which maintains that an objective reality exists apart from our ability to measure it. This fundamental disagreement between what is known to be true about the universe by quantum physics and classical physics created intense debates in the 1920s and 1930s between Albert Einstein and Niels Bohr regarding the nature of the universe (Issacson, 2007).

The goal of determining evidence-based interventions using research methodology is to design studies that reveal relations among variables that might not otherwise be obvious from casual observation. Research designs simplify complex situations to control and isolate variables of interest, ruling out alternative, competing explanations for the data collected in a study. The extent to which a research design is successful in ruling out plausible rival hypotheses is not absolute, but rather one of degree. Four types of validity are typically considered in this context: internal validity, external validity, construct validity, and statistical conclusion validity (Shadish et al., 2002).

Internal Validity

The degree to which an investigator can attribute changes in a dependent or outcome variable to systematic, manipulated changes in an independent (treatment) variable while simultaneously ruling out alternative explanations capture the notion of internal validity. Threats to internal validity include history, maturation, instrumentation, statistical regression, selection biases, and the interaction of selection biases with other threats to internal validity (Shadish et al., 2002). The RCT is the "gold standard" for protection against virtually all threats to the internal validity of a research study. Single-case experimental designs also provide protection against many, but not all, threats to internal validity. Quasi-experimental designs that do not involve random assignment do not provide this level of protection against internal validity threats and can sometimes lead to erroneous conclusions. Internal validity is the central concept in *efficacy studies* that investigate phenomena under tightly controlled experimental conditions.

External Validity

External validity refers to the generalizability of the results of a research investigation. It is concerned with the extent to which a study's findings can be generalized to other populations, participants, therapists/teachers, settings, treatment variables, and measurement variables. External validity is concerned with the boundary conditions or limitations of research findings. Whereas internal validity is concerned with attributing changes in a dependent variable to an independent variable, external validity focuses on the extent to which the same effect would be obtained with other populations, participants, therapists, settings, and with different methods for measuring outcomes. External validity is the core concept in *effectiveness studies* that investigate phenomena in real-world settings or conditions. Several threats to external validity have been noted and are classified into four broad categories: sample, stimulus, contextual, and assessment characteristics (Shadish et al., 2002).

Construct Validity

Construct validity establishes the basis for interpreting the causal relationship between an independent variable and a dependent variable. It deals with the extent to which generalizations can be made about higher-order constructs on the basis of research operations. There are several threats to the construct validity of a research study including inadequate explication of constructs, construct confounding, mono-operation bias, mono-method bias, and treatment diffusion. Each of these threats can compromise the interpretation or meaning of a particular research finding, thereby creating confusion about why treatments are successful or unsuccessful. Whereas internal validity is concerned with whether an independent variable was responsible for change in a dependent variable, construct validity concentrates on the *reason* or *explanation* for that change. The construct validity of a study is based on two questions: What is the intervention? What explains the causal mechanism for a change in the dependent variable?

Statistical Conclusion Validity

Statistical conclusion validity refers to threats in drawing valid inferences that result from random error and inappropriate selection of statistical analysis procedures. It deals with whether a presumed cause and effect covary and how strongly they covary. In the first case, statistical conclusion validity deals with the commission of *Type I errors* as false positive errors (falsely concluding an effect exists when it does not) and *Type II errors* as false negative errors (falsely concluding there is no effect when in fact there is). In the second case, we may overestimate the effects of an independent variable on a dependent variable.

Various threats to statistical conclusion validity exist and include low statistical power, violated assumptions of statistical tests, unreliability of measures, unreliability of treatment implementation (i.e., poor treatment integrity), and inaccurate effect size estimation. Although all of these treats are problematic, many group design studies of SEL interventions suffer from low statistical power because they use too few participants or fail to control for heterogeneity in experimental conditions.

STANDARDS FOR EVIDENCE-BASED TREATMENTS

Several professional organizations have proposed differing, but related, criteria and nomenclatures for the levels of scientific evidence necessary for determining whether or not a given treatment is evidence-based. Division 12 (Society of Clinical Psychology), Division 16 (School Psychology), Division 17 (Society of Counseling Psychology), Division 53 (Society of Clinical Child and Adolescent Psychology), and Division 54 (Society of Pediatric Psychology) of the American Psychological Association all have published separate position papers specifying criteria for classifying treatments based on the quality of research supporting those treatments. Although there is some variation among these divisions' documents, all have agreed upon the following criteria for the classification of scientific evidence.

• *Criterion 1: Well-established treatment.* There must be two good group design experiments, conducted in at least two independent research settings, and by independent research teams, demonstrating efficacy by showing the intervention to be (1) statistically superior to a pill or psychological placebo or another treatment, *or* (2) equivalent (i.e., not statistically different) to an already established treatment in experiments with sufficient statistical power to detect moderate differences, *and* (3) treatment manuals or their logical equivalent were used for implementation of the treatment, conducted with a target population, treated for specific problems, for whom inclusion criteria have been delineated, reliable and valid outcome measures were selected, and appropriate data analyses were used.

• *Criterion 2: Probably efficacious treatment.* There must be at least two good experiments showing that the treatment is superior (statistically significant so) to a wait-list control group, or one or more good experiments meeting the criteria for well-established treatments with the one exception of having been conducted in two independent research settings and by different investigatory teams.

• *Criterion 3: Possibly efficacious treatment.* There must be at least one good study showing the treatment to be efficacious in the absence of conflicting evidence.

• *Criterion 4: Experimental treatment.* The treatment has not yet been tested in trials meeting established criteria for methodology.

Nathan and Gorman (2002) developed a list of six types of treatment studies that vary along the levels of evidence each provides in support of a treatment. In their typology, *Type 1 studies* are the most rigorous and involved randomized, prospective clinical trial methodology. These types of studies include comparison groups with random assignment, blinded assessments, clear presentation of inclusion and exclusion criteria, state-of-the art diagnostic methods, adequate sample size with sufficient statistical power, and clearly described statistical methods. *Type 2 studies* are clinical trials in which an intervention is tested with at least one aspect of the Type 1 requirements missing. For example, a Type 2 study might not use blinded assessments or might not have adequate statistical power to detect a moderate effect. *Type 3 studies* are methodologically limited and involve open enrollment or trials aimed at collecting pilot data to determine if more rigorous designs are warranted. *Type 4 studies* are reviews with secondary data analyses such as meta-analyses. *Type 5 studies* are literature reviews that do not use secondary data analyses. *Type 6 studies* are case studies, essays, and opinion/position papers.

Single-Case Experimental Designs

The guidelines for well-established, probably efficacious, possibly efficacious, and experimental treatments specified by the various divisions of the American Psychological Association included only group experimental designs and did not specify what criteria should be used to evaluate the quality of studies using single-case experimental designs. This is a glaring omission that ignores a huge body of excellent research on SEL interventions using single-case experimental design methodology. For example, virtually all of the SEL intervention research literature for children with autism spectrum disorder (ASD) has used single-case research design methodology.

Single-case designs (SCDs) are interrupted time series designs that provide a rigorous experimental evaluation of intervention effects (Horner et al., 2005a; Kratochwill et al., 2010). SCDs have many variations, but always involve repeated, systematic measurement of a dependent variable before, during, and after the manipulation of an independent variable (i.e., a treatment). These designs provide a strong basis for establishing causal inferences and are widely used in clinical psychology, school psychology, special education, and applied behavior analysis. Experimental control in SCDs is established by replication of an intervention in an experiment using one of the following methods: (1) introduction, withdrawal, or reversal of the independent variable (e.g., ABAB designs); (2) iterative manipulation of the independent variable across different observational phases (e.g., multielement or alternating treatment designs); or (3) staggered introduction of the independent variable across different points in time or in different settings–contexts such as morning, noon, and afternoon recess (e.g., multiple baseline design) (Horner et al., 2005a).

SCDs answer the following questions using variations in the experimental design:

- Does an intervention (withdrawal, multielement, multiple baseline, and changing criterion designs) work?
- Does one intervention (reversal designs with a simple phase change, multielement designs, multiple baseline designs) work better than another?
- Do different intervention elements (reversal designs with complex phase changes, multielement designs, multiple baseline designs comparing different conditions) interact to produce behavior change?
- Do treatment effects maintain after treatment is withdrawn (sequential withdrawal design, partial-withdrawal design, partial sequential withdrawal design, multiple baseline designs with withdrawal of treatment)?

In SCD research, *replication* is a key mechanism for controlling threats to internal *validity*. Horner et al. (2005a) stated that replication is established when the design documents *three demonstrations* of the experimental effect at *three different points in time* with a single case. Experimental control is established when the predicted changes in the dependent variable covary with manipulation of the independent variable.

Three major criteria are used to establish an experimental effect: level, trend, and variability. "Level" refers to the mean score for the data within a phase. "Trend" refers to the slope of the best-fitting straight line for the data within a phase. "Variability" refers to the fluctuation of the data around the mean (e.g., range or standard deviation [SD]). In addition to these three criteria, four other criteria are used to determine an experimental effect: immediacy of the effect, the proportion of overlap in the data, the consistency of the data across phases, and comparing observed and projected patterns of the outcome variable.

Kratochwill et al. (2010) established the following rules to determine if a study's design meets evidence standards, meets evidence standards with reservations, or does not meet evidence standards. In order to meet evidence standards, the following design criteria must be present:

- The independent variable (i.e., the intervention) must be systematically manipulated with the researcher determining when and how the independent variable's conditions change. If this standard is not met, the study does not meet evidence standards.
- Each outcome variable must be measured systematically over time by more than one observer, and the study needs to collect interobserver agreement (IOA) in each phase and on at least 20% of the data points in each condition. IOA must meet minimal standards of 80% for percentage agreement or .60 using Cohen's kappa. If these standards are not met, the study does not meet evidence standards.

The study must include at least three attempts to demonstrate an intervention effect at three different points in time or with three different phase repetitions. If this standard is not met, the study does not meet evidence standards. For a phase to qualify as an attempt to demonstrate an effect, the phase must have a minimum of three data points.

Visual inspection of graphed data is by far the most common way researchers using SCDs analyze their data (Horner et al., 2005a; Kratochwill et al., 2010). Effects of intervention are determined by comparing baseline levels of performance to during and/or postintervention levels of performance to detect experimental treatment effects. Unlike statistical analyses, SCDs uses the "interocular" test of significance to determine an effect. Visual analysis typically takes place in four steps. First, a predictable baseline pattern is documented. Second, data within each phase is examined to assess within-phase patterns. Third, phase data are compared to data in the adjacent phases to assess whether manipulation of the independent variable is associated with an effect. Fourth, all information from all phases is integrated to determine if there are at least three demonstrations of an effect at a minimum of three different points in time.

Kratochwill et al. (2010) made the following recommendations for combining studies using SCDs:

- A minimum of five SCD research papers examining the intervention that meet evidence standards or meet evidence standards with reservations must be published in peer-reviewed jornals.
- The SCD studies must be conducted by at least three different research teams at three different geographic locations.
- The combined number of experiments (i.e., single-case design examples) across the papers totals at least 20.

THE VALUE OF META-ANALYTIC FINDINGS

The use of quantitative synthesis techniques, or meta-analyses, was relatively unknown in the social sciences prior to the 1970s. Three landmark meta-analyses squarely placed quantitative syntheses as a standard practice in psychology: Smith and Glass's (1977) meta-analysis of the psychotherapy outcome literature, Schmidt and Hunter's (1977) meta-analysis regarding validity generalization in the employment testing literature, and Rosenthal and Rubin's (1978) meta-analysis of the interpersonal expectancy effect in social psychology. By the early 1980s, several books devoted exclusively to meta-analytic methods appeared in the literature (Glass, McCaw, & Smith, 1981; Hedges & Olkin, 1985; Rosenthal, 1984).

A central goal of scientific research is to answer the question of causation. For example, we may want to know if a particular "dosage" of a SEL intervention makes a difference in children's social skill functioning. If most of the studies on this topic had high internal validity (i.e., random assignment to conditions), then the meta-analyst can ask questions about causation (higher doses of the intervention produces greater changes in social behavior). In contrast, if most of the studies in the meta-analysis have low internal validity (contrasting preexisting groups), then the meta-analysis can answer questions of covariation among variables, but not causation (correlation vs. causation).

The systematic quantitative integration over a number of primary studies allows one to get a notion of the external validity of an effect. For example, a researcher may be interested in the efficacy of SEL interventions with a particular diagnostic group such as children diagnosed with attention-deficit/hyperactivity disorder (ADHD). In this case, the efficacy of SEL interventions is more conceptually narrow than asking the question of whether SEL interventions are effective across diagnostic groups (ADHD, ASD, conduct disorder [CD], and oppositional defiant disorder [ODD]).

A major advantage of meta-analysis is that the primary studies being synthesized, by definition, involve multiple operationalizations of both independent and dependent variables. Aggregating results across multiple studies allows for the meta-analyst to capture different aspects of a given construct. For example, social skills outcome studies often involve multiple and different operationalizations of dependent variables. Some studies use systematic direct observations of social skills, other studies use peer sociometrics or acceptance ratings, and still other studies use teacher or parent ratings of social skills. The convergence of findings from studies varying in methodology increases confidence in the validity of an effect.

Both primary and meta-analytic research methods are complementary. Meta-analyses obviously cannot be conducted in the absence of primary studies and primary studies that are not properly integrated and quantified cannot inform theory and practice. Both forms of research inform future research and advance knowledge about phenomena. Subsequent chapters in this book on universal, selected, and intensive SEL interventions will review meta-analytic findings and make recommendations to readers based on this information.

- The primary goal of research methodologies is to allow professionals to draw valid inferences from controlled research that are not confounded or disconfirmed by plausible rival hypotheses.

- Some professionals choose from science those concepts and practices that are consistent with their preexisting beliefs, attitudes, and past practices and ignore scientific findings that are inconsistent with these beliefs.

- Different fields have different criteria and standards that they use to identify and establish acceptable levels of scientific evidence.

- Research evidence is best thought of as existing on a continuum anchored by evidence-based and non-evidence-based poles.

- The hierarchical method of evaluating scientific evidence is recommended because it considers a range of evidence generated by different research methods.

- EBPs involve making clinical decisions for treatments based on a review of information from rigorous research.

- Evidence-based treatments are treatments that have been shown to be efficacious through rigorous research methods that have good internal validity and can be considered efficacy-based research.

- EBPs are treatment approaches rather than a specific intervention applied to an individual and can be considered effectiveness-based research.

- Multiple types of research evidence varying in quality are used to support EBPs; they include observation, qualitative and mixed methods, single-case designs, epidemiological research, moderator–mediator analyses, randomized controlled trials, effectiveness studies, and meta-analyses.

- The IES supports research ranging from translational research to the evaluation of interventions implemented at scale.

- Goal 1 studies are termed exploration studies because they explore relations between educational outcomes and malleable factors, or those factors that can be changed.

- Goal 2 studies focus on developing educational interventions, programs practices, and products designed to improve existing education interventions.

- Goal 3 studies involve efficacy or replication studies using experimental and quasi-experimental designs.

- Goal 4 studies are designed to test interventions that have already demonstrated efficacy and are implemented at scale.

- Goal 5 studies are designed to develop and validate measurement instruments that are intended for use by practitioners for screening, progress monitoring, and outcome assessments.

- Four types of validity are considered in research studies: internal validity, external validity, construct validity, and statistical conclusion validity.

- Various divisions within the American Psychological Association have classified research studies on the basis of scientific evidence as follows: (1) well-established treatments, (2) probably efficacious treatments, (3) possibly efficacious treatments, and (4) experimental treatments.

- Nathan and Gorman (2002) classified research evidence into six types: Type 1 studies (randomized controlled trials), Type 2 studies (less rigorous than Type 1 studies), Type 3 studies (quasi-experimental designs), Type 4 studies (meta-analyses), Type 5 studies (narrative literature reviews), and Type 6 studies (case studies or position papers).

- SCDs consist of well-controlled research on a small number of individuals and are often used with low-incidence populations.

- Meta-analyses are a useful way of quantifying a literature by multiply operationalizing both independent and dependent variables.

CHAPTER THREE

Assessment of Social–Emotional Learning Skills

This chapter describes various types of assessment strategies that are important for understanding and dealing effectively with social skills deficits in children and youth. Effective SEL interventions must be based on psychometrically sound social skills assessment methods and strategies. The main purpose of social skills assessment is to gather information that will lead to correct decisions about targeted individuals. Five types of decisions are typically made in this assessment process: (1) screening decisions, (2) identification and classification decisions, (3) intervention decisions, (4) progress-monitoring decisions, and (5) evaluation of intervention outcome decisions.

One way of thinking about these various types of decisions is to conceptualize them as different types of "tests." For instance, a *screening test* looks for indicators of the possible presence of a specific problem or disease. A hearing screening test detects the possible presence of hearing loss. A *diagnostic test* looks for the presence of some problem or disease. A blood test for HIV is used to diagnose individuals suffering from this condition. A *treatment decision test* is designed to guide intervention decisions. A person with high blood pressure may be prescribed medication to control this condition. A *monitoring test* tracks the progress of a disease. Yearly blood work involving a cholesterol panel is used to monitor a patient's response to antistatin medication. Similar types of decisions are made in the assessment of social skills in children and youth.

SCREENING DECISIONS

The evaluation of an entire population to determine if they require more specialized, expensive, and comprehensive assessments is the goal of screening decisions. Screening tools have the advantage of being brief, inexpensive, and easy to administer and score. Screening for ESL skills deficits early in a child's school career is an essential aspect of prevention of more serious social difficulties later in the child's life. The longer children go without effective SEL interventions, the more resistant their social behavior will be to change later in their school careers (Bierman & Greenberg, 1996).

Screening tools must have reliable and valid cutoff scores to correctly identify children and youth who do and who do not have ESL skills deficits. Figure 3.1 shows the various decisions that can be made with screening tools. True positives reflect that an individual screened positive for ESL skill deficits and actually does have these deficits. This is called the *sensitivity* of the screening instrument. A false positive occurs when an individual screened positive for deficits, but in reality does not have these deficits. False negatives occur when a person screens negative for deficits, but actually does have these deficits. True negatives occur when an individual screens negative for deficits and does not have these deficits. This is termed the *specificity* of the screening instrument. It should be noted that in making screening decisions, it is more acceptable to make higher rates of false positive decisions than false negative decisions. This is because the consequences of overlooking children with social skills deficits are more serious than providing additional support to students who really do not need it (Lane, Oakes, Menzies, & Germer, 2014).

The Social Skills Improvement System Social–Emotional Learning Assessment System

The Social Skills Improvement System Social–Emotional Learning Assessment System (SELA) was inspired by the CASEL model of SEL competencies and provides multilevel performance rubrics to help educators systematically determine which students are likely to need SEL interventions. These criterion-referenced rubrics can also help to establish whether or not students who have received an intervention have improved in their personal and interpersonal behaviors and related academic skills. The SELA is a universal screening tool that can provide baseline information prior to or near the start of a program of instruction. It can be used to efficiently monitor

	Social Skill Deficit Present	Social Skill Deficit Absent
Screen +	True Positive (Sensitivity)	False Positive (False Alarm)
Screen −	False Negative (Broken Alarm)	True Negative (Specificity)

FIGURE 3.1. Screening decisions for SEL.

progress and rescreen students during and after completion of instruction. This helps track and monitor improvement for the skill areas targeted for instruction.

The SELA measures preschool through secondary level students' skills against age-level expectations in eight performance areas: *Self-Awareness, Self-Management, Social Awareness, Relationship Skills, Responsible Decision Making, Motivation to Learn, Reading,* and *Mathematics.* Internal reliability estimates based on coefficient alpha was .93, for the SELA Composite, and test–retest reliability for the SELA Composite was .89. Using receiver operator curve (ROC) analyses, the SELA discriminated socially at-risk from socially not-at-risk groups at a .92 level. Sensitivity (true positive) and specificity (true negative) were 60.5% and 92.4%, respectfully.

The BASC-3 Behavioral and Emotional Screening System

The BASC-3 Behavioral and Emotional Screening System (BASC-3 BESS; Kamphaus & Reynolds, 2015) is a brief universal screening system for measuring behavioral and emotional strengths and weakness in children and adolescents ages 2–19 years. The instruments are designed for use by schools, mental health clinics, pediatric clinics, and researchers for a variety of behavioral and emotional disorders that may lead to adjustment problems. The screening system includes three forms that can be used individually or in combination: Teacher, Parent, and Student Self-Report (grades 3–12) form. Each form ranges from 25 to 30 items, requires no formal training for raters, and is easy to complete, taking approximately 5–10 minutes of administration time. The BASC-3 BESS assesses a wide array of behaviors that represent both behavioral problems and social–emotional strengths and includes internalizing problems, externalizing problems, school problems, and adaptive skills (i.e., social skills). Spanish language versions are available for the Parent and Student Self-Report forms.

The BASC-3 BESS is a norm-referenced instrument and provides percentile ranks and T scores (mean = 50, SD = 10) that are used to determine level of risk. The scoring report yields cutoff points at three levels: *normal, elevated,* and *extremely elevated.* The scale has very good psychometric properties with test–retest reliability coefficients ranging from .80 to .91 across the three raters. Interrater reliabilities using mothers and fathers were around .83 and those for teachers were .80. Correlations between the BASC-3 BESS and the full-scale BASC-3 scale were .76 for externalizing problems, .52 for internalizing problems, .82 for school problems, and .82 for adaptive (social) skills. Overall, the BASC-3 BESS functions very well as a screening tool to identify children and youth who have both behavioral difficulties and adaptive social skill strengths.

IDENTIFICATION AND CLASSIFICATION DECISIONS

Assessment tools for making identification and classification decisions are necessarily more time-consuming and expensive than tools for making screening decisions. The most common types of assessment tools for making these decisions are behavior rating scales. Several social skills rating scales are currently available; however, only four of them have sufficiently large and representative standardization samples, adequate psychometric properties, and customer-friendly availability from reputable test publishers. These scales are (1) the Social Skills Improvement System Social–Emotional Learning Edition—Rating Scales (Gresham & Elliott, 2008); (2) the Walker–McConnell Scales of Social Competence and School Adjustment (Walker & McConnell, 1995); (3) the School Social Behavior Scales (Merrell, 1993); and (4) the Preschool and Kindergarten Behavior Scales (Merrell, 1994).

For a more comprehensive review of measures of children's social functioning, I recommend two recent reviews: Crowe, Beauchamp, Catroppa, and Anderson (2011) and Humphrey et al. (2011). Crowe et al. (2011) identified 86 measures in the research literature on social functioning assessment tools for children and adolescents, while Humphrey et al. (2011) identified 189 such measures, but focused on 12 that met rigorous psychometric criteria.

The Social Skills Improvement System Social–Emotional Learning Edition—Rating Scales

The Social Skills Improvement System Social–Emotional Learning Edition—Rating Scales SSIS-SEL Edition-RS (Gresham & Elliott, 2017) are a revision of the SSIS-RS (Gresham & Elliott, 2008). The SSIS-SEL-Edition RS is a multirater series of scales (teacher, parent, and student) and is standardized on a nationally representative sample of 4,700 children and adolescents ages 3–18 years. These rating scales are designed to assess each of the five SEL competencies identified by CASEL (2015): self-awareness, self-management, social awareness, relationship skills, and responsible decision making.

Each of the forms (teacher, parent, and student) can be completed in 10 minutes or less. The teacher form contains 51 SEL items distributed across the five CASEL domains and seven items that measure students' academic competence. The parent form contains 51 SEL items, and the student form contains 46 SEL items. Each item is rated on a 4-point Likert scale measuring the frequency of the SEL behavior (0 = "Never," 1 = "Sometimes," 2 = "Often," 3 = "Always"). Scores on the five CASEL subscales are expressed as standard scores (mean = 100, SD = 15). The teacher form is available in English and the parent and student forms are available in English and Spanish.

The SSIS-SEL Edition-RS teacher, parent, and student forms offer a Response Pattern Index to help detect a response set that might indicate inattentive or careless responding. This index is a count of the number of times a rating differs from the rating to the previous item. A very low count indicates the respondent tended to use the same rating across items. A very high count suggests that the respondent may have rated items in an alternating or cyclical pattern. Scores at the extremes are unusual and may signal a problem in the ratings.

The SSIS-SEL Edition-RS have strong psychometric properties in terms of internal consistency and test–retest reliability estimates. Median subscale reliabilities of the Social Skills and Academic Competence Scales are in the mid- to upper .90s for each age group on each form. Median subscale reliabilities are in the high .80s for the Teacher form, the mid-.80s for the Parent form, and .80 for the Student form. Test–retest reliabilities for the Composite Scale are .82 for the Teacher form, .84 for the Parent form, and .81 for the Student form.

Extensive data are presented in the SSIS-SEL Edition-RS manual for validity evidence including substantial correlations with the Behavior Assessment System–2, the Vineland Adaptive Behavior Scale, the Walker–McConnell Scale of Social Competence and School Adjustment, and the Home and Community Social Behavior Scales (Gresham & Elliott, 2017). The SSIS-SEL Edition-RS manual presents extensive evidence for the structural validity of the scales, as well as evidence showing that the scales differentiate between the standardization sample and special populations (e.g., ADHD, emotional disturbance, intellectual disability, speech/language impairment, and specific learning disabilities).

Some Considerations in Using the SSIS-SEL Edition-RS

In Chapter 1 I made an important distinction between social skills acquisition deficits and social skills performance deficits. Acquisition deficits can best be thought of as "can't do" problems and result from deficits in social-cognitive skills. They indicate a lack of knowledge regarding how to enact a given social skill. Performance deficits can best be thought of as "won't do" problems and result primarily from a lack of motivation to perform a social skill rather than a lack of knowledge concerning how to perform that skill. Dating back to the Social Skills Rating System (SSRS; Gresham & Elliott, 1990) and later with the SSIS-RS (Gresham & Elliott, 2008), we recommended using a combination of frequency and importance ratings to distinguish between social skills acquisition and social skills performance deficits.

The SSIS-SEL Edition-RS identifies social skills strengths, acquisition deficits, and performance deficits based on the standard scores of the five CASEL domains. A CASEL domain standard score of >115 and an item rating of 3 ("Always") identifies an SEL strength. A CASEL domain standard score of <85 and an item rating of 1 ("Sometimes") identifies a social skills performance deficit. A CASEL domain score of <85 and an item rating of 0 ("Never") identifies an SEL acquisition deficit.

The School Social Behavior Scales–2

The School Social Behavior Scales–2 (SSBS-2; Merrell & Candarella, 2008) is a 65-item teacher rating scale measuring two domains of social behavior: social competence and antisocial behavior. It was standardized on a sample of 2,280 children and adolescents ages 5–18 years. Each item on the SSBS-2 is rated on a 5-point Likert scale (from 1 = "never" to 5 = "frequently"). The total Social Competence and the total Antisocial Behavior scores are expressed as standard score (mean = 100, SD = 15) and percentile ranks.

The SSBS-2 has good psychometric properties with internal consistency estimates ranging from .91 to .98 and 3-week test–retest reliabilities ranging from .76 to .83. Interrater reliabilities between resource teachers and paraprofessional aides range from .72 to .83 for the Social Competence scale and from .53 to .71 for the Antisocial Behavior scale. The SSBS has been shown to correlate with several other social skills behavior rating scales including the Social Skills Rating System (Gresham & Elliott, 1990) and the Walker–McConnell Scales of Social Competence and School Adjustment (Walker & McConnell, 1995). The structural validity of the scale was established through confirmatory factor analyses.

The Preschool and Kindergarten Behavior Scales–2

The Preschool and Kindergarten Behavior Scales–2 (PKBS-2; Merrell, 2003) is a norm-referenced teacher or parent behavior rating scale that measures two dimensions of social behavior: *Social Skills* and *Social Behavior*. The scales were standardized on 3,315 children between the ages of 3 and 6 years. The Social Skills scale consists of three subscales: *Social*

Competence, Social Interaction, and *Social Independence.* The Social Behavior scale consists of seven subscales: *Self-Centered/Explosive, Attention Problems/Overactivity, Antisocial Aggression, Social Withdrawal, Anxiety/Somatic Complaints, Externalizing Problems,* and *Internalizing Problems.* Scores on the scales are expressed as standard scores (mean = 100, SD = 15) and percentile ranks. Internal consistency estimates for the scales range from .96 to .97 for the Social Skills and Social Behavior scales and from .81 to .95 for the subscales. Test–retest reliabilities range from .62 to .87 and interrater reliabilities range from .36 to .63. Validity evidence of the scales was established by correlations with other measures of social skills and factor analyses of the scales.

Sociometric Assessment

Early screening and identification of those children who are having difficulties with peers is an important consideration because of the long-term predictive validity of poor peer acceptance (Prinstein et al., 2009). A substantial research base shows that children who are strongly disliked by peers are less likely to complete secondary education, to develop long-term romantic relationships, or to demonstrate vocational competence as adults (Coie, Lochman, Terry, & Hyman, 1992; Connolly & Johnson, 1996; Nelson & Dishion, 2004). Longitudinal studies also have shown that children who are rejected by their peers have much higher rates of externalizing (aggression, delinquent, and oppositional behavior) and internalizing (social withdrawal, depression, and anxiety) behavior patterns (Hoza, Molina, Bukowski, & Sippola, 1995; Coie et al., 1990). Despite this well-established evidence base showing the importance of sociometric status, there are a number of practical and ethical concerns in using sociometric assessment procedures to identify children who have problematic interpersonal relationships with peers (Landau & Milich, 1990; Merrell, 1999; Walker et al., 2004).

There are two basic methods that have been used in the sociometric assessment literature: peer ratings and peer nominations. *Peer ratings* of social acceptance requires that children rate each other on a 3-, 5-, or 7-point Likert scale with the number of points on the scale being based on the child's age (Asher & McDonald, 2009). Typically, children are asked to rate their peers on these scales according to how much they would like to play with or work with each other in the classroom. These ratings are subsequently averaged and standardized using z scores within class or grade (mean = 0, SD = 1). These scores can be expressed as a continuous variable or children can be classified into low, average, and high acceptance groups.

Peer nominations require children to nominate peers according to liked most and liked least categories. Usually, children are asked to nominate three peers they like most and three peers they like least, although some studies have allowed for an unlimited number of nominations. One of the most innovative and influential use of peer nominations comes from the work of Coie, Dodge, and Coppotelli (1982) who developed a sociometric classification system that allows for five status groups: (1) popular, (2) rejected, (3) neglected, (4) controversial, and (5) average. This approach was largely based on earlier work by Peery (1979) who developed a similar system.

This classification system greatly increases the sensitivity and utility of sociometric assessment results. With this method, students are asked to select from a class roster three peers they like most and three peers they like least. For each student, the number of liked most (LM) and liked least (LL) choices received are summed, thereby creating LM and LL raw scores for each child. These raw scores, in turn, are standardized into z scores and used to calculate *social preference* (LM – LL) and *social impact* (LM + LL) scores. The five sociometric status groups are defined as follows: (1) popular (high social preference and high social impact), (2) rejected (low social preference and high social impact), (3) neglected (low social preference and low social impact), (4) controversial (mixed social preference and high social impact), and (5) average (average social preference and average social impact). Figure 3.2 shows the percentage of children who are typically classified into each of these five sociometric status groups.

Quite clearly, there is a large research literature that has established the importance of and predictive validity of low peer acceptance or peer rejection in a child's social development. Several characteristics of sociometric data, however, limit their routine use in identifying children with social skills deficits. First, it is important to distinguish between *peer-preferred* and *teacher-preferred* social skills. Walker et al. (1992) provided empirical data regarding specific adaptive and maladaptive behavioral correlates of peer-related and teacher-related adjustment. Peer-related adaptive behaviors include such things as defending peers, leading peers, complimenting peers, and affiliating with peers. These behaviors are related to a positive sociometric status and peer acceptance. However, teacher-related adjustment behaviors have a substantially different behavioral topography and outcomes. These behaviors include such things as compliance with teacher directives, following classroom rules, paying attention to instruction, and asking for help from adults. Gresham and Elliott (2008) have identified the top 10 teacher-preferred social skills, which are highly predictive of teacher acceptance and student academic performance.

Second, various meta-analyses of the social skills training literature show that sociometric measures are notoriously insensitive in detecting short-term treatment effects. Beelman, Pfingsten, and Losel (1994) showed the lowest effect sizes in SEL interventions for indices of sociometric status ($d = 0.13$) that is a very weak effect. Jiang and Cillessen (2005) in their

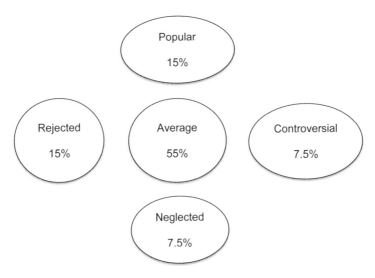

Popular: High Social Preference and High Social Impact
Rejected: Low Social Preference and High Social Impact
Neglected: Low Social Preference and Low Social Impact
Controversial: Mixed Social Preference and High Social Impact
Average: Average Social Preference and Average Social Impact

FIGURE 3.2. Classification of sociometric statuses.

meta-analysis of 77 studies involving 18,339 participants showed moderate-to-high stability of sociometric dimensions of acceptance, rejection, social preference, and peer ratings. This suggests that sociometric status is not likely to show responsiveness or sensitivity to change within the context of relatively short-term SEL interventions.

Third, although social skills deficits may be related to low sociometric status (at least for peer-preferred social skills), they are certainly not the only explanation for peer unpopularity (e.g., others include physical attractiveness vs. unattractiveness, positive or negative reputational biases, critical negative behavioral events, cross-sex nominations). Moreover, Newcomb, Bukowski, and Pattee (1993) in their meta-analysis showed relatively weak correlations (average $r = .20-.30$) between various sociometric statuses and specific behaviors measured by other methods such as teacher ratings, self-ratings, and systematic direct observations. In short, a consistent finding in the SEL intervention literature over the past 35 years demonstrates that sociometric status has been particularly resistant to change within the context of short-term interventions and is not strongly related to indices of prosocial behavior measured by other measurement methods (Beelman et al., 1994; Bierman & Powers, 2009; Cook, Browning-Wright, Gresham, & Burns, 2010; Gresham et al., 2004; Schneider, 1992).

Fourth, on an entirely practical level, most institutional review boards (IRBs) will most likely require that parental permission be obtained for each and every child in a classroom before administering sociometric measures. Obtaining such parental consent is untenable, expensive, and not a judicious use of resources. As many as 25% of students in classrooms may not have parental permission to participate in sociometric assessment activities. It is unclear how this might influence the accuracy of a sociometric assessment.

INTERVENTION DECISIONS

Although screening tools, behavior rating scales, and sociometric assessment methods can identify individuals having social skills deficits, these assessment methods do not inform the selection of intervention procedures. In other words, these methods can tell us *what* children have social skills deficits, but they cannot tell us *why* these deficits are occurring. An important consideration in the conceptualization of social skills deficits is the influence of *competing problem behaviors* on an individual's level of social skills. Recall in Chapter 1 I referred to these behaviors as being *academic disablers* because they interfere with the acquisition or performance of basic academic skills. These competing problem behaviors might also be thought of as *social disablers* because they compete with, interfere, or block the exhibition of a given social skill. Competing problem behaviors can be broadly classified as *externalizing* behavior patterns (e.g., noncompliance, aggression, impulsive behaviors) or *internalizing* behavior patterns (e.g., social withdrawal, anxiety, depression).

For example, a child with a history of noncompliance, oppositional behavior, and impulsive behavior may never learn prosocial behavior alternatives such as sharing, cooperation, and self-control because of the absence of opportunities to learn these behaviors caused by the competing *function* of these externalizing behaviors (Eddy, Reid, & Curry, 2002). Similarly, a child with a history of social anxiety, social withdrawal, and shyness may never learn appropriate social behaviors because of avoidance of the peer group, thereby creating an absence of opportunities to learn peer-related social skills (Gresham, Van, & Cook, 2006).

In Chapter 1, I also discussed the distinction between social skills *acquisition deficits* and social skills *performance deficits*. Acquisition deficits are "can't do" deficits that occur due to a lack of knowledge or learning concerning how to enact a given social skill. Earlier in this chapter, I described an assessment method for identifying these types of social skills deficits (i.e., scoring at the 10th percentile or below of a norm-referenced social skills rating scale). In contrast, social skills performance deficits are "won't do" deficits and are due primarily to motivational variables. I recommended that scoring between the 11th and 16th percentile on a norm-referenced social skills rating scale could identify these deficits.

One of the most conceptually powerful learning principles that can be used to explain the relationship between social skills performance deficits and competing problem behaviors is the m*atching law* described in Chapter 1 (Herrnstein, 1961, 1970), which states that the relative rate of a given behavior matches the relative rate of reinforcement for that behavior. In other words, response rate matches reinforcement rate.

Maag (2005) suggested that one way to decrease competing problem behaviors is to teach RBTs. The RBT concept may help solve many of the problems described in the social skills training literature such as poor generalization and maintenance, sometimes modest effect sizes, and the social invalidity of target behavior selection. The goal of RBT is to identify a prosocial behavior that will "replace" the competing problem behavior. Conceptually, RBT depends entirely on identifying *functionally equivalent behaviors*. Behaviors are said to be functionally equivalent if they produce similar amounts of relevant reinforcement from the environment (i.e., they follow the matching law). Table 3.1 shows some examples of competing problem behaviors and their positive replacement behaviors.

Functional Behavioral Assessment

Researchers and practitioners are increasingly using functional behavioral assessment (FBA) methods to match intervention strategies to behavioral function in order to enhance the effectiveness of interventions. Research over the past 30 years in the field of applied behavior analysis indicates that FBA methods contribute to beneficial outcomes for children and youth (Cooper, Heron, & Heward, 2007).

FBA can be defined as a systematic process for identifying events that reliably predict and maintain behavior. FBA uses a variety of methods for gathering information about antecedents (i.e., events that precede and trigger the occurrence of behavior) and consequences (i.e., consequent events that maintain behavior). Knowledge of the conditions maintaining problem behavior can be used to discontinue or control sources of reinforcement for that behavior and to teach adaptive, functionally equivalent behaviors instead (Cooper et al., 2007). It should be emphasized that FBA is not a single test or observation, but rather it involves a collection of assessment methods to determine the antecedents, behaviors, and consequences. The major goal of FBA is to identify environmental conditions that are associated with the occurrence and nonoccurrence of behavior.

The function of behavior refers to the *purpose* that behavior serves for an individual in a particular setting or situation. Fundamentally, there

TABLE 3.1. Replacement Behaviors for Disruptive Behavior Problems

Disruptive behavior	Replacement behavior
• Often bullies, threatens, or intimidates others.	• Acts responsibly when with others.
• Often initiates physical fights.	• Resolves disagreements calmly.
• Has been physically cruel to people.	• Is nice to others when they feel bad.
• Has deliberately destroyed others' property.	• Takes care when using other people's things.
• Often loses temper.	• Makes a compromise during a conflict.
• Is often touchy or easily annoyed.	• Takes criticism without getting upset.
• Often deliberately annoys others.	• Takes responsibility for his or her actions.
• Argues with adults (parents and teachers).	• Speaks in an appropriate tone of voice.
• Often blames others for his or her mistakes.	• Takes responsibility for his or her own mistakes.
• Is often angry and resentful.	• Interacts well with children and adults.

are only two functions of behavior: (1) positive reinforcement that involves anything that brings behavior into contact with a positively reinforcing stimulus and (2) negative reinforcement that involves escape from, avoidance of, delay of, or reduction of an aversive or negatively reinforcing stimulus. In other words, behaviors serving a positive reinforcement function allow the individual to "get something preferred" and behaviors serving a negative reinforcement function allow the individual to "get out of something nonpreferred." For example, if a child engages in disruptive classroom behavior and receives frequent peer attention for this behavior, it is likely being positively reinforced by contingent peer attention. In contrast, if a child engages in disruptive classroom behavior while he or she should be completing math work sheets, chances are that this behavior is being negatively reinforced by avoidance of math work sheet exercises.

The above two functions of behavior can be further divided into five categories: (1) access to tangible reinforcement or preferred activities (positive tangible reinforcement); (2) social attention/communication (positive social reinforcement); (3) escape from, avoidance of, delay of, or reduction of aversive tasks or activities (negative reinforcement); (4) escape from or avoidance of other individuals (negative social reinforcement); and (5) internal stimulation (automatic or sensory positive reinforcement).

FBA Process and Procedures

The FBA process takes place in the following sequence: (1) FBA interviews that are used to guide systematic direct observations of behavior; (2) systematic direct observations that can be done by teachers, behavior specialists, or school psychologists; (3) formulation of behavioral hypothesis statements that includes the conditions likely to produce the problem behaviors, delineation of the problem behaviors, identification of positive replacement behaviors, and consequent events that appear to maintain the behaviors; and (4) specification of behavioral interventions based on this information. These interventions might involve changing the conditions that evoke the problem behaviors, teaching positive replacement behaviors, and altering the consequences that are maintaining the problem behaviors.

FBA methods can be either indirect or direct procedures for determining behavioral function. Indirect methods are removed in time and place from the actual occurrence of behavior. FBA interviews with teachers, parents, and students, review of historical/archival records, and behavior rating scales or checklists are the most frequently used indirect FBA methods. Direct FBA methods assess behavior at the time and place of its actual occurrence and involve systematic direct observation of antecedents, behaviors, and consequences.

Direct observation is used to confirm the information obtained by indirect methods. A useful method for conducting a direct FBA is an antecedent–behavior–consequence, or A-B-C, analysis using a recording form such as the one shown in Figure 3.3. With this procedure, an individual's behavior is observed in naturalistic settings (classroom, playground, or other relevant setting) and the events occurring immediate prior to and following behavior are recorded. It should be noted that only immediate antecedent events can be assessed with this recording form.

Another important class of antecedent events, known as setting events, usually is obtained only through indirect assessment methods. Setting events are antecedents that are removed in time and place from the occurrence of behavior but are functionally related to that behavior. Setting events can exert potentially powerful influences on behavior. Examples of setting events include confrontations on the school bus with peers, physical abuse at home, sleep deprivation, and negative coercive social interactions with parents and siblings in the home.

Behavioral Hypotheses and FBA

Behavioral hypotheses are testable statements regarding the function(s) of behavior that are based on FBA information. There may be several

Time	Antecedent	Behavior	Consequence
9:30 A.M.	Teacher tells student to work quietly on math worksheets.	Student walks around the room and looks at other students.	Teacher says, "Everyone is working, but you. You need to sit down and work on your math worksheets."
11:30 A.M.	Teacher tells class to line up for lunch.	Student is rough housing in line with two other students.	Teacher tells student to stop rough housing.
1:15 P.M.	Teacher tells student to work quietly on language arts worksheets.	Student gets out of seat and wanders around the room.	Teacher tells student to go back to seat and work on worksheets.
2:45 P.M.	Teacher tells class to line up for the bus.	Student stays in seat and looks around the room.	Teacher tells student to line up for the bus.

FIGURE 3.3. A-B-C recording form.

behavioral hypotheses for a single problem behavior. At a minimum, behavioral hypotheses should include the following: (1) setting events, (2) immediate antecedent events, (3) problem behavior, and (4) maintaining consequences. Behavioral hypotheses should be observable, testable, and capable of being accepted or rejected. The following are examples of testable behavioral hypotheses for a child:

- "Frank is more likely to engage in disruptive and noncompliant behaviors when he comes to school without breakfast [setting event] and is asked to complete difficult math tasks [immediate antecedent]." *Hypothesized function: Escape from difficult, nonpreferred tasks.*
- "Frank is more likely to engage in disruptive and noncompliant behaviors during group instruction activities [immediate antecedent] when he has had an altercation with peers before school [setting event]." *Hypothesized function: Peer social attention for disruptive and noncompliant behaviors.*
- "Frank is more likely to engage in disruptive and noncompliant behaviors when he has not had enough sleep [setting event] and

is asked to complete tasks within a cooperative learning situation [immediate antecedent]." *Hypothesized function: Avoidance of nonpreferred activities involving cooperation.*

PROGRESS-MONITORING DECISIONS

To determine if an SEL intervention is being effective, one must collect reliable and valid data for measuring progress. *Progress monitoring* can be defined as a scientifically based practice that is used to assess behavioral performance and evaluate the effectiveness of intervention (Sprague, Cook, Browning-Wright, & Sadler, 2008). Progress monitoring requires frequent and repeated data collection using measures that are sensitive to change. Progress-monitoring tools must meet technical adequacy standards in terms of reliability and validity, must be sensitive to changes in behavior, and be time-efficient so professionals can monitor progress frequently (once or twice a week).

Progress monitoring, if done correctly, will result in desirable outcomes that include (1) data-based decision making, (2) improvements in social behavior, (3) greater accountability by the documentation of individuals' progress, and (4) efficient communication among teachers, parents, and children. Four methods have been frequently used to monitor children's progress in interventions in the area of social skills and problem behaviors: (1) systematic direct observations (SDOs), (2) direct behavior ratings (DBRs), (3) brief behavior ratings (BBRs), and (4) office discipline referrals (ODRs). There are various strengths and weaknesses for each of these methods that will be discussed in the following sections.

Systematic Direct Observations

SDOs are considered by many professionals to be the "gold standard" in the assessment of social skills because they provide a direct measure of an individual's actual behavior in a naturalistic setting (e.g., classroom or playground). SDOs can be used to measure various *dimensions* of behavior such as frequency/rate, temporality (e.g., duration, latency, interresponse times), intensity/magnitude, or permanent products (Cooper et al., 2007). The primary strength of SDOs is that they are *sensitive* to relatively short-term changes in behavior such as a prototypical SEL intervention.

SDOs are based on three fundamental assumptions. First, they are considered to be a sample of an individual's behavior in a specific situation or setting. Second, they involve repeated measurement of behavior over time to establish intraindividual variability that can be used to evaluate

Operational Definition of Prosocial Behavior: Prosocial behavior is defined as behavior directed toward other people that involve effective communication skills, cooperative acts, self-control in difficult situations, and empathic or supportive responses to others who experience a problem. Examples of prosocial behavior include compromising in conflict situations, interacting appropriately with other students, following classroom rules, showing concern for other students, and staying calm when disagreeing with other students.

15 sec.	30 sec.	45 sec.	60 sec.
X	0	0	X
0	0	0	X
X	X	X	0
0	X	0	0
X	0	X	0
0	0	0	0
X	X	X	0
X	0	0	0
0	0	X	0
0	0	X	X
X	0	0	0
0	X	X	0
0	X	0	0
X	X	0	0
0	0	X	0

Total Intervals: 60
Coding: X (behavior occurred in interval); 0 (behavior did not occur in interval)
Possible Scores: 0% to 100% of intervals
Score: 20/60 = 33.3%

FIGURE 3.4. 15-minute partial interval recording form: systematic direct observations.

an individual before, during, and after an SEL intervention. Third, they are considered to provide idiographic data about an individual rather than information about groups of individuals.

Although there are many ways to measure social skills using SDOs, I recommend that professionals consider using the following definition of prosocial behavior: *Prosocial behavior is defined as behavior directed toward other people that involve effective communication skills, cooperative acts, self-control in difficult situations, and empathic or supportive responses to others who experience a problem* (Gresham & Elliott, 2008). This definition of prosocial behavior was used successfully in a federally funded research grant (R324A08113, Frank M. Gresham, Principal Investigator) with high levels of interobserver agreement (average = .90). Employing this definition, prosocial behavior can be measured using a 15-second partial interval recording procedure. Partial interval recording involves observing a behavior for a period of time (e.g., 15 minutes) and if an occurrence of prosocial behavior occurs at any point in the interval, it is scored as having occurred. A 15-minute SDO using partial interval recording will yield 60, 15-minute intervals. An individual's score would be expressed as the percentage of the 60 intervals in which the behavior occurred. Figure 3.4 shows an example of a partial intervals recording procedure.

Although SDOs have several unique advantages, they also have several distinct disadvantages. First, SDOs are an extremely labor-intensive, expensive form of assessment requiring the use of highly trained observers. Second, there is little empirical guidance concerning the number or length of observation sessions needed to secure a representative sample of behavior. Third, SDOs can be influenced by the reactivity of individuals who realize they are being observed, thereby creating an inaccurate measure of behavior.

Direct Behavior Ratings

DBRs are a hybrid assessment tool that have characteristic of SDOs and behavior rating scales. They have been recommended as more practical alternatives to SDOs for progressmonitoring purposes (Cook, Volpe, & Delport, 2014). DBRs are observation tools that meet the following standards: (1) they specific the target behavior(s), (2), they rate behavior(s) at least once per day, (3) they share rating information across individuals (e.g., teachers, parents, and students), and (4) they monitor the effects of intervention (Chafouleas, McDougal, Riley-Tilman, Panahon, & Hilt, 2005; Chafouleas, Riley-Tilman, & McDougal, 2002). DBRs are being increasingly used as progress-monitoring tools because they are time- and resource-efficient methods for measuring behavior change.

DBRs are flexible and can be adapted to meet the needs of any measurement situation. They can vary across individuals, domains of behavior being assessed, the frequency with which behavior is rated (once or twice per day), and/or the rater (teacher, parent, or student). Figure 3.5 presents an example of a DBR for measuring social skills.

Student: ___Frank_____   Grade: _____   Teacher: _____

School: _____   Date: _____

Directions. Review each of the behaviors below. For each behavior, rate the degree to which the student showed the behavior in the classroom today. Please rate the student's behavior for today only.

1. Frank was compliant with teacher instructions today during the math lesson.

1	2	3	4	5	6	7	8	9
	Never/Seldom			Sometimes			Usually/Often	

2. Frank used an appropriate tone of voice during class.

1	2	3	4	5	6	7	8	9
	Never/Seldom			Sometimes			Usually/Often	

3. Frank interacted well with his classmates today.

1	2	3	4	5	6	7	8	9
	Never/Seldom			Sometimes			Usually/Often	

FIGURE 3.5. Direct behavior rating of social skills.

Brief Behavior Ratings

One drawback of relying exclusively on social skills behavior rating scales such as the SSIS-RS, SSBS, and PKBS is that these broadband measures may not be particularly sensitive in detecting short-term treatment effects. One approach in overcoming this limitation is to use *change-sensitive* BBRs to monitor how individuals respond to interventions. This was successfully completed on a federally funded research grant (R324A090098, Frank Gresham, Principal Investigator) and published by Gresham et al. (2010). Using an extant data set collected during a randomized controlled trial examining the effectiveness of an evidence-based intervention (Walker et al., 2009), a 12-item change-sensitive BBR was developed. The results showed that three of the four change-sensitive metrics agreed on the identification of change-sensitive items based on the SSRS (Gresham & Elliott, 1990).

A total of 12 SSRS-Teacher items (out of a total of 56 items) were identified as being the most change-sensitive while still maintaining an adequate level of internal consistency (alpha = .70) and test–retest reliability (r = .71). This 12-item set showed moderate correlation with the Teacher Rating Form (r = .51; Achenbach & Rescorla, 2001). These 12 items are rated on a 4-point scale (0 = "Never," 1 = "Seldom," 2 = "Sometimes," 3 = "Almost always") and are summed to yield a total BBR score. Based on these data, this BBR might be considered a useful General Outcome

Responds appropriately when hit or pushed.

| 0 (Never) | 1 (Seldom) | 2 (Often) | 3 (Almost Always) |

Follows your directions.

| 0 (Never) | 1 (Seldom) | 2 (Often) | 3 (Almost Always) |

Ignores peer distractions.

| 0 (Never) | 1 (Seldom) | 2 (Often) | 3 (Almost Always) |

Cooperates with classmates.

| 0 (Never) | 1 (Seldom) | 2 (Often) | 3 (Almost Always) |

Gives compliments to classmates.

| 0 (Never) | 1 (Seldom) | 2 (Often) | 3 (Almost Always) |

Volunteers to help classmates.

| 0 (Never) | 1 (Seldom) | 2 (Often) | 3 (Almost Always) |

Score Range: 0–18 points

FIGURE 3.6. Brief behavior rating scale.

Measure (GOM) for assessing the effects of SEL interventions (Gresham et al., 2010). Figure 3.6 shows an example of a BBR that could be used as a progress-monitoring tool.

Office Discipline Referrals

ODRs are disciplinary contacts between students and the principal's office that result in written records of the incidents in which the reasons for the referral are noted. Some schools computerize their recording procedures; others use standard referral forms for recording each ODR; still others document the incidents less formally (via narrative accounts). ODRs can be used as a progress-monitoring tool to track participants' behavior in SEL interventions and used as an index of behavioral improvement.

In many schools, it is not unusual for most ODRs to be accounted for by less than 10% of the school population. This indicates that most students receiving ODRs are "return customers." Generally speaking, elementary school students average between zero and one ODR each school year; the corresponding figure for middle school students is much higher at approximately 3.5 ODRs per student per year. McIntosh, Frank, and

Student: _____ Grade: _____

Date: _____ Time: _____ Referring Staff: _____

Location

Playground   Cafeteria   Library   Bathroom   Hallway   Classroom   Other

Minor Problem Behavior	**Major Problem Behavior**	**Possible Motivation**
Inappropriate language	Abusive language	Obtain peer attention
Physical contact	Fighting/physical aggression	Obtain adult attention
Defiance	Overt defiance	Avoid peers
Dress code	Harassment/bullying	Avoid adult
Property misuse	Tardy	Avoid task/activity
Electronic violation	Lying/cheating	Don't know
Other	Other	Other

Administrative Decision

Loss of privilege	Individualized instruction
Time in office	In-school suspension _____ hours/days
Conference with student	Out-of-school suspension _____ hours/days
Parental contact	Other _____

Others Involved in Incident: None   Peers   Staff   Teacher   Substitute   Other

Other Comments: _____

FIGURE 3.7. Office discipline referral form.

Spaulding (2010) analyzed ODRs in 2,500 schools involving more than 990,000 students and found an average ODR rate of 0.59 ($SD = 2.24$) with a range of 0–154 ODRs. Figure 3.7 shows an example of an ODR that can be used as progress monitoring tool.

INTERVENTION OUTCOME DECISIONS

Determining if SEL interventions produce desirable outcomes can be accomplished using various assessment methods. Perhaps the best way of making these intervention outcome decisions would be to use multiple informants of children's social skills to triangulate these outcomes. Presently, there is only one measure of children's and adolescents' social skills that provides information across the three primary informants of teacher, parent, and student; the Social Skills Improvement System—Rating Scales (SSIS-RS; Gresham & Elliott, 2008). This measure is recommended because it utilizes these multiple informants to measure both social skills and competing problem behaviors. The SSIS-Teacher rating scale also provides information on the child's academic performance. I have already reviewed the technical characteristics of the SSIS-RS in a previous section and will not repeat myself here.

The SSIS-RS are particularly well suited to recording specific and observable behaviors. Raters are not asked to interpret a child's thoughts, feelings, motives, or personality traits. As such, behavior rating scales yield more objective, reliable, and valid information than assessments based on high-inference projective techniques or clinical impressions. They also are less costly than individually administered tests and SDOs.

The SSIS-RS were designed with the knowledge that social behavior is influenced by the specific setting an individual is in, and that parents, teachers, and students often attribute different levels of importance to certain social behaviors. With its Teacher, Parent, and Student Forms, the SSIS-RS provide a broad picture of a child's behavior in various settings and from different perspectives.

CHAPTER SUMMARY POINTS

- Five types of decisions are typically made in the social skills assessment and intervention process: (1) screening decisions, (2) identification and classification decisions, (3) intervention decisions, (4) progress-monitoring decisions, and (5) evaluation of intervention outcome decisions.

- Screening decisions involve the evaluation of an entire population to determine if they require more specialized, expensive, and comprehensive assessments.

- True positive identification is the sensitivity of the screening tool and reflects that an individual screened positive for social skills deficits and actually does have these deficits.

- True negative identification is the specificity of a screening tool and reflects that the individual screened negative for social skills deficits and actually does not have these deficits.

- A false positive occurs when an individual screened positive for social skill deficits but does not have these deficits and a false negative occurs when the individual screened negative for social skills deficits but actually does have these deficits.

- Two screening tools that have adequate psychometric properties were discussed: (1) the SELA and (2) the BASC-3 BESS.

- Four social skills rating scales that have adequate technical characteristic and standardization samples were described: (1) the SSIS-SEL Edition-RS, (2) the Walker–McConnell Scales of Social Competence and School Adjustment, (3) the SSBS-2, and (4) the PKBS-2.

- Identification of social skills acquisition deficits using the SSIS-RS identifies those children and youth who score at or below the 10th percentile and identification of social skills performance deficits identifies these individuals who score between the 11th and 16th percentiles.

- Two basic methods are used in sociometric assessment: (1) peer ratings and (2) peer nominations.

- The sociometric classification system developed by Coie et al. (1982) uses social preference and social impact scores to classify children into one of five sociometric status groups: (1) popular, (2) rejected, (3) neglected, (4) controversial, and (5) average.

- Peer-preferred social skills are related to peer acceptance and adjustment whereas teacher-preferred social skills are not related highly to sociometric status.

- Although low sociometric status is predictive of long-term adjustment outcomes, it is expensive, time-consuming, and not a judicious use of resources.

- Acquisition deficits reflect "can't do" problems that occur due to a lack of knowledge or learning whereas performance deficits reflect "won't do" problems that are due primarily to motivational variables.

- A useful way of conceptualizing the relationship between social skill deficits and competing problem behaviors is the matching law, which states that the rate of a behavior will match the rate of reinforcement for that behavior.

- FBA is a systematic process for identifying environmental events that reliably predict and maintain behavior.

- There are two functions of behavior: (1) positive reinforcement (access to tangibles, social attention, automatic/sensory reinforcement) and (2) negative reinforcement (escape from, avoidance of, delay of, or reduction of aversive tasks or activities, escape from or avoidance of other individuals).

- A useful way of conducting an FBA is the use of an A-B-C analysis.

- Behavioral hypotheses are testable statements regarding the function(s) of behavior based on FBA information.

- Four types of progress-monitoring methods were described: (1) systematic direct observations, (2) direct behavior ratings, (3) brief behavior ratings, and (4) office discipline referrals.

- The SSIS-RS was recommended for making intervention outcome decisions because it is the only available measure to use multiple informants (teacher, parent, student) of social skills and problem behaviors.

CHAPTER FOUR

Universal Social–Emotional Learning Interventions

SEL interventions, by necessity, vary in terms of their intensity and duration because not all individuals will require the same "dosage" of an intervention. The U.S. Public Health Service developed a valuable classification system for different levels of intervention. This system classifies the intensity of interventions into three levels: *primary prevention, secondary prevention,* and *tertiary prevention.* Primary prevention refers to intervention approaches designed to keep problems from emerging and their goal is to *prevent harm.* Secondary prevention involves interventions whose goal is to *reverse harm* of children who exhibit social skills deficits. Tertiary prevention refers to interventions for the most at-risk children and youth and whose purpose is to *reduce harm.*

This three-level classification system served as the fundamental basis of what is known today as *response to intervention* (RTI; Gresham, 2002, 2007). RTI is an idea based on determining whether an adequate or inadequate change in behavior has been obtained via the implementation of an evidence-based intervention. In a RTI approach, professionals make decisions regarding changing or intensifying an intervention based on how well or poorly individuals respond to an intervention implemented with integrity. Professionals use RTI to select, change, or titrate interventions based on how individuals respond to those interventions. RTI assumes that if an individual shows an inadequate response to the best intervention available and feasible in a given setting, then that individual can and should be eligible for more intensive interventions.

Universal interventions are those designed to impact all students in the same manner under the same conditions. Each student receives the intervention at the identical "dosage" level, it is delivered in a common format, and is repeated on a daily or weekly basis. These interventions are ideally suited for classwide and schoolwide applications. Examples of universal interventions include vaccinations (for measles, whooping cough, mumps, polio), schoolwide discipline plans (positive behavioral support), and SEL interventions for all students in a school or classroom. In terms of universal, or Tier 1, school-based interventions such as social skills training, it is estimated that approximately 80% of students will respond adequately to these universal interventions.

In contrast, *selected,* or Tier 2, interventions are used for an identified or individually tailored intervention that is fine-tuned to meet the needs of a given student. Examples of selected interventions might include individualized programs designed to remediate oppositional–defiant behaviors or small-group SEL interventions for students who share common social skills deficits. It is estimated that approximately 15% of students will require these selected interventions.

Finally, a very small percentage of students (about 5%) will require the most intense level of intervention that is called *intensive,* or Tier 3, interventions. These interventions are very intense, expensive, and time-consuming and should be reserved for the most severe problems of, at-risk students. Examples of intensive interventions are function-based SEL interventions that will require a functional behavioral assessment (FBA) to design and implement the intervention (see Chapter 5). It is estimated that approximately 5% of students will require this level of intervention.

The aforementioned percentages at each level of intensity are used as a heuristic rather than an established fact. A heuristic can guide thinking but it is not necessarily a blueprint for action (Walker et al., 2004). The heuristic represented by the three levels or tiers and their respective percentages provides a conceptual roadmap for allocating resources, defining populations, and differentiating types of interventions that can be coordinated with each other. Three conclusions can be drawn from this logic: (1) no single tier solves all problems, (2) a well-designed multi-tiered system will have hierarchical tiers of increasing intensity, and (3) effective interventions at a lower-level tier will reduce continuing interventions at more than one level.

One should keep in mind that two sets of descriptors help in understanding the multi-tier model as a heuristic. First, *most, some,* and *few* are related to the commonly cited percentages of students (80%, 15%, 5%). The percentages are not specific numbers, but rather are a general concept. Tier interventions, if designed and delivered well, should meet the needs of *most* students. However, even with an effective universal intervention, *some* students will require more intensive interventions (i.e., Tier 2). If Tiers 1 and 2 are designed and delivered well, there will still be a *few* students who need Tier 3 interventions. The value of treating these numbers as a set of heuristics rather than as empirical criteria is that it allows for thinking about how multi-tiered services are structured and what the intended effect would be.

Second, the concept of *least, more,* and *most* is a way of thinking about the intensity of interventions. Tier 1 interventions should be scientifically based and appropriately intensive with the goal of promoting positive development and preventing problems. These SEL interventions are the focus of this chapter and represent the *least intensive* level of intervention. Tier 2 interventions are characterized by *more* intensive intervention and are the focus of Chapter 5. Tier 3 interventions are the *most* intensive intervention and are described in Chapter 6.

EVIDENCE-BASED UNIVERSAL INTERVENTIONS

SEL interventions involve SEL, in which children and youth acquire and effectively execute knowledge, skills, and attitudes to build and maintain positive interpersonal relationships and make responsible decisions. In 2013, the Collaborative for Academic, Social, and Emotional Learning (CASEL) published an intervention guide describing evidence-based universal SEL intervention programs for preschool through elementary school grades. In 2015, CASEL published a similar guide for middle school through high school; however, the studies reviewed in this guide focused almost exclusively on academic achievement outcomes and will not be reviewed in this chapter. The CASEL guides provide a systematic framework for evaluating the quality of classroom-based SEL programs. The goals of these guides are to give professionals information for selecting and implementing evidence-based SEL programs in schools. To be included in the CASEL guides, programs had to demonstrate the following characteristics: (1) be well-designed classroom-based programs that promote students' social and emotional competence, provide opportunities for practice, and offer multiyear programming; (2) deliver high-quality training and other implementation supports to teachers to ensure sound implementation; and (3) be evidence-based with at least one carefully conducted evaluation documenting positive impacts on student behavior and/or academic performance (CASEL, 2013, 2015).

Definition of SEL

SEL describes the process by which children and youth acquire and effectively enact knowledge and skills to build and maintain positive interpersonal relationships. Recall from Chapter 1 the five interrelated sets of cognitive, affective, and behavioral competencies that form the basis of

CASEL. SEL interventions were described as (1) *self-awareness* (the ability to recognize one's emotions and thoughts that influence social behavior), (2) *self-management* (the ability to regulate one's emotions, thoughts, and behaviors in different situations), (3) *social awareness* (the ability to take the perspective of and empathize with others), (4) *relationship skills* (the ability to establish and maintain healthy rewarding relationships with diverse individuals and groups), and (5) *responsible decision making* (the ability to make constructive and respectful choices about personal behavior and social interactions). These five CASEL competencies reflect both intrapersonal and interpersonal domains of functioning. Self-awareness and self-management are included in the intrapersonal domain whereas social awareness and relationship skills are dimensions within the interpersonal domain. Responsible decision making involves both intrapersonal and interpersonal skills.

Four of the five CASEL competencies are measured by the SSIS-RS (Gresham & Elliott, 2008). These scales were discussed extensively in Chapter 3 with respect to evaluation of SEL intervention outcomes. Table 4.1 shows how the SSIS-RS domains match up with four of the five CASEL domains. The CASEL domain of Self-Management is termed Self-Control on the SSIS-RS. Examples of Self-Control social skills include resolving disagreements calmly, staying calm when being teased, and making compromises in conflict situations. The CASEL domain of Social Awareness is called Empathy on the SSIS-RS and includes behaviors such as trying to understand the feelings of others, trying to make others feel better, and comforting others. The CASEL domain of Relationship Skills is measured on the SSIS-RS with the Communication and Engagement domains and includes behaviors such as making eye contact when talking, speaking in an appropriate tone of voice, and interacting well with others. The CASEL domain of Responsible Decision Making, which includes behaviors such as taking care of others' things, respecting the property of others, and taking responsibility for one's own mistakes, matches the SSIS-RS domain of Responsibility.

Table 4.1 clearly shows that there is at least an 80% overlap between the CASEL and SSIS-RS domains. The only domain not assessed by the SSIS-RS is the Self-Awareness domain, which involves behaviors such as recognizing how one's emotions and thoughts influence one's own behavior. Professionals implementing evidence-based SEL programs can feel confident that using the SSIS-RS would adequately assess most of the domains specified by CASEL.

Criteria for Evidence-Based Universal SEL Programs

CASEL's guide in identifying evidence-based universal SEL interventions has four goals: (1) to provide a systematic framework for evaluating the

TABLE 4.1. Comparisons of CASEL Competencies to SSIS-RS Domains

CASEL competency	SSIS-RS domain
Self-management	*Self-control*
	• Resolves disagreements calmly.
	• Stays calm when teased.
	• Makes compromise in conflict.
	• Responds appropriately when pushed/hit.
	• Takes criticism without being upset.
Social awareness	*Empathy*
	• Tries to understand others' feelings.
	• Tries to make others feel better.
	• Forgives others.
	• Tries to comfort others.
	• Shows concern for others.
Relationship skills	*Communication/engagement*
	• Makes eye contact when talking.
	• Speaks in an appropriate tone of voice.
	• Makes friends easily.
	• Interacts well with others.
	• Invites others to join activities.
Responsible decision making	*Responsibility*
	• Takes care of others' things.
	• Is well behaved when unsupervised.
	• Respects the property of others.
	• Takes responsibility for his or her own actions.
	• Does what he or she promised.
	• Takes responsibility for his or her own mistakes.

quality of classroom-based SEL programs; (2) to apply this framework to rate and identify well-designed, evidence-based SEL programs that can be widely disseminated across the United States; (3) to share best-practice guidelines for districts and schools regarding how to select and implement SEL programs; and (4) to suggest recommendations for future priorities to advance SEL research, practice, and policy (CASEL, 2013). An increasing body of research connects SEL interventions to improved attitudes toward school, increases in prosocial behavior, increases in academic achievement, reductions in aggressive behavior, decreases in mental health problems, and reductions in substance abuse (Durlak et al., 2011; Zins, Weissberg, Wang, & Walberg, 2004). CASEL specifies three criteria for selecting evidence-based SEL programs: (1) well-designed classroom-based programs that systematically promote students' social and emotional competence, provide opportunities for practice, and include multiyear programming; (2) delivery of high-quality training and implementation supports to ensure adequate treatment integrity; and (3) inclusion of at least one carefully conducted evaluation documenting positive effects on student behavior and/or academic performance.

The CASEL guide specifies that the criteria for evidence-based programs document improvement in student behavior by research that, at a minimum, includes a comparison group and pretest–posttest measurements of behavior. The research designs in these studies can be RCTs characterized by random assignment to treatment and comparison groups or high-quality quasi-experimental designs that do not use randomization of participants to groups (i.e., use of intact groups). The 2013 CASEL guide provides information on 23 SEL programs, with four targeting preschool-age children, 16 targeting children in grades K–5, and three targeting both preschool- and elementary school-age children. Some of these SEL programs teach social and emotional skills directly, while other programs target topics such as substance abuse prevention, violence prevention, health promotion, and character education.

These programs have five core characteristics: (1) they provide opportunities for *repeated practice* of newly acquired skills and behaviors within the program and beyond to real-life situations (Durlak et al., 2011), (2) they use a *sequenced* step-by-step training approach, (3) they emphasize *active* forms of learning requiring students to practice new skills, (4) they *focus* specific time and attention on skill development, and (5) they are *explicit* in defining the social and emotional skills they are attempting to promote.

Description and Outcomes of Evidence-Based SEL Programs

The 4Rs (Reading, Writing, Respect, and Resolution) Program

The 4Rs Program provides read-a-louds, book talks, and sequential, interactive skill lessons to develop social skills related to understanding and managing feelings, listening and developing empathy, being assertive, solving conflicts appropriately, and standing up to teasing and bullying. This program is intended for children in grades PreK–8 and is delivered in 35 period-long classroom sessions (one session per week throughout the school year) that are integrated with English/language arts classes. All 4Rs stories incorporate a variety of cultures, ethnicities, and backgrounds. Initial instructor training for the 4Rs Program typically lasts 25–30 hours and is required before using the program. The program offers a train-the-trainer system to support sustainability. The program has extensive evidence that it uses all five characteristics of an effective SEL program described earlier.

The 4Rs Program was evaluated in a large (N = 1,184) RCT of children in grades 3–4 and followed them over a 3-year period. Behavioral outcomes were improved academic performance for students at behavioral risk, increased positive social behavior, reduced conduct problems, and reduced emotional distress (Brown, Jones, LaRusso, & Aber, 2010; Jones, Brown, & Aber, 2011).

The Caring School Community Program

The Caring School Community (CSC) program is intended for use in kindergarten through sixth grade and is organized around four core educational practices: (1) class meetings (30–35 per grade), (2) cross-age buddies, (3) homeside activities, and (4) schoolwide community-building activities. Class meetings present a schedule of lessons and activities that are implemented throughout the school year. Forty cross-age buddy activities are designed to promote bonding between younger and older students while at the same time supporting exploration of a wide range of academic subjects. Homeside activities are implemented once or twice per month, are reviewed in class, are completed at home with caregivers, and then are reflected upon in class. Schoolwide community-building activities are implemented throughout the school year to build relationships, share knowledge, and promote pride in the school environment. The CSC program provides suggestions to support English language learners, and homeside activities are available in both English and Spanish. Instructor training for the CSC program lasts half a day to two full days, but is not required and offers a train-the-trainer system to support sustainability.

The CSC program has been evaluated in three randomized controlled trials and two quasi-experimental studies. (Battistich, 2000; Battistich, Schaps, Watson, & Solomon, 1996; Battistich, Schaps, Watson, Solomon, & Lewis, 2000; Battistich, Solomon, Watson, Solomon, & Schaps, 1989). The largest sample included 40 schools. Students have been followed over a 5-year period. Behavioral outcomes of the program included improved academic performance, increased positive social behavior, reduced conduct problems, and reductions in emotional distress.

I Can Problem Solve

The I Can Problem Solve (ICPS) program teaches students how to generate alternate solutions, anticipate consequences, and effectively solve problems. The program is designed for use in the prekindergarten through elementary grades and is divided into three sets of lessons for prekindergarten (59 lessons), kindergarten and primary grades (83 lessons), and intermediate grades (77 lessons). The scripted lessons take about 20 minutes to implement and focus on both pre-problem-solving skills and problem-solving skills. Dialoguing is a central component of this program. Beyond the lesson, teachers are encouraged to infuse the program methods to support positive teacher–student interaction into their regular classroom routines. To reinforce most lessons, the program provides parent pages as well as suggested strategies for connecting with core academic subjects. Training for the ICPS program usually lasts 1–2 days, is required, and offers a train-the-trainer system to support sustainability.

The ICPS program has been evaluated in two randomized controlled trials and one quasi-experimental study with the largest sample being 655 students who were followed over the course of 1 year (Feis & Simmons, 1985; Shure & Spivack, 1979, 1980, 1982).

The Incredible Years Series

The Incredible Years Series (TIYS) is a set of three curricula for children, teachers, and parents. The Child Training Program (Dinosaur Curriculum) focuses on developing skills to understand and recognize feelings, solve problems, manage anger, and develop and maintain friendships. The program is designed for children ages 3–8 years and includes approximately 60 lessons, depending on implementation, as the program provides multiple models for implementation in the classroom. Program content is delivered via puppetry or video vignettes followed by group discussion. Several activities reinforce the concepts learned and provide opportunities to practice skills. Parental involvement is strongly encouraged. Each lesson ends with an activity that is completed at home with parents or caregivers, and several letters to parents are sent home during the course of the program. Training for teachers focuses on developing classroom management skills and proactive teaching strategies. Training also emphasizes the importance of building positive relationships with students and teaching social skills and problem solving in the classroom. TIYS includes a separate training program for parents. Training typically lasts 3 days and is not required.

TIYS has been evaluated in two randomized controlled trials with the largest sample including 1,768 students and 153 teachers, with students being followed over 1 year (Webster-Stratton, Reid, & Hammond, 2001; Webster-Stratton, Reid, & Stoolmiller, 2008). Behavioral outcomes included increased positive social behavior and reduced conduct problems.

Promoting Alternative Thinking Strategies   ASK/NMSA TRANSITION PROGRAM

Promoting Alternate Thinking Strategies (PATHS) is a program that promotes peaceful conflict resolution, emotion regulation, empathy, and responsible decision making. The program is designed for students in kindergarten through sixth grade with separate sets of lessons for first through fourth grade and combined sets of lessons for use in preschool/ kindergarten and in fifth and sixth grades. Each lesson is scripted. Lessons begin with an introduction that includes a statement about background and goals, guidelines for implementation, suggestions for involving parents, a list of typical questions and answers, supplementary activities, and family handouts. Lessons end with reminders and suggestions for generalizing acquired skills beyond the lesson to the classroom. PATH lessons include a variety of cultures, ethnicities, and backgrounds. Parent letters and informational handouts are available in English and Spanish. Training for the PATHS programs lasts 2 days and is not required. The program offers a train-the-trainer system to support sustainability.

The PATHS program has been evaluated in multiple large RCTs in grades preschool through kindergarten and one quasi-experimental study (Conduct Problems Prevention Research Group, 1999a, 1999b, 2010; Greenberg & Kusché, 1998; Kam, Greenberg, & Kusché, 2004; Domitrovich, Cortes, & Greenberg, 2007). Students have been followed for up to 3 years. Behavioral outcomes include improved academic performance, increased positive social behavior, reduced conduct problems, and reduced emotional distress.

Positive Action

Positive Action is designed to promote a healthy self-concept and to establish positive actions for the body and mind for children and youth in grades PreK–12. The program focuses on effective self-management, social skills, character, and mental health as well as skills for setting and achieving goals. The Positive Action classroom curriculum contains separate sets of lessons. Each grade has approximately 140 sequenced lessons, all of which include step-by-step scripts organized around a different theme. The program is based on a single fundamental philosophy: You feel good about yourself when you do positive behaviors (positive self-concept) and there is a positive way to do everything. Supplemental program components support classroomwide, schoolwide, family, and community involvement. The program offers separate units for bullying preventions, drug education, conflict resolution, and promoting a positive school climate that can be added to the core program. Training for Positive Action lasts about one-half to 5 days, depending on the scope and sequence of implementation, and is not required. The program offers a train-the-trainer system to support sustainability.

Positive Action has been evaluated in two RCTs and two quasi-experimental studies, and students have been followed for up to 3 years (Beets et al., 2009; Flay & Allred, 2003; Flay, Allred, & Ordway, 2001; Li et al., 2011). Behavioral outcomes include improved academic performance and reduced conduct problems.

The Resolving Conflict Creatively Program

The Resolving Conflict Creatively Program (RCCP) includes sequenced, skill-building, classroom lessons (titled Connected and Respected) designed to encourage caring, peaceful, school learning communities for children in grades PreK–8. Lessons emphasize building relationships, understanding feelings, developing empathy, managing emotions, and developing social responsibility. The program contains 16 Connected and Respected lessons for each grade that are implemented in a workshop format. This approach includes a gathering, review of agenda, main activities and discussion, summary, and closing activities. Each lesson also includes suggestions for extension activities, infusion ideas, and connections to the literature. In addition to the classroom lessons, the program includes peer mediation and family components that are central to program implementation. A goal of this program is to address stereotyping and to reduce racial/ethnic/gender putdowns in the classroom. A checklist is provided for each grade level to assist in addressing these issues. Training for the program lasts 24–30 hours and is required. The program offers a train-the-trainer system to support sustainability.

The RCCP has been evaluated in two large RCTs and evaluations have followed students over 2 years (Aber, Jones, Brown, Chaudry, & Samples, 1998; Aber, Brown, & Jones, 2003). Behavioral outcomes include reduced conduct problems and reductions in emotional distress.

Second Step

Second Step provides instruction in SEL with units on skills for learning empathy, emotion management, friendship skills, and problem solving. The program contains separate sets of lessons used in grades PreK–8 that are implemented in 22–28 weeks each year. The Early Learning program also includes a unit for transitioning to kindergarten. Second Step uses four key strategies to reinforce skills development: (1) brain builder games designed to build executive function, (2) weekly theme activities, (3) reinforcing activities, and (4) home links. Teachers are encouraged to give children daily opportunities for practice. The first day contains a script and main lesson. The second day includes a story and discussion. The third and fourth days involve practice activities in small and large groups. The fifth day students read a book connected to the overall unit theme and teachers send home a "Home Link" activity that gives students an opportunity to practice new skills with caregivers. The Second Step lessons and accompanying photographs incorporate a variety of cultures, ethnicities, and backgrounds, and Home Link activities are available in English and Spanish. Training for the program lasts 1–4 hours and is not required.

Second Step has been evaluated in two RCTs and two quasi-experimental studies and students have been followed for up to 2 years (Frey, Nolen, Edstrom, & Hirschstein, 2005; Grossman et al., 1997; Holsen, Smith, & Frey, 2008; Holsen, Iversen, & Smith 2009). Behavioral outcomes include increased positive social behavior, reduced conduct problems, and reduced emotional distress.

Steps to Respect

Steps to Respect is a schoolwide program designed for use in grades 3–6. Implementation occurs in three phases: (1) school administrators take stock of their school environment and bullying issues, (2) all adults in the building are trained in the program, and (3) classroom-based SEL lessons are taught. The program includes 11 classroom lessons with two additional literature units that contain multiple lessons in each. These lessons focus on topics such as how to make friends, understanding and recognizing feelings, and dealing with bullying. Optional extension activities are provided at the end of each lesson for social and emotional skill areas as well as academic content areas. Family handouts are also provided for each lesson. The program attempts to eliminate any visibility of differences such that the materials can be applicable to a variety of cultures and ethnic backgrounds and can span a longer period of time and relevance. Training for Steps to Respect lasts 6–8 days and is not required.

The Steps to Respect program has been evaluated in two large RCTs with the largest study involving 33 schools and students being followed over a 2-year period (Brown, Low, Smith, & Haggerty, 2011; Frey et al., 2005). Behavioral outcomes include increases in positive social behavior and reduced conduct problems.

The Social Skills Improvement System Classwide Intervention Program

The Social Skills Improvement System Classwide Intervention Program (SSIS-CIP) is a universal SEL intervention program intended to facilitate the development of students' prosocial skills and reduce problem behaviors in the classroom. The program utilizes instructional strategies such as reinforcement, modeling, role playing, behavioral rehearsal, and problem solving. The SSIS-CIP is a brief curriculum that includes instructional units focused on 10 key classroom social behaviors that have been identified by teachers as important for classroom success. These skills include (1) listening to others, (2) following directions, (3) following classroom rules, (4) ignoring peer distractions, (5) asking for help, (6) taking turns in conversations, (7) cooperating with others, (8) controlling temper in conflict situations, (9) acting responsibly with others, and (10) showing kindness to others.

The SSIS-CIP has been evaluated in one large multisite cluster RCT (N = 432 students in 38 second-grade classrooms) (DiPerma, Lei, Bellinger, & Cheng, 2015). Behavioral outcomes of the program included improvement in overall teacher ratings of social skills, communication, cooperation, responsibility, and empathy, and decreases in internalizing behavior problems. The program has no effect on externalizing behavior problems or on social skills measured by systematic direct observations.

Summary of Universal SEL Programs

Based on the above reviews, it is clear that universal SEL programs have positive effects on increasing prosocial behaviors, reducing conduct problems, decreasing emotional distress, and increasing academic performance. All of the studies supporting the different programs were based primarily on RCTs (the "gold-standard" research design) and, to a lesser extent, quasi-experimental designs. However, the programs described in the CASEL guide (2013) do not tell us the *magnitude of effects* that are produced by these various programs.

To answer this question, one should read the meta-analysis by Durlak et al. (2011) of 213 school-based universal SEL programs involving 270,334 students in kindergarten through high school. This meta-analysis reported effect sizes (Cohen's d) across six areas: (1) SEL skills (d = 0.57), (2) attitudes (d = 0.23), (3) positive social behaviors (d = 0.24), (4) conduct problems (d = 0.22), (5) emotional distress (d = 0.24), and (5) academic performance (d = 0.27). With the exception of SEL skills that had a moderate effect size (0.57), the remaining five effect sizes (mean = 0.24) can be considered small using Cohen's (1988) standards. However, it should be noted that SEL programs produce effect sizes similar to and, in some cases, higher than other psychosocial and educational interventions.

A more practical way of interpreting the effect sizes in meta-analysis is to convert those effect sizes into a metric called the binomial effect size display (BESD; Rosenthal & Rubin, 1982). The BESD compares the percentage of individuals in the treatment group who improve to the percentage of those in the control group who improve. Using this metric, 64% of individuals in the treatment groups improved SEL skills compared to only 36% of individuals in the control groups. For attitudes and positive social behaviors, and emotional distress, 56% of individuals in the treatment groups improved compared to 44% of individuals in control groups. For conduct problems, 53% of people in the treatment groups improved compared to 47% of people in control groups. Finally, for academic performance, 57% of treatment group participants improved compared to 43% of participants in control groups. Thus, across the six domains targeted in SEL programs, an average BESD of 57% was obtained.

It certainly would be desirable to have higher effect sizes and BESDs across the six domains targeted by SEL programs. However, the meta-analysis clearly shows that SEL programs are associated with gains across several important behavioral, attitudinal, and academic domains that are comparable to other universal psychosocial and educational interventions (Durlak et al., 2011). Also, one should keep in mind the findings of DiPerma et al. (2015), who showed that the greatest changes in social skills occurred with students who exhibited lower skill proficiency prior to implementation of the program. This suggests that in many SEL studies, most students are already functioning quite well in SEL domains; therefore these studies are confounded by a ceiling effect that reduces the effect sizes one observes.

SAMPLE LESSON FROM THE SSIS-CI

Space considerations prevent an exhaustive description of the many SEL programs that were described in this chapter. However, I now provide a sample lesson using the SSIS-CIP that was reviewed earlier in this chapter. This sample lesson shows a step-by-step example of how social skills are taught in this program.

Take Turns When You Talk

Objective: The student will take turns in conversations with peers and adults. Specifically, the student will be able to focus on the skill learned in Unit 1, Listen to Others, because students cannot take turns in conversations unless they listen to what others are saying.

Tell

1. Introduce the Skill and Ask Questions about It.

Say: "Today we are going to talk about how we take turns when we talk to each other. When we talk to someone, we need to listen also. If we're talking to our friend, we say something and then we listen to what our friend says. Remember how we learned about listening to other people? Do you remember the three steps to listen to others? Step 1: Look, Step 2: Hear, Step 3: Do. We listen and then we talk. And we talk and then listen. Then we let the other person do that too."

Say: "Let's think of some things that you take turns doing:
- "Playing a game.
- "Getting a drink from the drinking fountain.
- "Answering a question at school.
- "Sharing a toy."

2. Define the Skill and Discuss Key Words.

Say: "First, you need to make sure you let someone know you want to talk to him or her. He or she needs to be ready to listen. Then, you can say what you want to say. Make sure you look at him or her. Then, it's the other person's turn to talk and your turn to listen. Look at who's talking and make sure you are being a good listener. Then, you can smile so he or she knows that you hear him or her."

Key words: *listen, hear, repeat, talk, take turns, wait.*

Say: "Look at the picture on the front of your book. What do you see? [Boy, girl.] What is the boy doing? [Talking.] What is the girl doing? [Listening.] The boy is talking and the girl is listening. The girl is waiting for her turn to talk."

Say: "When we take turns talking, we can hear what the other person is saying. Then he or she will listen to you too. It's not nice to talk when other people are talking. We need to listen when someone else is talking."

3. Discuss Why the Skill Is Important.

Say: "Taking turns and listening is important. It makes us better at listening and hearing other people and makes the people we are listening to and talking to happy:

- "Look at the person talking.
- "Be a good listener.
- "When he or she is done talking, then it's your turn to talk.
- "When you're talking, the other person will listen to you."

4. Identify the Skill Steps.

Say: "Now, open your book to page 2. Please look for the rainbow. Listen to me. I will tell you the steps to take turns when you talk:

- **"Step 1: Hear.** Use your ears to be a good listener and hear what the other person is saying.
- **"Step 2: Do.** Do something. Smile or nod your head to show that you are listening.
- **"Step 3: Talk.** When it's your turn to talk, the other person will listen.
- **"Step 4: Wait.** Wait to hear what the other person will say when you're done talking.
- **"Step 5: Repeat.** Do these steps again. Then you are taking turns!"

Summarize the skill steps. Say: "What are the steps again to take turns when you talk? Step 1: Hear, Step 2: Do, Step 3: Talk, Step 4: Wait, Step 5: Repeat."

Say: "Now we will draw a line between the picture and the words. Where is the word *hear*? [Have students point to the word.]

- "Step 1 is Hear. Where is the ear? Draw a line from the ear to the word *hear*.
- "Where is the word *do*? Step 2 is Do. Where is the smiling mouth? Draw a line from the smiling mouth to the word *do*.
- "Where is the word *talk*? Step 3 is Talk. See the dog talking? Draw a line from the dog talking to the word *talk*.
- "Where is the word *wait*? Step 4 is Wait. Do you see the stop sign? At a stop sign, we need to wait. Draw a line from the stop sign to the word *wait*.
- "Where is the word *repeat*? Step 5 is Repeat. See the arrows going around? That means 'do over,' 'do again,' or 'repeat.' Draw a line from the arrows to the word *repeat*."

Show

Say: "Please look at the rain cloud on page 2 again. Do you see the picture by the rain cloud? What do you see in the picture? [Boy, girl.] Who is talking? [Boy.] What is the girl doing? [She is not looking at the boy.] The boy is talking, but the girl is not looking. To talk together, the boy and girl both need to talk and listen to each other. It one doesn't listen, then they will not be able to take turns talking. Draw a circle around the boy. He is taking his turn. The girl is not."

Say: "Look at the boy. What steps can you see? [Step 2: Do, Step 3: Talk.] Look at the girl who is not looking. What steps are missing? What steps are not there? [Step 1: Hear, Step 2: Talk.]"

Show the video clips. Then talk about the skill steps.

Say: "Now let's watch a video and look for examples of students who are taking turns talking."

Say: "Are the boy and girl both talking and listening? [Yes.] What steps did you see? [Step 1: Hear, Step 2: Do, Step 3: Talk, Step 4: Wait, Step 5: Repeat.]"

Play the video again.

Say: "See the boy and girl taking turns. First, the boy talks, and then the girl listens. Then the girl talks, and the boy listens."

Say: "What happened when the boy and girl were talking? [The other boy started talking.] What steps were missing when the other boy started talking? [Step 1: Hear, Step 3: Wait.]"

Say: "See the boy and girls are taking turns talking. Then the other boy comes in and starts talking, but he doesn't listen and doesn't let others talk."

Say: "Does the boy with the toy listen to the other kids? [No.] He doesn't hear the other kids, and doesn't let them have a turn. What steps are missing? [Step 1: Hear, Step 4: Wait.]"

Play the video again.

Say: "See the girl and boy try and talk to each other and take turns, but the boy with the toy doesn't take turns. He doesn't listen and keeps talking."

Model and role play.

Positive Model: **Show a positive model of taking turns for one of the following situations:**

- Demonstrate politely standing in line at the sink or drinking fountain. Wait patiently until the person before you finishes. Then, take your turn.
- Demonstrate talking to a friend. Show that you are listening by giving eye contact and nodding your head. When the speaker is finished, the listener will take a turn talking. The new listener will give eye contact, smile, and listen.

Assign roles. Remind listeners to show as many skill steps as possible. Have volunteers demonstrate.

Negative Model: **Show a negative model for one of these same situations.** For negative models, consider the same situations, but this time don't model good listening skills, don't say anything, don't do anything, or don't wait patiently.

Do

Say: "Now, let's see what it looks like when listeners don't use the skill steps to take turns."

Say: "Let's go over what we just talked about:

- "What do we take turns doing? [Listening, playing a game, talking.]
- "How do we show we are listening? [Smiling, looking at the person talking.]
- "Why is it important to take turns? [So we can hear what the person is saying. It's nice to share.]
- "What are the five skill steps to take turns when we talk? [Step 1: Hear, Step 2: Do, Step 3: Talk, Step 4: Wait, Step 5: Repeat.]"

Monitor Progress

Say: "Now, let's use our books again. Look for the star. ['How am I doing?,' on page 3.] Now you know the five steps to take turns when you talk. Now, think how well you take turns when you talk. See the ladder? If you take turns very well, you are at the top of the ladder. If you need to practice more, then you are down the ladder."

Say: "How well do you take turns when you talk? Think about the five steps to take turns when you talk: hear, do, talk, wait, and repeat. Do you use these five steps well? If yes, find the number 4 at the top of the ladder. Draw a circle around the 4. You are doing great! If you do not know these five steps well, or if it is hard for you to take turns when you talk, find the number 1. Draw a circle around the 1. You are doing okay. Sometimes it's hard to take turns when talking. You just need to practice. If you are in the middle, draw a circle around number 2 or 3. You may be good or doing better. However, we can all practice to be better at taking turns when we talk."

Practice: Taking Turns When We Talk Exercise

Say: "Now, let's find the rain cloud on page 2 again. See these lines? For these [upper] lines I will spell four words. Write the letters of the words on these lines.

"The first word is T-A-L-K-I-N-G [pause about 3–5 seconds between each letter]. What does this spell? [Talking.]. The second word is T-O. What does this spell? [To] The third word is T-H-E. What does this spell? [The.] The fourth word is G-I-R-L. What does this spell? [Girl.] Who can read this sentence? [The boy is talking to the girl.]"

Say: "Now for this lower line, I will spell five more words."
"The first word is N-O-T. What does this spell? [Not.] The second word is L-O-O-K-I-N-G. What does this spell? [Looking.] The third word is A-T. What does this spell? [At.] The fourth word is T-H-E. What does this spell? [The.] The fifth word is B-O-Y. What does this spell? [Boy.] Who can read this sentence? [The girl is not looking at the boy.]"

Generalize

Say: "Let's talk about places where we could take turns when we talk."
Brainstorm places where we can take turns when we talk, for example:
- Home
- School
- At lunch

Say: "Go to the back page. Look for the soccer ball at the top. Look at the pictures. These are places where we can take turns taking with others. What are these pictures? [Classroom, play area, lunch area, home, car/bus.] Today, we all did it in class.

"This week, we are practicing the five steps that help us take turns when we talk. The five steps are: Step 1: Hear, Step 2: Do, Step 3: Talk, Step 4: Wait, Step 5: Repeat. Today, we all practiced in class. Everyone draw a smiley face in this box next to the picture of the classroom. This box says 'I did it!'

"During the week, I will ask where you practiced the five steps. Did you practice on the playground? Did you practice at lunch? Do you practice at home? Did you practice in the car or bus? If you answer yes, then you can add a smiley face to the other boxes."

CHAPTER SUMMARY POINTS

- SEL interventions vary in terms of their intensity and duration and can be characterized as primary prevention (universal interventions), secondary prevention (selected interventions), and tertiary prevention (intense interventions).

- In a response to intervention approach, the intensity of the intervention is matched to the responsiveness an individual shows to that intervention.

- Universal interventions are designed to impact all students in the same manner under the same conditions.

- Selected interventions are individually tailored interventions that are fine-tuned to meet the needs of a given student.

- Intensive interventions are intense, expensive, and time-consuming and should be reserved for the most at-risk students.

- Estimates are that about 80% of students will respond adequately to universal intervention, 15% will respond adequately to selected interventions, and the remaining 5% of students will require intensive interventions.

- CASEL (2013) published an intervention guide of evidence-based universal SEL programs.

- CASEL focuses on five, interrelated sets of cognitive, affective, and behavioral competences: (1) self-awareness, (2) self-management, (3) social awareness, (4) relationship skills, and (5) responsible decision making.

- There is about an 80% overlap between the CASEL domains and the SSIS-RS domains.

▪ The CASEL guide specifies that the criteria for evidence-based programs document improvement in student behavior by research that includes a comparison group and pretest–posttest measurement of behavior using randomized controlled trials or high-quality quasi-experimental designs.

▪ The universal SEL programs reviewed by CASEL have five core characteristics: (1) they provide opportunities for repeated practice of newly acquired skills and behaviors, (2) they use a sequenced step-by-step training approach, (3) they emphasize active forms of learning, (4) they focus specific time and attention on skill development, and (5) they are explicit in defining social and emotional skills they are promoting.

▪ This chapter reviewed 10 high-quality evidence-based SEL universal intervention programs: (1) 4Rs, (2) Caring School Community, (3) I Can Problem Solve, (4) The Incredible Years Series, (5) the PATHS curriculum, (6) Positive Action, (7) Resolving Conflict Creatively, (8) Second Step, (9) Steps to Respect, and (10) SSIS-Classwide Intervention Program.

▪ Intervention outcomes for virtually all of these programs are increases in positive social behavior, reduction of conduct problems, decreases in emotional distress, and improved academic performance.

▪ A recent meta-analysis of 213 studies involving 270,334 children from kindergarten through high school showed effect sizes across five areas: (1) SEL skills (0.57), (2) attitudes (0.23), (3) positive social behavior (0.24), (4) conduct problems (0.22), and (5) academic performance (0.27).

▪ These effect sizes show that 64% of persons in treatment groups improve in SEL skills, 56% of people in treatment groups will improve in attitudes and positive social behaviors, 53% of treatment group members will show reductions in conduct problems, and 57% of persons in treatment groups will show improved academic performance. One reason for the relatively small effect sizes is that most persons in SEL programs already have good SEL skills and thus do not have room for improvement.

▪ These effects sizes are consistent with the effect sizes found in many other psychosocial and educational interventions.

IMPLICATIONS FOR PRACTICE

• Use universal SEL interventions as the first step in remediating social skills deficits to prevent the harmful effects of social skills deficiencies.

• Universal SEL interventions are designed to impact *all students* under the exact same conditions (i.e., they all receive the same "dosage" of the intervention).

- Expect that, on average, universal SEL interventions should be effective with about 80% of any given school population.

- Good SEL programs should be based on the CASEL model.

- The CASEL model identifies five SEL competencies: self-awareness, self-management, social awareness, relationship skills, and responsible decision making.

- Consider using one of the following SEL curricula:
  - 4 Rs (Reading, Writing, and Resolution)
  - Caring School Community
  - I Can Problem Solve
  - The Incredible Years
  - Promoting Alternative Thinking Strategies
  - Positive Action
  - Resolving Conflict Creatively Program
  - SSIS-Social Emotional Learning Classwide Intervention Program

CHAPTER FIVE

Selected Social–Emotional Learning Interventions

The last chapter described a number of universal, or Tier 1, SEL interventions that have been shown to be evidence-based. These were defined as interventions that *all* students receive at the same "dosage" level. Recall that a heuristic I used estimated that approximately 80% of students will respond adequately to a Tier 1 SEL intervention and therefore will not require additional social skills instruction. The 20% of students that do not respond adequately to a universal intervention will require additional instruction and supports to improve social skills performances. Tier 2, or *selected*, interventions are more intense (i.e., more time, narrower focus of instruction) than Tier 1 interventions. Tier 2 interventions can be provided by a variety of professionals such as general education teachers, remedial education teachers, behavior specialists, school psychologists, or school counselors.

Tier 2 selected interventions can be differentiated from Tier 1 universal interventions by the intensity of the intervention provided. These interventions are provided for *some* students who do not adequately responds to a universal intervention. *Intensity* is defined as the number of minutes and the focus of the intervention. In general, a four-step process helps define Tier 2 selected SEL interventions: *how much* additional intervention time is needed, *what* will occur during that time, *who* is the most qualified person to deliver the instructional strategy, and *where* will that additional intervention occur.

Tier 2 selected SEL interventions have several critical features. One, these interventions are continuously available to the student and students have rapid access to the intervention. Two, these interventions require relatively low effort on the part of the individual delivering the intervention with maximum benefits to the students. Three, these interventions are consistent with schoolwide expectations and are implemented uniformly by all staff in the school. Four, these interventions are flexible based on student need and the degree of social skills deficits. Finally, continuous progress monitoring of the student's response to these interventions is used in the decision-making process.

ADVANTAGES OF TIER 2
SELECTED SEL INTERVENTIONS

There are several advantages of Tier 2 selected SEL interventions. First, the intensity of the intervention is matched to the degree of responsiveness the student shows in the intervention. Most students will respond adequately to these interventions and will require no further services. Second, providing these Tier 2 interventions allows for the early identification of behavior problems that have a better chance of being effective than social skills problems identified later in a child's school career. In the absence of these interventions, these social skills problems will likely escalate and morph into more serious and debilitating social behavior patterns. Third, these selected interventions focus on positive student outcomes and emphasize *direct measurement* of social behavior and the instructional environment. These interventions are concerned primarily with measureable and changeable aspects of the instructional environment that are related to positive student outcomes. Fourth, these selected interventions increase reinforcement for appropriate social behavior and are applied across school settings. Subsequently, these interventions can be changed from external reinforcement interventions to self-management interventions that will require even less staff time to implement and monitor.

TYPES OF TIER 2
SELECTED SEL INTERVENTIONS

There are two basic approaches to delivering Tier 2 selected SEL interventions: (1) problem-solving approaches and (2) standard protocol approaches (Gresham, 2007).

Problem-Solving Approaches

Problem-solving approaches can be traced back to the behavioral consultation model first described by Bergan (1977) and later revised and updated by Bergan and Kratochwill (1990). Behavioral consultation takes place in a sequence of four steps: (1) problem identification, (2) problem analysis, (3) plan implementation, and (4) plan evaluation. Specifically, the behavioral consultation model answers the following four questions: What is the problem? Why is the problem occurring? What should we do about it? Did we solve the problem?

The goal in behavioral consultation is to define the problem in clear, unambiguous, and operational terms; to identify environmental conditions related to the problem; to design and implement an intervention plan with integrity; and to evaluate the effectiveness of the intervention plan. Problems are defined in a problem-solving approach as a discrepancy between current and desired levels of performance; the larger this discrepancy, the larger the problem. For example, if a child cooperates with others in the classroom only once per day and the desired level of performance for this behavior is five times per day, then there is an 80% discrepancy between current and desired levels of performance.

Another important aspect of problem solving is to determine why the problem is occurring. At this stage, the distinction between "can't do" problems and "won't do" problems becomes important. Can't do, or acquisition, deficits occur because the individual does not have the necessary skill or behavior in his or her repertoire. For instance, if a child never engages in appropriate social interactions on the playground with peers, then it may be that the child lacks appropriate peer group entry strategies. In this case, the acquisition deficit must be remediated by directly teaching the child appropriate peer group entry strategies.

Won't do problems are considered to be performance deficits, meaning that the child knows how to perform the behavior or skill, but does not do so at an acceptable level. Reasons for not performing the behavior or skill may be due to the lack of opportunities to perform the skill (i.e., antecedent reasons) or the lack of or low rate of reinforcement for performing the behavior (i.e., consequent reasons). In this case, remedial interventions would involve providing multiple opportunities to perform the behavior and increasing the rate of reinforcement for performing the behavior or skill.

The final stage of a problem-solving model involves determining whether or not the intervention was effective in changing behavior to desired levels. This process involves *data-based* decision making in which effectiveness is determined empirically by direct measurement of intervention outcomes. For example, if the child's level of social skills prior to intervention was at the 10th percentile on a teacher rating of social skills and the level subsequent to an intervention is at the 25th percentile, then one could conclude that the intervention was effective. The decision in this case would probably be to continue the intervention with the eventual goal of lifting the child's level of social skills to the 50th percentile.

Standard Protocol Approaches

Standard protocol approaches involve the use of manualized treatments in which the components of the intervention are written in specific detail. A good example of a standard protocol Tier 2 selected intervention is the *SSIS—Intervention Guide* (SSIS-IG; Elliott & Gresham, 2008). The SSIS-IG is a research-based instructional program that addresses basic social competencies and promotes the use of prosocial behaviors. It is designed for those students who demonstrate social skills deficits and who have failed to respond adequately to a Tier 1 universal SEL intervention such as the ones described in Chapter 4. Students with social skills acquisition deficits will benefit most from this program, however, the program also includes strategies to target social skills performance deficits once the acquisition deficits have been remediated. These strategies, which focus on increasing prosocial behaviors in the classroom and other school settings, are intended to be used in the problem-solving framework described earlier in this chapter. This program is described in much greater detail later in this chapter.

QUESTIONS TO BE ANSWERED FOR TIER 2 SELECTED INTERVENTIONS

Tier 2 selected interventions are likely to be varied for different student needs. The following questions should be answered by using evidence-based social skills assessment strategies such as the ones described in Chapter 3. Assessments at Tier 2 should be able to answer specific questions such as:

- Which students require supplemental social skills instruction or practice based on an analysis of their current needs in relation to Tier 1 standards of performance?
- How should students receiving supplemental social skills instruction be grouped together for small-group social skills instruction?
- Which students will be provided with a standard protocol social skills approach to address common and recurring concerns for which there is ample evidence-based options for intervention?
- Which students will need modified SEL interventions or more in-depth problem solving (especially problem analysis) in order to ensure an appropriate match between the intervention supports and the students' needs?
- Which students are demonstrating a positive response to the supplemental intervention provided to them?
- Which students are demonstrating moderate-to-poor responses to the intervention?

- Are the majority of students within the supplemental social skills instruction group demonstrating a positive response to the intervention?
- What modifications are needed to increase positive student responses to the intervention at Tier 2 (increased "dosage" of the intervention)?
- Which students may need more intensive SEL interventions (i.e., Tier 3 interventions)?
- Which students are ready to transition back to Tier 1 instruction?
- Are students who are demonstrating progress at Tier 2 based on progress-monitoring data also demonstrating progress on their Tier 1 assessments (why or why not)?

ASSESSMENT OF TREATMENT INTEGRITY AT TIER 2

The accuracy with which SEL interventions are implemented as planned, intended, or programmed is known as *treatment integrity*. The implementation of evidence-based SEL interventions is predicated on the assumption that demonstrable changes in social behavior (i.e., the dependent variable) are related to systematic, manipulated changes in the environment (i.e., the independent variable) and are not due to extraneous variables. The absence of objective and measured specification of an operationally defined independent variable (i.e., the intervention) and its subsequent measured application in a natural environment (e.g., a classroom or therapy room) compromises any incontrovertible conclusions that might be drawn concerning the relation between an intervention and behavior change (Gresham, 1989; McIntyre, Gresham, DeGennaro, & Reed, 2007).

Establishing the accuracy of treatment implementation is a critical aspect of both scientific and practical application of behavior change strategies. The ineffectiveness of many social–behavioral interventions is likely due to the low accuracy or inconsistency with which these interventions are implemented rather than the inert or weak nature of these interventions in changing behavior. This becomes particularly problematic with problem-solving based SEL interventions that must be implemented by third parties (e.g., teachers or parents) rather than therapists.

The treatment integrity construct is currently thought of as multidimensional, in contrast with its initial conceptualization as being unidimensional (Gresham, 1989). Treatment adherence represents a quantitative dimension of treatment integrity because it can be measured in terms of the number or percentage of critical treatment components that are implemented over the course of a treatment. Treatment adherence can be thought of as the *accuracy* and *consistency* with which a treatment is implemented. In this view, there are two aspects of treatment adherence: (1) treatment component adherence and (2) session/daily adherence.

Figure 5.1 depicts an example of how one might present data on these two dimensions of treatment adherence for an SEL intervention implemented twice per week. As shown in Figure 5.1, the overall component adherence was 64.3% with three components being implemented half the time and one component never being implemented. Figure 5.1 also shows that the daily adherence to the treatment protocol was inconsistent (71.4% vs. 57.1%). Measuring these two aspects of treatment adherence allows one to assess which components are being implemented inconsistently on which days or in which sessions.

More recently, other dimensions of treatment integrity have evolved in the literature: interventionist competence and treatment differentiation. *Interventionist competence* refers to the skill and experience of the interventionist in delivering the treatment. Competence in this sense might be best conceptualized as a qualitative dimension of treatment integrity because it reflects judgments of how well a treatment is delivered. Figure 5.2 shows how interventionist competence might be assessed using objective ratings of how well a social skills group leader implemented an SEL intervention.

Treatment differentiation represents theoretical distinctions between different aspects of two or more treatments and how those theoretical differences are represented in treatment delivery. For example, cognitive-behavioral theory posits that the mechanism accounting for the reduction of aggressive behavior and the increase in socially appropriate behavior

	Monday	Tuesday	Wednesday	Thursday	Friday	
Introduces the skill and asks questions about it.	X	X	X	X	X	100%
Defines the skill and discusses key words.	X	O	X	X	X	80%
Discusses why the skill is important.	X	X	O	X	O	60%
Identifies the skill steps and has students repeat them.	X	X	X	O	O	60%
Repeats the skill steps.	X	O	X	O	O	40%
	100%	60%	80%	60%	40%	

Daily Integrity = 68%; Component Integrity = 68%

FIGURE 5.1. Two dimensions of treatment adherence in an SEL intervention skill: Getting along with others.

Introduces skills and asks questions about it.	0	1	2	3
Defines skill and discusses key words.	0	1	2	3
Discusses why skill is important.	0	1	2	3
Identifies skill steps; has students repeat them.	0	1	2	3
Models and role-plays the skill.	0	1	2	3
Reinforces occurrences of the skill throughout the session.	0	1	2	3
Corrects inappropriate demonstrations of the skill.	0	1	2	3

Rating Descriptors

0—Not Implemented
1—Limited Implementation
2—Partial Implementation
3—Full Implementation

Score Range: 0–21 points

FIGURE 5.2. Interventionist competence scale.

pivots on how an individual thinks about or perceives conflict situations and intensions of peers. A common technique in cognitive-behavioral therapy is to challenge thoughts that magnify negative outcomes in conflict situations and to replace them with more effective, realistic thoughts. In contrast, social learning theory posits that observational learning or viewing an adaptive, socially appropriate response in conflict situations should reduce aggressive behavior and increase socially appropriate behaviors. A common technique based on social learning theory is coping modeling in which the model initially demonstrates aggressive behavior and then gradually more comfortable engaging in prosocial behavioral alternatives.

An additional dimension of treatment integrity is termed *treatment receipt,* which is conceptualized as the *dose* or *exposure* of the treatment, participant comprehension of the treatment, and participant responsiveness to the treatment. Exposure or dose of a treatment refers to the amount of treatment received by the participant. For example, the "dose" of a treatment might be the number of times per day or per week the participant is exposed to the treatment. Exposure to a treatment can also be conceptualized as the *duration* of a treatment regimen for a particular problem. Some problems might require only 3 weeks of exposure to a treatment whereas other problems might require a considerably longer time to reconcile a particular problem (e.g., 10–15 weeks).

Participant comprehension refers to the degree to which a participant understood or comprehended the content or rationale of a treatment. For example, in problem-solving replacement behavior intervention, a teacher's understanding of the difference between attention-maintained and escaped-maintained behaviors would constitute participant comprehension. *Participant responsiveness* refers to the extent to which a participant is engaged in treatment and finds it relevant.

PROBLEM-SOLVING SEL INTERVENTIONS

Problem-solving SEL interventions are based on the behavioral consultation model described earlier in this chapter. Recall that this model has four distinct phases: (1) problem identification, (2) problem analysis, (3) plan implementation, and (4) problem evaluation. SEL interventions based on this approach can be virtually unlimited and can include a variety of intervention strategies. It is important to keep in mind that problem-solving SEL interventions are targeted toward the remediation of social skills *performance deficits* or so-called "won't do" problems. Recall that these types of deficits are due primarily to a lack of motivation for performing appropriate social behaviors and are often accompanied by competing problem behaviors. Typically, problem-solving SEL interventions involve *replacement behavior training* in which competing problem behaviors are "replaced" by prosocial behaviors by manipulating the schedules of reinforcement for these two types of behavior patterns. This procedure was described in Chapter 1 as the use of the matching law, which states that the rate of a behavior will match the rate of reinforcement for that behavior.

Problem Identification

Problem identification, the first step in the problem-solving process, plays an important role in designing an intervention. Chances are very good that if a problem has been clearly defined, then an intervention is likely be successful. Problem identification involves five steps: (1) establishment of objectives, (2) establishment of measures for objectives, (3) establishment and implementation of data collection procedures, (4) presentation of data, and (5) definition of a problem by establishing a discrepancy between current and desired level of performance (Bergan & Kratochwill, 1990).

Establishment of Objectives

Performance objectives have several core characteristics. First, objectives must specify the behavioral performance required to achieve the objective.

For example, a teacher might have the objective for a student "to get along better" with classmates. Although the phrase "get along better" is unclear, it does point toward the direction that the teacher wants the behavior to change (increase a behavior). Second, an objective must specify the level of performance that will be required for the attainment of the objective. For example, the teacher might specify that "getting along better" would be indicated by increases in positive social interactions with peers by 50%. Third, an objective should specify the conditions under which performance of the objective is expected to occur. For instance, "getting along better" with classmates might be expected to occur during unstructured activities in the classroom.

Establishment of Measures for Objectives

Assessment of social skills was discussed extensively in Chapter 3. In terms of problem identification, a number of the assessment techniques for progress-monitoring decisions described in Chapter 3 can be used as measures for objectives. These include systematic direct observations, direct behavior ratings, brief behavior ratings, ODRs, and norm-referenced social skills rating scales. Each of these measures has distinct advantages and disadvantages.

Implementation of Data Collection Procedures

Decisions concerning how data will be collected are an essential aspect of problem identification. These decisions can be guided by answering the following questions concerning data collection:

1. What should be assessed? (direct observations, direct behavior ratings, brief behavior ratings, etc.)
2. How often should behavior be assessed? (once per day, three times per week, etc.)
3. How long should behavior be assessed? (over 2 weeks, 1 month, etc.)

Answering these questions will lead to an informed decision regarding a proper assessment of social behavior.

Presentation of Data

After data have been collected by one or more assessment methods, they should be summarized in a manner that can easily be understood. Perhaps the easiest and most useful way of displaying data is through the use of a line graph. Visually depicting behavioral performance in the form of a graph is easier to understand than data presented verbally or in a table. In a graph, one can easily gauge the *level* (increases or decreases over time), *trend* (upward or downward), and *variability* (fluctuations) occurring over successive time periods. Variations of graphs can also include bar charts (histograms), pie charts, or cumulative frequency graphs.

Discrepancy between Current and Desired Levels of Performance

In a problem-solving approach, the magnitude of a problem is defined as a discrepancy between current and desired levels of performance. The larger this discrepancy, the larger the problem. For example, if systematic direct observations of cooperative behavior showed a current level of twice per day and the desired level is eight times per day, then the discrepancy would be six times per day. Another example might be if a norm-referenced social skills rating scale showed that a child was functioning at the 10th percentile and the desired level would be at the 50th percentile, then the discrepancy would be 40 percentile ranks.

Problem Identification Interview

In a problem-solving approach, the problem identification process is initiated via a *problem identification interview* (PII). In a PII, a consultant (psychologist, counselor, or behavior specialist) guides a consultee (parent, teacher, or other school staff members) through the problem-solving process that results in specification of objectives to be accomplished. The primary goal of the PII is to obtain a precise description of the current behavior of concern to the consultee. The consultant obtains behavioral descriptions that specify exactly what the child does and does not do. Additionally, another goal is to specify the conditions under which the behavior is and is not occurring by focusing on the antecedent, consequent, and sequential events surrounding the behavior. Finally, the consultant gathers tentative information about the severity of the problem in terms of specifying the discrepancy between current and expected levels of performance. The following outline provides an illustration of a PII that is typically used in a problem-solving approach to SEL intervention.

1. Determine the behaviors and the strengths of the behaviors of concern.
   a. Introduce discussion about the child's problem behaviors. *"Tell me about Frank."*
   b. Obtain a precise description of the child's behavior. *"Tell me about Frank's problems in getting along with others in your classroom."*
   c. Continue asking the consultee to give you a behavioral definition

of the problem. *"What does Frank do when he does not get along with others?"*
- *"Give me some examples of situations where Frank does not get along with others."*
d. Get an estimate of the severity of the behavior. *"How often during the day does Frank not get along with others?"*; *"You have said that Frank does not get along with others about five times per day. Is that right?"*
2. Determine the conditions under which the behaviors of concern occur.
   a. Determine the antecedent conditions of the behavior. *"What is usually going on right before Frank is having problems in getting along with others?"*
   - *"What are you doing just before Frank is not getting along with others?"*
   - Determine the consequent conditions of the behavior. *"What do you do just after Frank has problems in getting along with others? What are his peers doing when this happens?"*
   - Determine the sequential conditions related to the behavior. *"Are there any days where this is more of a problem than other days?"*; *"You said that Frank has difficulty in getting along with others when some of his peers tease him. Is that right?"*
3. Establish performance assessment procedures.
   a. *"We need to get a record of how often Frank does not get along with others."*
   b. Tell the consultee why we are collecting these data. *"This record will tell us how much of a problem Frank is having with others."*
   - Establish data collection procedures. *"Could you record the number of times per day that Frank has problems in getting along with others?"*; *"Can you also note what happens just before and just after Frank has these problems?"*
   - *"We agreed that you could record the number of times per day that Frank has difficulty in getting along with others. Is that right?"*; *"We also agreed that you could note what is going on just before and just after Frank has these difficulties. Is that right?"*
4. Make arrangements for subsequent contacts with the consultee.
   a. Arrange for the next interview. *"Could we meet next Wednesday or Thursday to discuss Frank's problems?"*
   b. *"Would you prefer to meet with me briefly after school?"*
   - Arrange for a contact to monitor data collection procedures. *"Would it be OK if I dropped by to see how your data collection is going?"*

As you can see from the above questions in the PII, the consultant is trying to get a precise specification of behavior and its possible maintaining conditions. You will also note that at times the consultant summarizes the information the consultee has provided to make sure that they are on the same page. A good PII contains a lot of questions on the part of the consultant and a lot of answers that provide information on the part of the consultee. The way the consultant elicits information from the consultee is through the frequent use of questions ("How often or how much") and imperatives ("Tell me" or "Describe"). These questions and imperatives keep the PII on track and do not allow the consultee to "wander" of the topic.

Problem Analysis

The goal in problem analysis is to help the consultee identify factors or conditions that influence the problem to be solved in consultation. The consultant must have the necessary knowledge and skills to analyze problems presented by the consultee and be able to communicate this knowledge to the consultee. Problem analysis consists of two distinct phases: (1) *an analysis phase* and (2) *a plan design phase.*

Analysis Phase

In the analysis phase, one approach would be for the consultant to focus on external and internal factors that may affect the accomplishment of consultation goals. For example, the consultant may focus on the antecedent and consequent conditions surrounding the behavior. A second approach in the analysis phase is to analyze the skills that the child and consultee needs to achieve the consultation goals. An example might be that a child does not have the necessary social skills to get along with others in the classroom. In this case, these social skills must be directly taught to the child before he or she can successfully interact with peers. In the case of the consultee, a teacher might not have the skills to create an instructional environment that would be conducive to the facilitation of positive social behaviors among students. In this case, the consultant would have to work with the consultee in developing these skills.

The initial step in problem analysis is to determine whether to focus on the analysis of skills or on the analysis of conditions, or on both. For example, a child may have problems in self-control of anger in social interactions with peers. In this case, there should be consideration of the skills the child would need for anger management and then teach these skills directly to the child.

If the goal of consultation is to increase or maintain behavior, problem analysis should focus on the conditions that may influence the frequency of behavior. This would necessitate consideration of the antecedent, sequential, and consequent conditions surrounding behavior. From a behavior analytic perspective, this would involve a thorough A-B-C (antecedent–behavior–consequence) analysis that could be used to design an SEL intervention. Antecedent conditions are events that occur prior to behavior and can be either stimulus events (occurring immediately prior to behavior) or setting events (temporally and situationally removed from behavior). Consequent events occur immediately after a behavior and cause the behavior to increase (reinforcement) or decrease (punishment). Sequential events indicate the patterning of events across a period of time.

Plan Design Phase

The plan design phase consists of two parts: (1) development of plan strategies and (2) development of plan tactics. *Plan strategies* are broad strategies that can be used to attain the goals of consultation. For example, a consultant might recommend to a teacher that he or she use differential reinforcement of alternative behavior to increase the level of a student's prosocial behavior. *Plan tactics*, on the other hand, describe the specific procedures to be used to implement the plan strategy. For example, a consultant might instruct a teacher to reinforce prosocial behavior with attention using a variable ratio schedule (e.g., VR-5). The essential difference between plan strategies and plan tactics is that the former indicates what principles may be useful in changing behavior and the latter translates these principles into specific actions.

Problem Analysis Interview

The problem analysis process is initiated via the problem analysis interview (PAI) in which a consultant and a consultee decide if a problem exists that would call for a problem analysis. If so, the consultant and consultee discuss the conditions and/or skills that may be influencing a child's behavior and they subsequently design a plan to remediate the problem. The following is an example of a PAI for a social skills problem.

1. Validate the problem.
   a. *"Let's look at Frank's data on his not getting along with others."*
   b. If data are not sufficient, then tell the consultee to collect more data. *"Since Frank was sick most of last week, we need to get some more data before we can proceed."*
   c. If data are sufficient, ask questions about the data. *"According to the data you have here, Frank had difficulty in getting along with others, on average, about five times per day. Is that correct?"*

    d. Set goals for intervention outcomes. *"About how many times per day would you like to see Frank get along with others?"; "You said last week you would like to see Frank get along with others about five times per day. Is that correct?"*

    e. Discuss the discrepancy between current and expected levels of performance. *"It looks like there is a discrepancy of about five times per day between how Frank is behaving now and how you would like to see him behave. Is that correct?"*

2. Conduct a conditions analysis.

    a. *"What generally happens just before Frank has difficulty in getting along with others? What were his classmates doing when this happens?"*

    b. *"What happens right after Frank has these problems with his peers? How do you react? How do they react?"*

    c. Determine the sequential conditions of the baseline behavior. *"When during the day does Frank have the most difficulty in getting along with peers?"; "Is this more of a problem in the morning or the afternoon?"; "What are you teaching in the morning and afternoon?"*

    d. Focus attention on those conditions that may be involved in plan design and establish agreement regarding these conditions. *"You said sometimes you ignored Frank when he had these problems and sometimes you reprimanded him. Is that right?"; "You also said that Frank's peers sometimes ignored him and other times that did not. Is that right?"*

    e. Design a plan to attain problem solution. *"Let's come up with a plan to solve Frank's problem with getting along with his peers. One thing we could do is to use a procedure called precorrection. Precorrection involves taking Frank aside before class and instructing him about situations where he is likely to have problems in getting along with peers. You would discuss these situations and tell him what to do instead of being uncooperative."; "You could also reinforce Frank for getting along with peers by verbal praise and letting him have access to preferred activities."*

    f. Establish agreement regarding the plan. *"We agreed that you would use both precorrection and reinforcement for getting along with peers. Is that correct?"*

    g. Reaffirm data collection procedures. *"You said you could count the number of times per day Frank got along with his peers. Is that correct?"*

3. Make arrangements for subsequent contact with the consultee.

    a. Arrange for a problem evaluation interview. *"When could we meet next week to see how things are going? Where would be a convenient place for us to meet?"*

b. Arrange for monitoring the plan implementation. *"Can I stop by next Wednesday and see how things are going? When would be the best time for me to stop by?"*

c. Set up training if necessary. *"When would be the best time for me to show you how to use the precorrection and reinforcement procedures?"*

Plan Implementation

Plan implementation is the third stage of the problem-solving process. At this stage the plan designed in problem analysis is implemented. The effectiveness of a plan depends directly on how well a plan is implemented. The consultee is usually responsible for implementing the plan that was developed in problem analysis. It should be noted that consultees (e.g., teachers or parents) have very little training in the application of psychological principles for changing behavior. It is the consultant's responsibility to ensure that consultees know how to implement the plans developed in problem analysis. This may require the consultant to conduct training sessions in the intervention prior to plan implementation.

There are two types of monitoring that occur during plan implementation: (1) monitoring of child behavior and (2) monitoring of treatment integrity. Teachers can monitor child behavior on a daily basis by using simple frequency counts of the target behavior. Teachers can also use DBRs or brief behavior rating scales to monitor child behavior (see Chapter 3). Monitoring of treatment integrity requires the consultant to observe the actual implementation of the treatment plan. Assessment of treatment integrity is a critical aspect of intervention because poorly or inconsistently implemented plans have very little chance of being effective in changing behavior (Gresham, 1989, 2014). Treatment integrity was discussed extensively earlier in this chapter.

There are three categories of objectives that should take place during plan implementation: (1) skill development objectives, (2) implementation monitoring, and (3) plan revision. These objectives are listed below.

Skill Development Objectives

• Determine if the consultee has the skill to implement the plan correctly.
• Determine the feasibility of skill training in plan implementation.
• Develop procedures to increase skill mastery.
• Evaluate skill training.

Implementation Monitoring

• Monitor the child's target behavior(s).
• Monitor the treatment integrity of the plan.

Plan Revision

- Determine the need for a plan revision.
- Develop a revised plan if needed.

Problem Evaluation

The purpose of problem evaluation is to determine if the goals of consultation have been satisfactorily met. Three decisions can be made in problem evaluation concerning the plan: (1) continue the plan, (2) terminate the plan, or (3) change the plan. Problem evaluation typically takes place by the visual inspection of graphical data to determine changes in level (average amount of behavior change), trend (upward or downward change in behavior), and variability (fluctuations in behavior over time). The process of problem evaluation takes place through the problem evaluation interview (PEI) described below.

Problem Evaluation Interview

The PEI is used to evaluate plan effectiveness. Two procedural details should be noted in the PEI: (1) to schedule additional interviews or (2) to terminate consultation. If one or more goals have not been met, then it will be necessary to schedule additional interviews. If the goals have been achieved, then the consultant should formally terminate consultation. An example of a PEI is presented below.

1. Evaluate goal attainment.
   a. Initiate the evaluation process. *"Show me the data on Frank's getting along with peers from last week."*
   b. Describe the child's behavior during plan implementation. *"It looks like Frank got along much better with his peers last week."*
   c. Establish recall of the specific behavioral goal under consideration. *"In our first meeting, you said that Frank had problems in getting along with peers about five times per day. You also said you would like for him to interact appropriately with peers about five times per day. Is that right?"*
   d. Evaluate the goal under consideration. *"Do we agree that Frank has met his goal in getting along better with peers?"*
2. Decide whether to move to the next phase of problem solving or to return to earlier stages of consultation.
   a. Determine whether to move to the next phase of consultation. *"Let's discuss the effectiveness of our plan to help Frank get along better with his peers."*

    b. Evaluate whether to go back to earlier phases of consultation. *"Since Frank has met his goal, we can now move on to the next phase of the problem-solving process."*

3. Evaluate plan effectiveness.
    a. Evaluate whether the plan was responsible for behavior change. *"Do you think the plan was responsible for the changes in Frank's behavior with his peers?"*
    b. Evaluate whether the consultee thinks the plan would work with other children or in other situations. *"Do you think this plan would be effective with other children in your classroom?"; "Do you think the plan would work on the playground?"*

4. Carry out postimplementation planning.
    a. Initiate a consideration of a postimplementation plan alternatives. *"We may want to consider gradually reducing the amount of the plan that Frank receives."*
    b. Talk about plan modifications. *"We could reduce the amount of your social praise and the number of precorrection sessions over the next 2 weeks."*
    c. Establish postimplementation data collection procedures. *"We could reduce the number of times you tracked Frank's behavior to three times per week."*
    d. Terminate consultation. *"Since our goal for Frank has been met, this will be our last meeting. I have enjoyed working with you on this. If you have additional concerns about Frank or other students, give me a call."*

SOME TIER 2 INTERVENTIONS FOR PERFORMANCE DEFICITS

A number of antecedent- and consequence-based strategies can be used to remediate social skills performance deficits using Tier 2 selected interventions. Recall that the basis for social skills performance deficits can often be traced to antecedent and/or consequent conditions surrounding behavior. These procedures are used to enhance the performance of social skills and to reduce competing problem behavior. The following sections review these antecedent- and consequence-based strategies.

Antecedent-Based Strategies

Antecedent-based strategies focus on modifying or creating social environments that will lead to increases in appropriate social behavior. These strategies are presented within four intervention approaches: peer-mediated strategies, cuing/prompting, precorrection, and check-in/check-out.

Peer Initiations

Peer initiations involve the recruitment and training of a child's peers to engage that individual in prosocial interactions. This approach has been used primarily with socially isolated or neglected children who tend to engage in social withdrawal behaviors (Kohler & Strain, 1990). It should not be used with aggressive or oppositional–defiant children. It also should not be used with children who have social skills acquisition deficits. Table 5.1 presents guidelines for using peer initiations to facilitate positive social interactions of socially isolated or neglected children.

Cuing/Prompting

Stimuli that precede a behavior (i.e., antecedent stimuli) acquire an evocative effect on a given behavior. Reinforcement of behavior in the presence of certain stimuli, over time, makes those stimuli become discriminative stimuli. Discriminative stimuli signal that a behavior will be reinforced in their presence and will not be reinforced in their absence. Response prompts are supplementary antecedent stimuli used to cue a behavior in the presence of a discriminative stimulus.

There are three types of response prompts: verbal instructions, modeling, and physical guidance. Verbal instruction response prompts involve either verbal or nonvocal verbal (written words, pictures, manual signs) instruction. An example of a verbal response prompt might be to tell a child, "Look at the other person when you are talking to him." An example of a nonvocal verbal instruction might be a posted classroom rule that states: "Be nice to your classmates." Verbal response prompts are an easy and efficient way to prompt appropriate social behavior.

Modeling can be used as a response prompt to evoke a behavior. Modeling can effectively prompt behaviors and is an easy and practical way of teaching a complex social skill by showing children how to execute a

---

TABLE 5.1. Guidelines for Using Peer Initiations

- Recruit peer helpers who display a high degree of self-confidence and are well liked by peers.

- Train peer helpers in social-initiation strategies. Use modeling, behavioral rehearsal of peer initiation strategies, feedback on behavioral rehearsal, reinforcement for competent performances, and direct instruction in specific behaviors required to initiate a social interaction.

- Using procedures in Guideline 2 above, prepare peer helpers for initial rejection or being ignored.

- Periodically conduct booster sessions to retrain peer helpers and to discuss unique problems they may be having in conducting social initiations.

behavior. In using modeling, the learner must observe the model and be able to imitate the behavior of the model. Modeling can be used to teach a host of social skills ranging from appropriate peer group entry strategies to dealing with teasing and name calling.

Physical guidance is a response prompt that is used primarily with young children or children with severe disabilities. In physical guidance, the teacher partially physically guides the student through then entire movement of the behavior. Physical guidance functions as an effective response prompt, but it is more intrusive than verbal instruction and modeling because it requires direct physical involvement between the teacher and the student. If physical guidance is used, it is important to remember that at some point this prompt should be faded and ultimately eliminated.

Precorrection

Precorrection is a useful antecedent approach that facilitates prosocial behavior. In precorrection, a problem behavior is presented and a prompt is given for an appropriate social behavior alternative. Precorrection typically occurs in seven steps.

- Specify the context for the expected behavior. This context could be any situation, circumstance, setting, or occasion in which the target behavior is expected to occur.
- Specify the expected behavior to the student. Typically, the expected behavior is incompatible with a problem behavior (e.g., compromising in conflict situations vs. fighting with others).
- Modify the situation in which a problem behavior is more likely to occur. For example, if two students frequently argue with each other in class, the teacher might move them across the room from each other (proximity control of behavior).
- Practice behavioral rehearsal of the expected target behavior. For example, if the target behavior is taking turns in conversations, the student would be asked to role-play a conversation in which taking turns could be rehearsed.
- Reinforce the student's appropriate performance of the behavior to ensure its reoccurrence.
- Prompt the expected behavior throughout the day.
- Monitor the student's performance of the expected behavior, using teacher reporting, *self*-monitoring, or peer reporting.

Check-in/Check-out

Check-in/check-out (CICO) is a school-based Tier 2 selected intervention that provides daily support to students who are at risk for developing more serious behavior problems. CICO is based on three "big ideas" discussed by Crone, Hawken, and Horner (2010):

1. At-risk students will benefit from clearly defined expectations, frequent feedback, consistency, and positive reinforcement that is contingent on meeting goals.
2. Social skills, problem behaviors, and academic performance are linked.
3. Behavior support begins with the development of effective adult–student relationships.

CICO promotes increased collaboration between school and home and provides for increased opportunities for self-management. Although a major component of CICO is positive reinforcement (a consequence strategy), I placed it under the heading of antecedent interventions because it relies heavily on the communication of behavioral expectations and consistency (antecedent conditions).

CICO contains a number of elements and procedures that are required for its successful implementation. A general overview of these key elements is provided below.

Personnel

CICO is managed by a school-based coordinator who can be a behavior specialist, school psychologist, or school counselor. The intervention is also managed by the classroom teacher who provides consistent feedback and praise.

Student Identification

A student can be identified as a candidate for the CICO intervention in one of four ways: (1) the behavior support team in the school screens students' behaviors that put them at risk (e.g., increases in ODRs or school absences), (2) the systematic screening of all students for behavior problem and social skills deficits, (3) teacher nomination, and (4) the student did not respond adequately to a Tier 1 universal SEL intervention.

Process

The CICO intervention involves a daily cycle and a weekly cycle (typically every 2 weeks). The daily cycle involves the following elements:

- The student arrives at school and checks in with an adult (the CICO coordinator).
- At this check-in, the student receives a daily progress report (DPR).

- The student carries the DPR throughout the school day and hands it to the teacher at the start of each class period.
- The student retrieves the DPR after each class period and receives feedback from the teacher related to his or expected social behaviors.
- At the end of the day, the student returns the DPR to the CICO coordinator, who determines whether the student's daily point goals were met, and then the student carries a copy of the DPR home.
- Family members receive the DPR, deliver praise for success, and sign the form. The student returns the signed DPR to school the next day.

The CICO intervention is appropriate for students who are at risk for developing more serious social skills deficits and problem behaviors. These students typically engage in low-level problem behaviors such as coming to school unprepared, talking out in class, and exhibiting minor disruptive behaviors in the classroom. The CICO intervention is predicated on the assumption that students engage in problem behaviors in order to obtain adult attention. The CICO intervention is *not appropriate* for students who engage in serious or violent behaviors. These types of students might benefit from CICO, but they will require much stronger (Tier 3 intensive) interventions to address their behavior problems. Chapter 10 provides several examples of CICO SEL intervention for various types of social skills problems.

Consequence-Based Interventions

Differential Reinforcement of Incompatible Behaviors

The application of differential reinforcement involves reinforcement of one response class and withholding reinforcement for another response class. Differential reinforcement consists of two components: (1) providing reinforcement contingent on a behavior that is incompatible with the problem behavior and (2) withholding reinforcement as much as possible for the problem behavior. Differential reinforcement is one of the most effective and widely used techniques to reduce problem behavior and to increase socially skilled behavior (Cooper et al., 2007). Recall the description of the matching law earlier in this book.

The matching law is based on the notion of differential reinforcement. It states that the rate or frequency of behavior will match the rate or frequency of reinforcement for that behavior. For example, talking aggressively to others is reinforced every five times it occurs and talking nicely to others is reinforced every 15 times it occurs, talking aggressively will occur three times more frequently than talking nicely (15/5 = 3).

Differential reinforcement of incompatible behavior (DRI) reinforces a behavior that cannot occur simultaneously with the problem behavior and withholds reinforcement following occurrences of the problem behavior. In the above example of the matching law, a DRI intervention would increase the frequency of reinforcement for talking nicely to others and decrease the frequency of reinforcement for talking aggressively to others. If you reinforced talking nicely every time it occurred and reinforced talking aggressively every five times it occurred, talking nicely would be five times more frequent than talking aggressively (5/1 = 5).

The following guidelines have been shown to increase the effectiveness of DRI:

- Select an incompatible behavior that is already in the child's repertoire.
- Select reinforcers that are powerful and can be delivered consistently.
- Reinforce incompatible behavior immediately and consistently.
- Withhold reinforcement for the problem behavior.
- Consider combining DRI with other intervention procedures (e.g., response cost, time-out, stimulus fading).

Chapter 10 provides a case study example of using DRI as a tool in replacement behavior training.

Behavioral Contracts

Behavioral contracts (sometimes called contingency contracts) are documents that specify a contingent relationship between the completion of specified behaviors and access to a reinforcer. Usually, behavioral contracts specify how two or more people will behave toward each other. Unlike verbal agreements, behavioral contracts have a high degree of specificity in designing, implementing, and evaluating an intervention. Behavioral contracts have been used successfully to modify a variety of behaviors such as homework completion, school grades, completion of chores in the home, and improvement of social skills (Cooper et al., 2007).

Behavioral contracts consist of three major components: (1) a task description, (2) a specification of the reinforcement contingency, and (3) a task record. The task aspect of a behavioral contract has four parts: *who* (the person who will perform the task), *what* (the behavior to be performed), *when* (the time when the task must be completed), and *how well* (a list of steps detailing how to perform the behavior. The specification of the reinforcement contingency specifies *who* will judge the completion of the task. *What* is the reinforcement that will be delivered after successful task completion. *When* specifies the time that the reinforcement can be received by the target student. *How much* is the amount of reinforcement that can be earned by completing the task. The task record is used to progress-monitor behavioral performance specified in the contract. Guidelines for writing behavioral contracts for social skills are listed below. Chapter 10 shows an example of an SEL intervention using a behavioral contract.

- Clearly specify in the written contract what you and the child expect to gain from the agreement to participate in the contract. For example, you may want a child to increase the frequency of compromising in conflict situations with others. In return, the child may want to have more computer time. Note that you can also write a behavioral contract with the entire classroom in which you would specify participation in role-playing activities and compliance with group rules as things you want to gain. In return, you can specify a group-preferred reinforcer that students will gain when they comply with the contract.
- Specify only observable behaviors that you can easily monitor.
- Specify the negative consequences for failure to meet the terms of the contract.
- Include a bonus clause to reinforcement consistent compliance with the contract over an extended period of time.
- Have all parties sign the contract.
- Keep the contract simple so that children fully understand what is expected of them.
- If the contract does not seem to be influencing behavior or if you want to change the target behavior or the reinforcers, renegotiate the contract.

Positive Practice

Positive practice is a behavior reduction technique based on the principle of overcorrection. Overcorrection involves the child having to engage in effortful behavior that is directly related to the problem. In positive practice overcorrection, contingent on the occurrence of a problem behavior, the child would be required to perform the correct form of the behavior or a behavior that is incompatible with the problem behavior. For example, if a child insulted a classmate (e.g., said "You're really stupid!"), the child would have to practice saying nice things to the insulted classmate, to each person in the classroom, and to the teacher. Because positive practice serves an educational function by teaching the appropriate behavioral alternative to the inappropriate one, this practice is useful in SEL interventions. Guidelines for implementing positive practice are listed below.

- Determine what interfering problem behaviors will result in the use of positive practice.
- Identify a socially skilled alternative appropriate behavior that a student will practice after exhibiting an inappropriate behavior.
- Apply positive practice to behavioral incidents that occur naturally in the classroom (e.g., teasing, name calling, bullying).
- Apply positive practice immediately after the student exhibits the inappropriate behavior.
- Before applying positive practice, ask the student what he or she did that was inappropriate and what would be a better thing to do.
- Have the student practice the appropriate behavior four or five times.
- Note the function that positive practice is serving. If inappropriate behavior increases subsequent to your use of positive practice, discontinue the practice because it is serving as a reinforcer for inappropriate behavior.

Positive Peer Reporting

Positive peer reporting (PPR) is a classwide intervention strategy that is designed to address the poorly accepted child who disrupts the class by seeking negative attention. Some students thrive on peer attention and often do whatever they have to in order to get it. Many of these students attempt to intentionally irritate their classmates in an attempt to be noticed. These students often bother others to get attention although they may find themselves either socially isolated or overtly socially rejected.

PPR is based on the notion of reporting to the class something nice or socially appropriate a selected student did that day. The targeted student is the student who, in the past, engaged in disruptive behavior for negative peer attention. In PPR, classmates provide positive peer attention for socially appropriate behavior. In a very real sense, PPR involves "tattling" on a student for exhibiting appropriate behavior. Listed below are several guidelines that can be used in setting up a PPR SEL intervention.

- Select one or more group rewards. Students will earn a point every time they successfully praise the target student.
- Decide how many points the class must earn collectively to be able to trade them in for a group reward.
- Choose students who are the target of the PPR intervention (one or two students at most).
- Teach students how to praise each other. Set aside 10–20 minutes to review fundamentals of praise statements with students.
- Post examples of What Is Praise? and Examples of Praise posters on the wall.

- Introduce the PPR intervention by telling students that they will all be contributing toward earning a group reward by using PPR.
- Implement the PPR intervention and keep track of points earned by the class.
- Tally the number of compliments given and add that number of points toward the class group reward.
- If the class meets their point goal, give the class their group reward.

A TIER 2 INTERVENTION FOR SOCIAL SKILLS ACQUISITION DEFICITS

The SSIS-IG

The SSIS-IG is a highly structured and detailed manualized, commercially available Tier 2 selected intervention program (Elliott & Gresham, 2008). The SSIS-IG is conceptualized as teaching social skills across seven domains: Communication, Cooperation, Assertion, Responsibility, Empathy, Self-Control, and Engagement. These seven domains were derived, in part, from research using the *Social Skills Rating System—Rating Scales* (Gresham & Elliott, 1990) and, more recently, the revision of the SSRS entitled as the SSIS-Rating Scales (Gresham & Elliott, 2008).

Instructional strategies in the SSIS-IG are based on principles derived from social learning theory and cognitive-behavioral therapy. Specifically, instructional strategies rely on modeling, coaching, behavioral rehearsal, performance feedback, and social problem solving. The theory of change for these intervention procedures and how they impact intervention outcomes is presented in Figure 5.3.

The theory-of-change model derives from social learning theory (Bandura, 1977, 1986), which utilizes the concept of vicarious learning and the role of cognitive-mediational processes in determining which environmental events are attended to, retained, and subsequently performed. Social learning theory is based on the idea of reciprocal determinism, which describes the role of an individual's behavior has on changing the environment and vice versa. The model utilizes strategies from social learning theory including modeling (vicarious learning), coaching (verbal instruction), behavioral rehearsal (practice) to enhance fluency of instructed social skills, and feedback/generalization programming strategies to facilitate transfer of taught social skills to naturalistic environments and situations outside of the group instructional setting.

Social skills are taught in this theory-of-change model using a six-step instructional sequence: tell (coaching), show (modeling), do (role playing), practice (behavioral rehearsal), monitor progress (feedback and self-assessment), and generalize (generalization programming). It is important

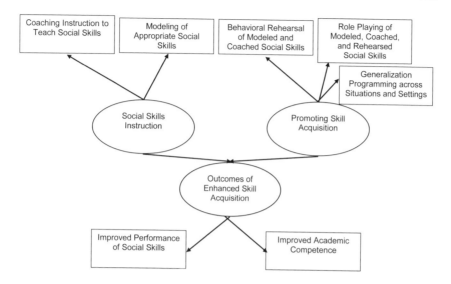

FIGURE 5.3. Theory of change: acquisition.

to note that in each phase, while one strategy provides the basis for instruction, other strategies may be concurrently used to augment learning. For example, in the *tell* phase, while coaching is the focal point of the lesson, elements of modeling may be used to illustrate examples of the featured skill, and social problem solving can help students to discuss and understand the importance of learning the skill.

The outcomes of this six-step instructional model lead to improved acquisition and performance of social skills and their generalization to other settings and social situations. Additionally, based on the earlier discussion of social skills as *academic enablers*, improved social skill performance is expected to lead to improved academic performance because it enables students to benefit from academic instruction (Caprara et al., 2000; DiPerma & Elliott, 2002; Malecki & Elliott, 2002; Wentzel, 2009).

The SSIS-IG remediation program for social skills deficits is delivered in a small-group setting (four to five children) conducted by a group leader experienced in working with small groups of children. The SSIS-IG is implemented for two sessions per week for 45 minutes per session (90 minutes per week) over a period of approximately 12 weeks. Approximately two social skills per week are targeted for instruction. The program takes advantage of well-established and effective teaching models, including situated learning, positive peer models, behavioral rehearsal, and specific performance feedback (see discussion of the theory of change above). In addition to the skills taught, the SSIS-IG offers materials that support home–school communications and student self-assessment to enhance generalization of instructed social skills outside of the school setting.

Skills Taught in the SSIS-IG

The social skills taught in the SSIS-IG program are derived from the SSIS-RS items (Gresham & Elliott, 2008). Twenty social skills are taught in the program. The conceptual foundation for these 20 social skills is based on the notion of *keystone behaviors*. Keystone behaviors are those behaviors that, when changed, are likely to lead to changes in other behaviors not targeted for change. Keystone behaviors form a response class that describes how behaviors are organized into more complex units that become functionally equivalent (Maag, 2006). Instructionally, it is more efficient and effective to identify and teach behaviors at the level of a response class rather than teaching numerous, unrelated separate behaviors. For example, out of 50 separate behaviors that might be targeted for intervention, it may be that only 10–15 behaviors need to be directly taught, if these behaviors were organized into a functionally equivalent response class. The previous discussion of the relationships among social skills, social tasks, and social competence captures this notion of response class. Social tasks such as playing a game, joining a peer group, and having a conversation are all examples of behaviors organized into a response class.

Remediation of Social Skills Deficits

The SSIS-IG for social skill deficits is delivered in small pullout groups (four to five students) in two 45-minute sessions per week resulting in 90 minutes of weekly social skills instruction over 12 weeks for a total of approximately 18 hours of SEL intervention. Students stay in the same group for the duration of the intervention. Instructional strategies involve a six-step instructional sequence involving: coaching, modeling, role playing/problem solving, behavioral rehearsal, progress monitoring/feedback, and generalization programming.

In the *coaching phase*, the group leader presents and defines the social skill, discusses its importance, and outlines the steps in performing the target social behavior. Coaching teaches general principles of social interaction, allows for integration of behavioral sequences in performing a social skill, sets appropriate goals for accomplishing social interactions, and enhances students' awareness of the impact of their social behavior on others (Oden & Asher, 1977).

The *modeling phase* depicts positive and negative social behaviors using pictures, video clips, and role plays as well as discussion of alternatives to accomplish the social–behavioral objective. It utilizes principles of vicarious learning and observational learning as described by Bandura (1977, 1986) in his classic work on social learning (social cognitive) theory.

Modeling is one of the most efficient and effective methods of teaching social skills because it does not require that every behavioral component be individually taught in a given behavioral sequence. Much of the research in SEL interventions utilizes modeling as an essential treatment strategy (Bierman & Powers, 2009; Cook et al., 2008; Gresham, Van, & Cook, 2006; Walker et al., 2004).

The *role-playing* and *social problem-solving phase* directs students to review the social skills definition, describe its importance, review the skill step components, and then enact the social skill in a role-play situation. Social problem solving teaches students how to resolve interpersonal conflicts and problems using a general strategy (general case programming) rather than specific skills. It involves many of the techniques and strategies used in the coaching, modeling, and behavioral rehearsal phases.

The *behavioral rehearsal phase* requires students to practice the skills presented in the social skills lessons in contexts outside of the setting of the lesson. This phase incorporates behavioral rehearsal, which is the repeated practice of social skills that enhances retention of the concepts and processes. Behavioral rehearsal is important for the acquisition of social behavior (Bandura, 1977).

The *progress monitoring/feedback phase* requires students to reflect on their own progress. The group leader encourages this reflection using the Social Skills Progress Chart. In addition, the group leader monitors and documents student progress and provides specific performance feedback to students during the lessons.

The *generalization phase* requires students to apply their skills in a variety of settings and social situations, and the group leader encourages students to practice outside the group situation. Generalization might be defined as the occurrence of relevant behaviors under different nontraining conditions without the specific scheduling of those same events or conditions (Stokes & Baer, 1977). The SSIS-IG incorporates generalization into every phase of social skills training (see Elliott & Gresham, 2008). Unlike many social skills programs, the SSIS-IG teaches students that there is more than one way to attain social goals. This program utilizes the generalization procedures outlined by Stokes and Osnes (1982, 1989) using procedures of training diversely, teaching relevant behaviors, and teaching functional mediators

CHAPTER SUMMARY POINTS

- Tier 2 selected interventions are provided for *some* students (about 20%) who do not respond adequately to Tier 1 universal interventions.

- Tier 2 selected intervention decisions consist of four steps: (1) *How much* intervention time is needed?, (2) *What* will occur during that time?, (3) *Who* will deliver the intervention?, and (4) *Where* will the intervention take place?

■ There are several advantages of Tier 2 selected interventions: (1) the intervention's intensity is matched to the degree of a student's responsiveness to that intervention, (2) Tier 2 interventions allow for early identification of behavior problems, (3) these interventions focus on positive student outcomes and emphasize direct measurement of social behavior and the instructional environment, and (4) these interventions increase reinforcement for appropriate social behavior and are applied across school settings.

■ There are two basic approaches to deliver Tier 2 selected interventions: (1) problem-solving approaches, and (2) standard protocol approaches.

■ Problem-solving approaches are based on the behavioral consultation model and take place in a sequence of four steps: (1) problem identification (What is the problem?), (2) problem analysis (Why is the problem occurring?), (3) plan implementation (What should we do about it?), and (4) problem evaluation (Did we solve the problem?).

■ Problem-solving approaches are most appropriate for social skills *performance deficits.*

■ Standard protocol approaches involve the use of manualized or scripted treatments and are most appropriate for the remediation of social skills *acquisition deficits.*

■ Establishing the accuracy of treatment implementation or treatment integrity is an essential aspect of Tier 2 selected interventions.

■ Problem identification is initiated via a problem identification interview that involves five steps: (1) establishment of objectives, (2) establishment of measures for objectives, (3) establishment and implementation of data collection procedures, (4) presentation of data, and (5) establishment of a discrepancy between current and desired levels of performance.

■ Problem analysis is initiated via a PAI consisting of two distinct phases: (1) an analysis phase (determining factors or conditions influencing the problem to be solved) and (2) a plan design phase (developing general plan strategies and specific plan tactics).

■ Plan implementation is the point at which an intervention is implemented and consists of two types of monitoring: (1) monitoring of child behavior (the target behavior to be changed) and (2) monitoring of treatment integrity (the degree to which the plan is implemented as intended).

■ Problem evaluation is used to evaluate a plan's effectiveness and occurs via a problem evaluation interview that results in two decisions: (1) to schedule additional interviews and/or to revise the plan or (2) to terminate consultation.

▪ Problem-solving consultation uses a variety of antecedent-based and consequence-based intervention strategies to facilitate the performance of social skills.

▪ Antecedent-based strategies focus on modifying or creating social environments that will lead to increases in prosocial behavior and include (1) peer-mediated strategies, (2) cuing/prompting, (3) precorrection, and (4) check-in/check-out.

▪ Consequence-based strategies focus on changing the consequent conditions surrounding behavior and include (1) differential reinforcement of incompatible behavior (DRI), (2) behavioral contracts, (3) positive practice, and (4) positive peer reporting.

▪ The SSIS-IG is a manualized SEL intervention designed to remediate social skills acquisition deficits.

▪ The SSIS-IG teaches social skills using a six-step instructional model: (1) tell (coaching), (2) show (modeling), (3) do (role playing), (4) practice (behavioral rehearsal), (5) monitor progress (feedback and self-assessment), and (6) generalize (generalization programming).

IMPLICATIONS FOR PRACTICE

• Expect that Tier 2 or selected SEL interventions will be needed by about 15% of the school population because they responded inadequately to the universal, or Tier 1, SEL intervention.

• Keep in mind that Tier 2 or selected SEL interventions are continuously available to the student, require low effort on the part of the person delivering the intervention, are consistent with schoolwide expectations, and are flexible based on student need.

• Remember that Tier 2 or selected SEL interventions focus on positive student outcomes and emphasize the *direct measurement* of social behavior and the instructional environment.

• Be aware that there are two fundamental types of Tier 2 selected SEL interventions: (1) problem-solving approaches and (2) standard protocol approaches.

• Know that problem-solving approaches are based on the behavioral consultation model consisting of four phases: (1) problem identification (What is the problem?), (2) problem analysis (Why is it occurring?), (3) plan implementation (What are we going to do about it), and (4) plan evaluation (Did we solve the problem?).

- Remember that standard protocol approaches involve the use of scripted or manualized treatments in which the components are written in specific detail.

- Be sure to assess the integrity with which any SEL intervention program is implemented to ensure the accuracy of program delivery using direct observation and/or permanent products.

- Use established antecedent-based SEL intervention strategies such as peer initiations, curing/prompting, check-in/check-out, and/or pre-correction.

- Use established consequence-based SEL intervention strategies such as differential reinforcement of incompatible behavior, behavioral contracts, and positive peer reporting.

CHAPTER SIX

Intensive Social–Emotional Learning Interventions

The last chapter described a number of problem-solving Tier 2 interventions and a standard protocol selected intervention (the SSIS-IG). Tier 2 interventions are designed for *some* students (about 20% who do not respond to Tier 1 universal interventions. However, not all of these students will respond adequately to these Tier 2 selected interventions either. It is estimated that approximately 3%–5% of children will require much more intensive Tier 3 interventions. These interventions are designed for a *few* students and are targeted toward children who are considered to be at high risk for the most serious social–emotional behavior problems.

Tier 3 intensive interventions have several features that differentiate them from Tier 2 selected interventions. One, these interventions are much more intense in terms of time, "dosage," and response effort than Tier 2 interventions. Two, these interventions are highly individualized and tailored to the specific needs of a particular child. Three, these interventions are based on a functional behavioral assessment (FBA) that reveals the function of problem behaviors and replaces them with a socially skilled alternative behavior that would serve the same function. Four, Tier 3 interventions take place over a considerably longer period of time that Tier 2 interventions.

The goal of Tier 3 intensive interventions is remediation of existing social–emotional problems and prevention of more severe problems. Chronic nonresponders to Tier 1 and Tier 2 interventions are candidates for Tier 3 interventions. However some students may have learning gaps so severe that the problem-solving team will recommend Tier 3 interventions without first trying Tier 2 intervention support. There is considerable increase in intensity with Tier 3 interventions, namely:

- The group size is only one to three students.
- The time per week is 150–300 minutes.
- The duration of service is 15–20 weeks.
- Progress monitoring is conducted at least twice per week.
- The level of intensity usually requires a full period of intervention held outside of the general education classroom.
- The professional responsible for intervention sessions, such as a school psychologist, behavior specialist, counselor, or school social worker, requires specialized training.

TIER 3 STRUCTURE AND CRITERIA

Tier 3 interventions need to be fast paced, with good modeling followed by focused guided practice. Ongoing positive corrective feedback is needed to maintain student interest and involvement. The intervention sessions are more intense because of the smaller group size and longer sessions. The intervention routine needs to be so familiar that the students are able to follow the lessons with little time wasted explaining basic directions. Lessons should reinforce old skills while modeling and teaching new ones. Tier 3 interventions should involve:

- Systematic and explicit instruction that includes modeling and direct teaching using multiple examples.
- Specialized programming that focuses on just a few key skills at a time.
- Mirroring of skills being taught in the general education classroom, as well as attention to filling gaps that are causing difficulty in the general education classroom.
- A variety of practice opportunities that coordinate with identified classroom skills but use different approaches.
- Continuous corrective feedback, encouragement, and self-monitoring activities.

REPLACEMENT BEHAVIOR TRAINING

An important consideration in the conceptualization of Tier 3 interventions is the contribution of *competing problem behaviors* that prevent children from acquiring or performing prosocial behaviors. Children and youth who require Tier 3 interventions often display high rates of competing problem behaviors such as aggression, noncompliance, defiance, and impulsivity that effectively compete with prosocial behavior patterns. For example, a child with a behavioral history of impulsivity and oppositional defiant behavior may never learn prosocial behavior alternatives such as cooperation and self-control because of the absence of opportunities to learn these behaviors (Eddy et al., 2002).

In the last chapter, I discussed the importance of the matching law in using an intervention known as differential reinforcement of incompatible behavior (DRI). Recall that the matching law states that the relative rate of a behavior will *match* the relative rate of reinforcement for that behavior. In other words, if one behavior is reinforced at a higher rate than another behavior, it will be "chosen" more frequently than the other behavior (i.e., the response rate matches the reinforcement rate). Many children requiring Tier 3 intensive SEL interventions have a learning history in which competing problems behaviors are "chosen" more frequently than prosocial behaviors because the reinforcement rate is higher for these behaviors. In short, these competing problem behaviors have greater *utility* in producing reinforcement to an individual than prosocial behaviors (Snyder & Stoolmiller, 2002).

Maag (2005) suggested that an effective way of decreasing competing problem behaviors is to teach positive replacement behaviors, or what has been called replacement behavior training (RBT). RBT is based on the matching law described above with the goal of identifying a prosocial behavior that will result in more frequent reinforcement relative to a competing problem behavior. Table 6.1 shows potential positive replacement behaviors for competing problem behaviors. RBT depends on identifying *functionally equivalent behaviors*. Behaviors are considered to be functionally equivalent if they produce similar amounts of reinforcement from the environment.

The functional equivalence of behavior is based on the notion of DRI in which a behavior that is incompatible with a problem behavior is reinforced. Behaviors are considered to be incompatible if they cannot occur simultaneously. For instance, following teacher directions and talking back to the teacher are incompatible because they cannot occur at the same time. A practitioner using DRI in this case would increase the rate of reinforcement for following directions and decrease the rate of reinforcement for talking back to the teacher.

It is important to remember that RBT based on DRI is only useful for the remediation of social skills *performance deficits* because the prosocial behavior chosen to replace the competing problem behavior must already be in the child's repertoire. It is not an appropriate intervention in remediating social skills *acquisition deficits* because if a prosocial behavior is not in a child's repertoire, it cannot be reinforced. Remediation of social skills

TABLE 6.1. Replacement Behaviors for Problem Behaviors

Problem behavior	Replacement behavior
• Disobeys rule or requests.	• Follows your directions.
• Is aggressive toward peers.	• Interacts well with peers.
• Breaks into or stops group activities.	• Waits his or her turn when playing games.
• Withdraws from others.	• Makes friends easily; introduces him- or herself to others.
• Is inattentive.	• Pays attention to your instructions.
• Bullies others.	• Acts responsibly with others.
• Acts anxious with others.	• Starts conversations with peers.
• Talks back to adults.	• Follows classroom rules.
• Blames others for his or her mistakes.	• Takes responsibility for his or her own behavior.

acquisition deficits will necessarily require an intensive Tier 3 standard protocol SEL intervention.

FACTORS CONSIDERED IN TIER 3 INTENSIVE INTERVENTIONS

A host of factors are related to a behavior's response or lack of response to intervention. Six factors that appear to be the most relevant for school-based interventions are (1) severity of behavior, (2) chronicity of behavior, (3) generalizability of behavior change, (4) treatment strength, (5) treatment integrity, and (6) treatment effectiveness. Each of these factors is discussed in the following sections.

Severity of Behavior

Behavioral severity can be defined using objective dimensions of behavior such as frequency, rate, duration, intensity, and permanent products (Cooper et al., 2007). Behavioral severity that is operationalized by high frequencies, durations, and/or intensities is more resistant to intervention than behaviors occurring at lower levels of these behavioral dimensions (Gresham, 1991; Nevin, 1988). These behaviors are not only more resistant to interventions, but also tend to produce high rates of positive reinforcement (e.g., social attention or access to tangible reinforcers) and/or negative reinforcement (e.g., escape or avoidance of task demands) for the student.

The net result is that these behaviors continue and even escalate despite interventions designed to reduce them. Using an analogy to physics, the "force" (strength of the intervention) is insufficient to change the "momentum" (severity) of behavior. Given this logic, it is clear that Tier 1 and Tier 2 interventions do not have sufficient "force" or strength to change severe behavior problems.

Chronicity of Behavior

One definition of *chronic* is "habits that resist all efforts to eradicate them" or "deep-seated aversion to change" (*Webster's New World College Dictionary, 4th Edition*). This use of the term *chronic* is directly related to the concept of response to intervention or, more accurately, resistance to intervention. One distinguishing feature of severe behavior problems is that they represent a pattern of behavior that continues despite interventions designed to change them (Gresham, 1991, 1999). Also, another use of the term *chronic* is "the recurrence of behavior problems" once they have been changed by an intervention. This use of the term *chronic* represents a problem in the *maintenance* of behavior change over time.

Children and youth requiring Tier 3 intensive interventions have a long history of serious behavior problems that are highly resistant to intervention. In addition, if a powerful Tier 3 intervention changes these behaviors, they are likely to recur in the absence of behavior supports to keep these behaviors at acceptable levels. As mentioned earlier, these children have been resistant to Tier 1 and Tier 2 interventions because they are not strong enough to change behavior. Also, some children may be "fast-tracked" into Tier 3 interventions without going through earlier tiers of an intervention program.

Generalizability of Behavior Change

Generalization and maintenance of behavior change is directly related to a behavior's resistance to intervention. If a behavior pattern is severe (i.e., in terms of frequency, intensity, and/or duration) or chronic (i.e., it has been resistant to intervention), it will tend to show less generalization across different, nonintervention conditions and will show less generalization over time when intervention conditions are withdrawn. Children who demonstrate severe behavior patterns over an extended period of time are quick to discriminate intervention from nonintervention conditions, particularly when intervention conditions are vastly different from nonintervention conditions. For example, when students are exposed to a highly structured point system that uses a response–cost component for inappropriate behaviors and a reinforcement component for prosocial behaviors, they will easily discriminate when the program is not in effect. Since discrimination is the polar opposite of generalization, behaviors under these conditions are likely to deteriorate to baseline levels of performance when one returns abruptly to preintervention conditions (withdrawal of the point system).

Children with severe behavior patterns often show excellent initial behavior change, particularly in terms of behavioral excesses, but fail to show generalization and maintenance of these behavior changes. A reason for this lack of generalization and maintenance is that interventions often exclusively target decreasing inappropriate behaviors at the expense of targeting the establishment of appropriate or prosocial behaviors. Furthermore, to ensure generalization and maintenance of intervention effects, these effects should be actively programmed (Cooper et al., 2007). Recent advance in positive behavior support in which entire schools recognize and abide by a common set of behavioral expectations for students should enhance the generalization and maintenance of individualized intervention effects (Sugai, Horner, & Gresham, 2002).

Treatment Strength

The strength of a treatment reflects the ability of a given treatment to change behavior in the desired direction. Strong treatments produce greater amounts of behavior change than weaker treatments. Treatment strength is not absolute, but rather situationally, behaviorally, and individually specific (Gresham, 1991). Some treatments are strong in some situations or settings, but not for others (e.g., home vs. school). Some treatments are strong for some behaviors, but not for others (e.g., work completion vs. physical aggression). Some treatments are strong for some individuals, but not for other individuals (typically developing children vs. children with ASD). In short, treatment strength is determined by the interaction of situational, behavioral, and individual factors.

In behavioral interventions, treatment strength is not always clearly quantifiable a priori as in other fields. For example, a 500-mg antibiotic is chemically twice as strong as a 250-mg antibiotic for treating bacterial infections. In contrast, four points awarded for prosocial behavior is not necessarily twice as strong as two points awarded. The fundamental difference between a specification of treatment strength in medical and behavioral treatments is that the form specifies treatment strength a priori (e.g., drug dosage) and the latter specifies treatment strength a posteriori (e.g., magnitude of behavior change). Treatment strength for Tier 3 SEL interventions, in part, can be specified a priori by intensity (twice a day, 5 days per week, for 15 weeks). However, one can only know the true strength of a treatment by the magnitude of behavior change that it produces.

Treatment Integrity

The degree to which a given treatment is implemented as planned or empirically validated describes the concept of treatment integrity (Gresham, 1989, 2014). Treatment integrity involves the accuracy and consistency with which an intervention is implemented. Treatment integrity is an essential ingredient of all interventions because effective treatments can be rendered ineffective simply because they were either implemented poorly or not implemented at all. It is also possible for ineffective treatments to be implemented with perfect integrity but have no effect on behavior change. Many SEL interventions designed in a problem-solving behavioral consultation model produce ineffective results because of the poor integrity with which these interventions are delivered.

The level of integrity with which SEL interventions are implemented in applied settings is likely to be lower than what is reported in the research literature. The integrity of interventions depends on several factors such as the complexity of the intervention, the time required to implement the intervention, the materials and resources required to implement the intervention correctly, and the perceived and actual effectiveness of the intervention (Gresham, 2014).

Treatment Effectiveness

The idea behind multi-tiered interventions is based on the notion that if an individual shows an inadequate response to intervention at lower tiers, then he or she will require a more intense intervention. If a behavior pattern continues at an unacceptable level, then it will require a more time-consuming, expensive, and intense intervention to change the behavior. Four approaches have been discussed to quantify whether or not treatments are effective or ineffective: (1) visual inspection of graphed data, (2) reliable changes in behavior, (3) changes on social impact measures, and (4) social validation.

Visual inspection of graphed data is perhaps the most straightforward way of quantifying the effect of an intervention. In this approach, an individual's level and trend of behavior in the intervention phase is compared to the level and trend of behavior in the baseline or pretreatment phase. Unlike traditional statistical analyses, visual inspection relies on the "interocular test" of significance. That is, if a meaningful effect was produced by the treatment, then it should be obvious or noticeable by simply viewing graphed data. A drawback in using this approach, however, it that there are no standards or benchmarks for deciding if behavior change is clinically or educationally significant.

Another approach to quantifying an effect of an intervention is to determine if the intervention has produced reliable changes in behavior.

Four metrics have been proposed to quantify the extent to which changes in behavior are reliable: (1) absolute change index, (2) reliable change index, (3) percent nonoverlapping data points, and (4) percent change from baseline.

An *absolute change index* is the degree or amount of behavior change an individual makes from baseline to postintervention phases of a treatment. Absolute change is straightforward, intuitively logical, and easy to calculate. It is also consistent with a problem-solving approach to defining behavior problems because of the discrepancy between current and desired levels of performance discussed extensively in Chapter 5. Using this approach, a problem is considered "solved" if the degree of absolute change is large relative to desired levels of performance.

There are some problems with using absolute change to quantify the effects of an intervention. For example, an individual might show a relatively large amount of behavior change from baseline to postintervention levels of performance, but this change might not be large enough to allow that individual to function within a particular setting. Absolute change also interacts with tolerance levels for problem behaviors at the classroom and school levels. That is, even though a change in behavior is large, the behavior pattern still might not be tolerated by significant others in the school environment.

The *reliable change index* (RCI) is calculated by subtracting an individual's posttest score on an outcome measure from his or her pretest score and dividing this difference by the standard error of difference between posttest and pretest scores (Nunnally & Kotsche, 1983). The standard error of difference represents the variability in the distribution of change scores that would be expected if no change had occurred. A RCI of +1.96 ($p < .05$) would be considered a reliable change in behavior.

The RCI has the advantage of quantifying reliable changes from baseline to postintervention levels of performance and confidence intervals can be placed around change scores to avoid overinterpretation of results. The RCI, however, is affected by the reliability of the outcome measures used. For example, if a measure is highly reliable (0.90 or greater), then small changes in behavior might be considered statistically reliable, but not socially or clinically important. In contrast, if a measure has relatively low reliability, then large changes in behavior might be socially important, but not considered statistically reliable. Also, the interpretation of RCI is clouded when using direct observations measures (e.g., frequency or duration) because "reliability" has a different meaning for these measures. As such, calculation of RCI does not have the same meaning because the data are nonparametric (i.e., they are not based on a normal distribution of test scores).

Percent nonoverlapping data points (PND) is a metric computed by calculating the percentage of nonoverlapping data points between baseline and intervention phases (Mastropieri & Scruggs, 1985–1986). If the goal is to decrease problem behavior, one computes PND by counting the number of intervention data points exceeding the highest baseline data point and dividing by the total number of data points in the intervention phase. For example, if 9 of 10 treatment data points exceed the highest baseline data point, the PND would be 90%. Alternatively, if the goal is to increase prosocial behavior, then one calculates PND by counting the number of intervention data points that are below the lowest baseline data point and dividing by the total number of data points in the intervention phase. PND provides a quantitative index to document the effects of an intervention that is easy to calculate.

Several drawbacks to using this method should be noted. One, PND often does not reflect the magnitude of an effect of an intervention. That is, one can have 100% nonoverlapping data points in the treatment phase yet have an extremely weak treatment effect. Two, unusual baseline trends (high and low data points) can skew the interpretation of PND. Three, PND is greatly affected by floor and ceiling effects. Four, aberrant outlier data points can make the interpretation of PND difficult (Strain, Kohler, & Gresham, 1998). Five, there are no well-established empirical guidelines for what constitutes large, medium, or small effects using PND.

An alternative to the PND statistic is to calculate the *percent change in behavior from baseline* to postintervention levels of performance. This metric involves comparing the median level of performance in baseline to the median level of performance in intervention. For example, if the median frequency of a behavior was 2 and the median frequency of a behavior after intervention was 8, then the percent change in behavior would be 75% (8–2/8 = .75, or 75%). The advantage of the percent change metric is that outliers or aberrant data points or floor and ceiling effects do not as greatly affect it as the PND index. Percent change is often used in medical treatments to evaluate the effects of drugs that reduce cholesterol or blood pressure. There are well-established medical benchmarks for desirable levels of blood cholesterol (<200 dl) and blood pressure (120/80). Unfortunately, there are no such benchmarks for many behaviors targeted for intervention in the area of social skills. Also, like with the PND, there are no clear guidelines for determining the magnitude of behavior change that are sufficient to indicate that an individual has demonstrated an adequate response to intervention. As such, this metric must be supplemented by other measures such as social validation measures that are described later in this chapter.

Changes on Social Impact Measures

The ultimate goal in intervention for children and youths with severe problems in social–emotional functioning is to change their standing on measures of social impact. A social impact measure is characterized by changes that are recognized to be critically important in everyday life. These measures represent socially valued intervention goals because social systems such as schools and mental health agencies utilize them to index the success or failure of interventions. Examples of social impact measures include sociometric status, friendship status, arrest rates, school dropout, and school suspensions/expulsions. These measures might be considered criterion measures against which behavior changes can be validated.

The drawback of using social impact measures is that they are not particularly sensitive in detecting short-term intervention effects. Many treatment consumers consider these social impact measures to be the bottom line in gauging successful intervention outcomes. However, exclusive reliance on these measures might ignore a great deal of behavior change (Kazdin, 1999). It is often the case that rather large and sustained changes in behavior are required before these changes are reflected on social impact measures. Sechrest, McKnight, and McKnight (1996) suggested using the method of *just noticeable differences* (JND) to index intervention outcomes. The JND approach answers the question: How much of a difference in behavior is required before it is "noticed" by significant others or reflected on social impact measures?

Social Validation

Social validity addresses three fundamental questions asked by professionals: What should we change? How should we change it? How will we know it was effective. There are often disagreements among professionals and between professionals and treatment consumers on these three fundamental questions. Wolf (1978) described the social validation process as involving the assessment of the social significance of intervention goals, the social acceptability of intervention procedures, and the social importance of intervention effects. This last aspect of the social validation process is most relevant in quantifying treatment effectiveness of Tier 3 intensive interventions.

Establishing *the social importance* of the effects of an intervention attests to the practical or educational significance of behavior change for a student. Do the quantity and quality of the changes in behavior make a difference in the student's behavioral functioning and adjustment? In short, do the changes in behavior have *habilitative validity* (Hawkins, 1991)? Is the student's behavior now in a functional range subsequent to the intervention? These questions capture the essence of establishing the social importance of intervention effects.

A way of establishing the social importance of intervention effects is to view behavioral functioning as belonging to either a functional or a dysfunctional distribution. An example might be socially validating an SEL intervention by showing that the student's social behavior moved from a dysfunctional to a functional range of performance. Using teacher and parent ratings on nationally normed social skills rating scales is one means of quantifying the social importance of intervention effects. Moving a student's social skills ratings from the 10th percentile to the 40th percentile would represent a socially important change. Similarly, changing a target behavior measured by systematic direct observations into the range of non-referred peers would also corroborate the behavior ratings and therefore could be considered socially important.

The social importance of effects is perhaps best conceptualized and evaluated on several levels: proximal effects, intermediate effects, and distal effects (Fawcett, 1991). Proximal effects are changes in target behaviors produced by an intervention such as increases in social skills or decreases in competing problem behaviors. Proximal effects can be evaluated using visual inspection of graphed data or percent change in behavior from baseline to intervention. Intermediate effects can be evaluated by more molar assessments such as substantial changes in social skills and problem behavior ratings on nationally normed behavior rating scales. Distal effects can be evaluated by changes on social impact measures such as ODRs, improvements in peer acceptance and friendships, reduced suspension/expulsion rates, and decreases in school absences.

FUNCTIONAL BEHAVIORAL ASSESSMENT

Definition of Functional Behavioral Assessment

Functional behavioral assessment (FBA) can be defined as a collection of techniques for gathering information about antecedents, behaviors, and consequences in order to determine the reason (*function*) of behavior (Gresham, Watson, & Skinner, 2001). Once the function of a behavior is determined, this information is used to reduce the problem behavior and facilitate prosocial behavioral alternatives. FBA is not a single test or observation, but rather a multimethod strategy involving observations, interviews, checklists, and review of records regarding student behavior, its antecedents, and its consequences. The central goal of FBA is to identify environmental conditions that are associated with the occurrence and nonoccurrence of behavior. In this approach, the function of behavior is represented by a change in an independent variable (environmental conditions) and the effect is represented by a change in a dependent variable (behavior). It should be noted that there are different kinds of functional relationships. Some functional relationships are *correlational,* meaning that certain environmental events co-occur with the occurrence of behavior. Other functional relationships may be *causal* in the sense that these environmental events are both necessary and sufficient to explain the occurrence of the behavior.

The function of behavior refers to the purpose that behavior serves for the individual. Behavioral functions typically fall into five categories: (1) social attention/communication (positive reinforcement); (2) access to tangibles or activities (positive reinforcement); (3) escape from, delay of, reduction in, or avoidance of aversive tasks or activities (negative reinforcement); (4) escape from or avoidance of other individuals (negative reinforcement); and (5) internal stimulation or automatic reinforcement (positive reinforcement). Note in the above categories, there are only two main functions of behavior: *positive reinforcement* and *negative reinforcement*.

Behavior analysts often make a distinction between *functional assessment* and *functional analysis*. Functional assessment describes the full range of procedures that can be used to identify the antecedents and consequences associated with the occurrence of behavior. Functional analysis refers to the experimental manipulation of environmental events in a highly controlled setting to assess the controlling functions these events have on behavior. Functional analysis uses experimental manipulations to make "causal" rather than descriptive or correlational statements about the operant function of behavior.

Treatment matched to the operant function of behavior may follow one of two strategies: (1) weakening the maintaining response–reinforcer relationship for problem behaviors (e.g., punishment or extinction) or (2) establishing or strengthening a response–reinforcer relationship for prosocial behavior that replaces the current function of problem behavior (e.g., DRI). Treatments based on the latter form the fundamental basis for replacement behavior training in the remediation of social skills performance deficits.

Principles Underlying FBA

In order to apply FBA principles in replacement behavior training, a basic understanding of contingencies is required. Contingencies describe a relationship between behavior (B) and its antecedent (A) and consequent (C) conditions. Although specific antecedent conditions precede and can be associated with a behavior, they do not describe the function of behavior. Rather, from an operant learning perspective, behaviors are maintained by (are a function of) consequences that occur contingent upon those behaviors.

Consequent Events

In the operant paradigm, there are only two broad functions of behavior: (1) positive reinforcement and (2) negative reinforcement. When a behavior is positively reinforced, the function of behavior is to bring the behavior into contact with a stimulus. Positive reinforcement can be in the form of social attention, which includes praise, sympathy, reprimands, redirection, consolation, restraint, smiles, frowns, or eye contact. Positive reinforcement can also result in access to tangible or material reinforcers (e.g., toys, food, clothing) or access to preferred activities (e.g., watching television, listening to music, playing video games).

Another source of positive reinforcement for a small number of individuals is known as nonsocial automatic or sensory reinforcement. This typically occurs in cases of self-injurious behavior (SIB) and/or stereotypic behaviors in which the effects of social reinforcement are inconclusive. In these cases, the effects of controlling variables are unclear, therefore leading some professionals to postulate that the behavior may be maintained by self-produced sensory, perceptual, or biological reinforcers.

When a behavior is negatively reinforced, the function of behavior is to remove, avoid, delay, or reduce contact with a stimulus. Engaging in behaviors that result in task demands being removed or modified is an example of a behavior resulting in negative reinforcement. Negative reinforcement, unlike positive reinforcement, involves the removal or modification of a stimulus that results in an increase in behavior.

In summary, a key principle in FBA is that positive reinforcement always involves either the presentation or contact with an event that increases the probability of behavior and negative reinforcement always involves the removal, avoidance, delay, or reduction of an event that increases the probability of behavior. Thus, when conducting FBAs, one should identify the positive and/or negative reinforcement contingencies and the specific antecedent conditions under which a behavior occurs.

Antecedent Events

As previously mentioned, the central tenet of operant learning theory is that behavior occurs or does not occur as a function of its consequences. As such, FBA seeks to identify reinforcement and punishment contingencies rather than antecedent events for which behavior is viewed as both secondary to and derived from its consequences. Antecedent events, however, can be classified as discriminative stimuli, establishing operations, or setting events. Each of these antecedent events are discussed briefly in the following paragraphs.

A *discriminative stimulus* or S^D is an antecedent event that is associated with or otherwise signals that a behavior will be reinforced. Almost all operant behavior is under stimulus control and, if this were not the case, all behavior would be equally likely on all occasions to result in chaos. Therefore, behavior that is reinforced in the presence of a given stimulus and not other stimuli is said to be under *stimulus control*. For example, the recess bell at school is a S^D for the class to go outside and play (presumably a reinforcing event). Operant intervention procedures relying on differential reinforcement are based on the principle of stimulus control (e.g., DRI).

Another antecedent event that has an influence on behavior is an *establishing operation* or EO. An EO is defined as a variable that temporarily alters the effectiveness of a reinforcer for behavior (Smith & Iwata, 1997). EOs do two things: (1) they increase the momentary salience of a stimulus as a reinforcer and (2) they increase the probability of behaviors that are associated with contacting that stimulus. For example, not drinking fluids and exercising heavily for a period of time are EOs for increasing the effectiveness of water as a reinforcer for drinking behavior and other behaviors associated with obtaining water.

EOs do not derive their functional properties through the process of differential reinforcement (i.e., via stimulus control), but rather their presence or absence mediates the effectiveness of stimuli as reinforcers to increase (establishing operation) or decrease (abolishing operation) the frequency of behavior. Northrup, Fusilier, Swanson, Roane, and Borrero (1997) showed that methelphenidate administered to children with ADHD functioned as an EO to alter the effectiveness of commonly used classroom reinforcers such as peer social attention and avoidance of task demands. Knowledge of EOs such as in the above study can substantially impact the effectiveness of a given intervention because of the different functions of the behavior in the presence of an EO.

Setting events are antecedent events that are removed in time and place from the occurrence of behavior, but are functionally related to that behavior. Given a particular setting event, a particular behavior is more likely to occur than if the setting event is absent. For example, getting into a fight on the bus on the way to school can serve as a setting event for noncompliance to teacher instructions later in the school day. Setting events, unlike discriminative stimuli, are removed in time and place from behavior (i.e., behavior is not under stimulus control of the setting event). Setting events, unlike EOs, do not necessarily alter the momentary effectiveness of a reinforcer.

FBA Methods and Procedures

FBA methods can be categorized as (1) *indirect,* using interviews, historical/archival records, checklists, and rating scales; (2) *direct,* using systematic direct observations in naturalistic settings; and (3) *experimental,* using standardized experimental protocols that systematically manipulate and isolate contingencies maintaining problem behavior using single-case experimental designs. Experimental methods are usually reserved for special populations and unusual behaviors and will not be discussed in this chapter.

Indirect FBA Methods

Indirect FBA methods involve the assessment of behavior that is removed in time and place from its actual occurrence. Functional assessment interviews, historical/archival records, and behavior rating scales or checklists are the most commonly used indirect FBA methods.

Functional Assessment Interviews

A functional assessment interview (FAI) has four primary goals: (1) to identify and operationally define the problem behavior, (2) to identify antecedent events (discriminative stimuli, setting events, and establishing operations), (3) to obtain preliminary information concerning the hypothesized function served by the problem behavior, and (4) to identify appropriate prosocial replacement behaviors that will serve the same function as the problem behavior. The problem analysis interview discussed extensively in Chapter 5 is actually an FAI. FAIs may be conducted with teachers, parents, and students to obtain preliminary information about behavioral functions. During the initial stages of functional assessment, it is important for interviewers to obtain information that is as precise as possible from third parties to assist in functional assessment. It should be noted that FAIs provides only one person's perception of a problem that will yield only partial information about behavioral function.

Historical/Archival Records

School records often contain a great deal of useful information for FBA. A first step in conducting an FBA should be a systematic review of these school records. One useful school record kept by all schools is an office disciplinary referral that contains the number of suspensions, the behaviors resulting in the suspensions, and the discipline action taken other than a suspension.

School record searches are an efficient use of time and can eliminate unnecessary redundancies in the FBA process. School records are one of the most valuable FBA methods for severe, low-frequency behaviors that are not amenable to direct observation such as physical assaults, bringing weapons to school, or destruction of school property. Also, along with FAIs, school records may provide one of the only ways to obtain information on students who have been suspended or expelled from school.

Behavior Rating Scales/Checklists

Behavior rating scales and checklists can be used as an adjunct to other FBA methods, serving as a brief initial method of identifying target behaviors for more in-depth functional assessment methods. Behavior rating scales do not provide information on the antecedents and consequences of target behaviors. Commonly used behavior rating scales include the *Teacher Rating Form, Child Behavior Checklist, Youth Self-Report* (Achenbach & Rescorla, 2001a, 2001b), *Conners Rating Scales* (Conners, 1997), and the *Social Skills Improvement System—Rating Scales* (Gresham & Elliott, 2008). Rating scales can also be adapted to include specification of antecedents and consequences as well as ratings of possible functions served by behavior.

Readers are cautioned not to rely exclusively on indirect FBA methods such as FAIs, archival records, and rating scales to determine behavioral function. It may be tempting to rely on these methods because of their relative brevity and efficiency. However, they are inadequate for conducting a comprehensive FBA.

Direct FBA Methods

Systematic direct observation of antecedents, behaviors, and consequences is the hallmark of FBA. Direct observation should be used to confirm the information obtained from the indirect assessment procedures described earlier. A useful method of conducting direct observation is an antecedent–behavior–consequence (A-B-C) recording form. In using this procedure, a student's behavior is observed in the classroom, playground, or other relevant setting. The behavior is observed and the events occurring immediately prior to and following the behavior are recorded.

The A-B-C procedure can lead to a determination of the plausible function of behavior. For example, while watching a student during independent seat work for reading (antecedent condition), an observer may notice a student leaving his seat, talking with other students, throwing materials at others, putting his head on his desk, and scribbling graffiti on his desk. Clearly, these behaviors have a different topography (form), but their description and recording does not explain the most important thing we want to know: What function(s) are these behaviors serving?

For each of these behaviors, the student's teacher may react with a verbal reprimand, repeated instruction to begin work, offering help to get started with the assignment, or ignoring these behaviors. Furthermore, the student's peers may react by ignoring these behaviors, laughing at these behaviors, throwing materials back at the student, and so forth. By observing and recording the sequence of events that surround target behaviors, an observer can form hypotheses regarding the antecedent and consequent conditions that may be prompting and maintaining the student's problem behaviors.

Summarizing FBA Data

When enough data have been collected for an FBA, the information must be summarized in a fashion to be useful in making intervention decisions.

This summary has three steps: (1) formulation of behavioral hypotheses, (2) constructing a competing behavior pathways model, and (3) comprehensive intervention planning based on behavioral hypotheses and competing behaviors pathways.

Behavioral hypothesis statements are testable conjectural statements about the presumed function of behavior. Behavioral hypotheses have three criteria: (1) they must be based on information from earlier assessments (records, interviews, observations); (2) they must specify variables that are testable, measureable, and can be manipulated by teachers or others in the classroom or other settings; and (3) consultees and consultants must agree that hypotheses represent reasonable syntheses from accumulated assessment information. Examples of behavioral hypotheses were presented in Chapter 3.

The next step in summarizing FBA information is to construct a competing behaviors pathway model, a graphic description of variables (antecedent and consequent) associated with the occurrence of problem behavior. Such a model is useful because it: (1) links behavioral intervention procedures to FBA data; (2) matches values, skills, and capacity of people who will implement the intervention plan; (3) enhances treatment integrity; and (4) increases the logical consistency among different procedures in the comprehensive intervention plan.

Figure 6.1 provides a graphical display of externalizing and internalizing domains and subdomains. Four components are necessary for diagramming the model: (1) conditions or situations leading to the problem behavior (setting events, establishing operations, and/or discriminative stimuli), (2) specification of the desired prosocial behavior, (3) specification of the competing problem behavior, and (4) analysis of the consequences maintaining the desired and competing problem behaviors. An extremely important concept in behavior change is that inappropriate problem behaviors are performed instead of the desired behavior because the former successfully competes with the latter because the former behaviors are more *reliable* (they result in the same consequence most of the time) and are more *efficient* (they require less response effort).

The final step in the FBA process is to select an intervention procedure based on the competing behaviors pathway model. There are several general considerations in designing these intervention procedures. The first consideration in intervention planning is to focus on changing antecedent events that will make the problem behavior less likely. Recall that antecedent events can be setting events, establishing operations, or discriminative stimuli. A number of antecedent event changes can be used including (1) altering schedule of activities, (2) changing the size and composition of groups, (3) shortening task length, (4) interspersing easy and difficult tasks, (5) providing precorrections for appropriate behaviors, and (6) taking a break.

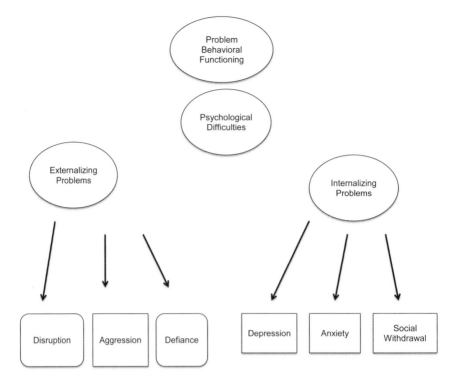

FIGURE 6.1. Domains and subdomains of externalizing and internalizing problems.

The second consideration is to consider changing the consequent events to make appropriate behavior more likely and competing problem behaviors less likely. There are two general strategies for altering consequent events: (1) increase the value of the consequence for the desired behavior and (2) decrease the value of the consequence for the competing problem behavior (i.e., the matching law). The principle of DRI is based entirely on this logic.

Additional Considerations

When target behaviors and reinforcing events are clear, discrete, and immediate, an A-B-C analysis based on systematic direct observations may allow for a relatively straightforward determination of the function served by competing problem behaviors. However, several properties of reinforcement, including delayed reinforcement, intermittent reinforcement, and reinforcement for competing behaviors, can compromise the effectiveness of direct observation in the natural environment.

Systematic direct observations are based on a sequence of events and, as such, are based on *contiguity* (correlational proximity) rather than *contingencies* (cause–effect relationships). For instance, the sequence could be that a student misbehaves and the teacher reprimands the student for this misbehavior. Because the teacher reprimand is the event that immediately follows the behavior (i.e., a contiguous event), this sequence suggests that the reprimand is positively reinforcing the inappropriate behavior. Although immediate reinforcement tends to be stronger than delayed reinforcement, it is not always the case that events occurring immediately following a behavior are actually controlling the behavior. For example, it could be that the misbehavior is not being positively reinforced by the teacher reprimand. Instead, the event actually reinforcing the behavior may be peer attention that the student receives during recess or after school (delayed reinforcement).

Another limitation of direct observation in the natural environment is related to *schedules of reinforcement* as opposed to the immediacy of reinforcement. We know that intermittent schedules of reinforcement are very effective in maintaining behavior. Even when behaviors are reinforced by events that occur immediately after those behaviors, those reinforcers may not be delivered very often (i.e., intermittently). For example, a school psychologist may observe a student engaging in inappropriate behaviors that are reinforced by intermittent teacher attention. However, because the teacher may ignore the behavior the majority of the time it occurs (a thin variable schedule of reinforcement), the school psychologist observing the student may never see the teacher reinforce the behavior. Thus, the school psychologist may conclude erroneously that teacher attention is not reinforcing the behavior.

Classroom environments are complex situations where students can engage in a variety of competing behaviors. Students' aberrant behaviors are functionally related reinforcement contingent upon those aberrant behaviors and reinforcement for competing problem behaviors. Although an A-B-C analysis may indicate plausible reinforcing events for inappropriate behaviors, it may also be necessary to collect data on reinforcement procedures (e.g., rates of reinforcement, quality of reinforcement, immediacy of reinforcement) for competing behaviors to accurately determine behavioral function. Chapter 10 presents several examples of FBAs and how they can be used to design intensive Tier 3 interventions.

REMEDIATION OF ACQUISITION DEFICITS

Remediation of social skills acquisition deficits focuses on directly teaching alternative prosocial behaviors. According to this logic, some behaviors are not performed because the student does not have the desired behavior in his or her repertoire (i.e., an acquisition deficit). As such, problem behaviors occur because the student has no other acceptable or appropriate behavioral alternatives. Intervention strategies in these cases utilize modeling, coaching, role playing, and behavioral rehearsal (Elliott & Gresham, 2008).

The Social Skills Improvement System—Intervention Guide

I discussed the use of the SSIS-IG (Elliott & Gresham, 2008) in Chapter 5 as a Tier 2 selected intervention. This intervention targets 20 social skills and is delivered in a small-group setting with four to six students that takes place twice per week (45 minutes per session or 90 minutes per week) over a period of about 15 weeks. This intervention consists of about 22 hours of social skills instruction for Tier 2 students requiring the program.

The SSIS-IG can also be used as a Tier 3 intensive SEL intervention program but with some key differences. One, it should be delivered to one or two students rather than four to six students as is the case in the Tier 2 intervention program. Tier 3 students require much more individually focused instruction to remediate their social skills acquisition deficits. Two, the intervention should take place 45 minutes per session for 3 days per week. Three, the program should be delivered over a period of about 20 weeks (45 hours of intense social skills instruction). Other than these three key differences, the instructional approach and strategies remain the same as in the Tier 2 program.

Fast Track

Fast Track is a comprehensive remediation strategy for children and youth having severe and chronic conduct problems. It was developed by the Conduct Problems Prevention Research Group (1992). Fast Track consists of five integrated components including parent training, home visiting, academic tutoring, classroom interventions, and social skills training group (Friendship Groups). The social skills component takes place 1 hour per week over a period of 22 weeks and focuses on improving peer relations, reducing aggressive interactions with peers, and interpersonal social problem-solving skills. Like the SSIS-IG, the SEL intervention consists of modeling, coaching, performance feedback, and role playing.

Outcome research on Fast Track showed that participants had lower rates of aggressive behaviors, improved social-cognitive skills, increased prosocial behaviors, and fewer children enrolled in special education. Effect sizes were moderate but consistent across measures for the participants in the intervention group.

Problem-Solving Skills Training

The problem-solving skills training (PSST) intervention is designed for children who engage in aggressive behavior patterns and who have characteristics of children with CD. (Kazdin, 2003a). Aggressive behavior for these children is not so much triggered by environmental events, but rather via the way in which these events are perceived and processed. Attribution of intent to others represents an important cognitive disposition that is critical in understanding aggressive behavior. Aggressive children often attribute aggressive intent to others in social situations in which the actual intent of others is unclear.

The PSST focuses on teaching cognitive problem-solving skills in weekly sessions with each session lasting between 30 and 50 minutes over 12–20 sessions. A central aspect of the intervention is the development of problem-solving steps that are designed to break down interpersonal situations into units that allow for the identification and use of prosocial behaviors. The problem-solving steps are as follows:

1. What am I supposed to do? (identify and define the problem)
2. I have to look at all my possibilities. (delineate or specify alternative solutions to the problem)
3. I'd better concentrate and focus in. (concentrate and evaluate the solutions you generated)
4. I need to make a choice. (choose the action that you think is correct)
5. I did a good job or I made a mistake. (verify whether the solution was the best choice or not)

Typically, PSST addresses interpersonal problems. The therapist models the application of the steps to one situation, identifies alternative solutions, and selects one of them. The therapist and the child role-play that solution. In all sessions, the therapist prompts the child verbally and non-verbally to guide performance, provides contingent social reinforcement, delivers specific performance feedback, and models ways of improving performance. A critical aspect of PSST is the application of the problem-solving steps in real-life situations by systematic programmed assignments designed to have the child generalize the problem-solving steps to everyday situations.

Studies have shown that PSST produces significant improvements in prosocial behavior and reductions of aggressive behaviors with the magnitude of these changes being rather large ($d = 1.20$). PSST has shown that after the program, children are returned to normative levels of functioning for same-age and same-sex children (Kazdin, 2003a).

THE ANGER COPING PROGRAM

The Anger Coping Program (ACP) was designed to address anger arousal and social-cognitive processes associated with aggressive behavior in children (Lochman, Barry, & Pardini, 2003). The ACP is designed for five to seven children in a group therapy format, although for a Tier 3 intervention, the program should be implemented for one or two children. The program has been successfully implemented in both school and clinic settings. The program consists of 18 sessions and meets weekly for 60–90 minutes in a large room. The entire program consists of about 20 to 27 hours of intensive Tier 3 SEL intervention.

The ACP focuses on anger arousal and social-cognitive processes and targets a number of skills that have been found to be deficient in angry and aggressive children. These skills include awareness of negative feelings, use of self-talk, distraction techniques, strategies to decrease anger arousal, perspective taking, goal setting, and social problem-solving skills. Research findings suggest that specific client characteristics are associated with greater improvement in the ACP. Aggressive children who are poor problem solvers, who have lower perceived levels of hostility, and who are more rejected by peers exhibit better treatment outcomes (Lochman, 2002). Also, children with a more internalized attributional style and higher levels of anxiety tend to benefit more from the ACP intervention. Approximately two-thirds of children undergoing the ACP show significant improvement, with the remaining one-third of the children requiring some type of continued involvement following the conclusion of the program.

CHAPTER SUMMARY POINTS

- Tier 3 intensive SEL intervention are designed for the *few* students who do not respond to Tier 1 or Tier 2 interventions (3–5%).

- Tier 3 interventions are much more intense in terms of "dosage," time, and response effort; are highly individualized and tailored to the specific needs of children; are based on an FBA; and take place over a considerably longer period of time than Tier 2 interventions.

- Tier 3 intensive SEL interventions have the following characteristics:
  - Group size is only one to three students
  - Time per week is from 150 to 300 minutes
  - Duration if over 15 to 20 weeks
  - Progress monitoring is conducted at least twice per week
  - Level of intensity usually requires a full period of intervention held outside the general education classroom

- Professionals responsible for intervention sessions require specialized training, such as a school psychologist, behavior specialist, counselor, or school social worker.

Remediation of social skills performance deficits involves RBT, in which competing problem behaviors are replaced with socially skilled alternative behaviors that serve the same function.

- RBT involves teaching functionally equivalent behaviors using principles derived from the matching law (behavior rate matches reinforcement rate).

- Several factors should be considered in Tier 3 intensive interventions:
  - Severity of behavior
  - Chronicity of behavior
  - Generalizability of behavior change
  - Treatment strength
  - Treatment integrity
  - Treatment effectiveness

Functional behavioral assessment (FBA) is a collection of techniques for gathering information about antecedents, behaviors, and consequences to determine the reason or function of behavior.

- Behavior function is either positive reinforcement (social attention, access to tangibles/activities, or automatic/sensory reinforcement), or negative reinforcement (escape, delay, reduction, or avoidance of aversive tasks or activities or escape or avoidance of other individuals).

- Behavior analysts make a distinction between functional behavioral assessment (correlational) and functional analysis (causal).

- Antecedent events can be discriminative stimuli (immediately prior to behavior), setting events (removed in time and place from behavior), or establishing operations (a variable that alters the temporary effectiveness of a reinforcer).

- FBA methods can be indirect (functional assessment interviews, historical/archival records, checklists, and rating scales) or direct (systematic direct observations in naturalistic settings).

- FBA data are summarized in three steps: (1) formulation of behavioral hypotheses, (2) constructing a competing behavior pathways model, and (3) comprehensive intervention planning based on behavioral hypotheses and competing behaviors pathways.

- Remediation of social skills acquisition deficits focuses on directly teaching alternative prosocial behaviors.

■ Several Tier 3 standard protocol approaches target remediation of social skills acquisition deficits: (1) Social Skills Improvement System-Intervention Guide, (2) Fast Track, (3) problem-solving skills training, and (4) Anger Coping Program.

IMPLICATIONS FOR PRACTICE

• Know that chronic nonresponders to Tier 1 (universal) and Tier 2 (selected) SEL interventions are prime candidates for Tier 3 (intensive) SEL interventions.

• Realize that there is considerable increase in intensity, time, and expense in delivering Tier 3 interventions.

• Plan to organize your Tier 3 intensive SEL intervention around the following:
  ◦ Group size of one to three students.
  ◦ About 150–300 minutes of training per week.
  ◦ Length of intervention should be about 15–20 weeks.
  ◦ Progress-monitor the effects of the intervention at least twice per week.
  ◦ These interventions require a full period of intervention outside of the general education classroom.
  ◦ Professionals responsible for delivering these interventions should be school psychologists, behavior specialists, counselors, or school social workers.

• Note that Tier 3 intensive interventions should involve the following basic principles:
  ◦ Use systematic and explicit instruction that includes modeling and direct teaching employing multiple examples.
  ◦ You should focus only on a few key skills at a time.
  ◦ Identify the gaps that are causing difficulty in the general education classroom.
  ◦ Use a variety of practice opportunities that coordinate with classroom skills.
  ◦ Use continuous corrective feedback, encouragement, and self-monitoring activities.

• Conceptualize your Tier 3 intensive SEL intervention as an exercise in RBT in which competing problem behaviors are "replaced" with social-skilled alternative behaviors.

- Consider the following factors before implementing a Tier 3 intensive SEL intervention:
  - Severity of behavior
  - Chronicity of behavior
  - Generalizability of behavior change across settings and situations
  - Treatment strength
  - Treatment integrity
  - Treatment effectiveness
- Conduct an FBA to identify the function the competing problem behavior serves (attention, escape/avoidance, access to tangible reinforcement, escape or avoidance of other individuals, or automatic or sensory reinforcement).
- Use the following FBA methods:
  - Functional assessment interviews
  - Historical/archival records
  - Behavior rating scales or checklists
  - ABC recording
- Construct a competing behavioral pathways model to conceptualize your Tier 3 intervention.
- To remediate social skills acquisition deficits, consider the following manualized SEL intervention programs:
  - Fast Track
  - Social Skills Improvement System—Intervention Guide
  - Problem-solving skills training
  - Anger Coping Program

CHAPTER SEVEN

Social–Emotional Learning Interventions for Specific Populations

with Paula Rodriguez

The previous chapters described multi-tiered SEL interventions that vary in cost, time, and intensity for *all* (Tier 1 universal interventions), *some* (Tier 2 selected interventions), or *few* (Tier 3 intensive interventions) children. This multi-tiered system of supports is predicated on the idea that if a child does not respond to less intense interventions, then he or she should be given more intense interventions until an adequate response can be obtained.

This chapter focuses on SEL interventions for children and youth with *developmental disorders* such as intellectual disability (ID), ASD, and social (pragmatic) communication disorder (SPCD). (Chapter 6 described Tier 3 intensive interventions appropriate for children with externalizing disorders [CD, ODD, and ADHD] and internalizing disorders [anxiety disorders and major depressive disorder].) This chapter also describes intensive

---

Paula Rodriguez, LCSW, is the founder and Director of Deaf Focus Services, which provides community, communication, and counseling support for the deaf community and families who have children who are deaf or hard of hearing. She specializes in child and family therapy and behavior management and intervention.

SEL interventions for children and youth who are deaf/hard of hearing (D/HOH).

Developmental disorders are a group of conditions with onset in the developmental period that are manifested early (prior to school entry) and that produce impairments in social, personal, academic, and occupational functioning. Children diagnosed as having ASD, ID, and SPCD can be characterized in this way. Although being D/HOH is not a psychological disorder, children and youth who are D/HOH have social skills challenges due to their deficits in language and verbal communication skills. These social skills deficits involve having fewer opportunities to access social language (pragmatics), deficits in affective vocabulary, poor understanding of conversational rules, poor social problem-solving skills, and difficulties in empathizing with others. Most individuals who are deaf use some form of sign language (e.g., American Sign Language [ASL], Signed Exact English, cued speech) that makes it extremely difficult to socially interact with their hearing peers.

SEL INTERVENTION STRATEGIES

ID and ASD

SEL interventions for children and youth with ID and ASD are similar in terms of teaching strategies and target behaviors. In fact, approximately 75% of children diagnosed with ASD have IQs in the range of persons with ID. Comorbid diagnosis of ID and ASD is based on social communication abilities being below that expected for general developmental level (American Psychiatric Association, 2013). Because individuals in these two diagnostic categories share similar types of social skills deficits, they are discussed together in this chapter.

ID refers to a condition characterized by significant limitations both in intellectual functioning and in adaptive behavior as expressed in conceptual, social, and practical adaptive skills. This condition has an onset prior to age 18 years (American Association on Intellectual and Developmental Disabilities, 2010). Historically, persons were defined as having ID because they failed to adapt socially to their environment. The oldest historical approach to defining ID emphasized social behavior in describing the condition (Greenspan, 2006).

ID has four levels of severity: (1) mild, (2) moderate, (3) severe, and (4) profound. The various levels of severity are defined on the basis of *adaptive functioning* and not IQ because adaptive functioning determines the level of supports that are required (American Psychiatric Association, 2013). Adaptive behavior functioning can be impaired in at least one of three domains: (1) conceptual, (2) social, and (3) practical. Adaptive behavior functioning must be sufficiently impaired that ongoing support is needed in order for the individual to perform adequately in one or more life settings at school, work, home, or the community.

Most persons diagnosed with *mild ID* have adaptive behavior deficits primarily in the conceptual and social domains. When compared to typically developing peers, these individuals are immature in their social interactions. The have difficulty in accurately perceiving peers' social cues. Their communication, conversation, and language skills are more concrete than expected for their age. They have a limited understanding of risk in social situations, their social judgment is immature for their age, and they are prone to being manipulated by others (gullibility).

Persons diagnosed with *moderate ID* show marked differences from peers in social and communicative behavior across development. Their spoken language is the primary tool for social communication but it is much less complex and more concrete than that of their peers. The ability to read and interpret social cues is substantially impaired and their social judgment and decision-making skills are very limited. Friendships with typically developing peers are adversely affected by communication and social limitations.

Individuals diagnosed with *severe ID* have spoken language skills that are extremely limited in terms of vocabulary and grammar. Their speech often consists of single words or phrases, and language used for communication is focused on the present and with concrete everyday events. These individuals can understand simple speech and gestural communication (e.g., gestures, pantomime, or simple ASL signs).

Persons diagnosed with *profound ID* have extremely limited understanding of symbolic communication in speech or gestures. They may understand a few basic simple instructions or gestures. They typically express their needs or desires through nonverbal, nonsymbolic communication. Many of these individuals have comorbid sensory and physical impairments that may prevent many social activities.

Persons with ASD exhibit persistent deficits in social communication and social interaction across multiple contexts. These individuals have:

- Deficits in social–emotional reciprocity ranging from abnormal social initiations and substantial limitations in reciprocal conversational skills.
- Deficits in nonverbal communication (pragmatics) used for social interaction as evidenced by (1) poorly integrated verbal and nonverbal communication, (2) abnormalities in eye contact and body language, (3) deficits in the understanding and use of gestures, and (4) a lack of facial expressions and nonverbal communication.
- Deficits in developing, maintaining, and understanding relationships that include adjusting behavior to suit social contexts, difficulties in sharing and imaginative play, and absence of interests in peers.

ASD has three levels of severity that are used to describe current symptomatology with the understanding that severity can vary by context and fluctuate over time:

1. *Level 3:* "Requiring very substantial support" that is characterized by severe deficits in verbal and nonverbal social communication skills that create very limited social initiations.
2. *Level 2:* "Requiring substantial support" that is characterized by marked deficits in verbal and nonverbal social communication skills, social impairments even when supports are in place, and abnormal responses to social overtures from others.
3. *Level 1:* "Requiring support" that is characterized by deficits in social communication skills in the absence of supports and difficulties in initiating social interactions and difficulties in making friends with peers.

Young children with ASD lack social communication abilities that limit learning, especially learning via social interactions or in settings with peers. Adaptive skills are usually below measured IQ and they have extreme difficulties in planning, organization, and coping with environmental changes. Adults with ASD have poor psychosocial functioning and have marked limitations in independent living and obtaining gainful employment.

Social (Pragmatic) Communication Disorder

SPCD is characterized by a central difficulty with pragmatics, or the social use of language and communication. Individuals with SPCD have deficits in understanding and following the social rules of verbal and nonverbal communication in naturalistic contexts, altering language to meet the needs of the listener or situation, and following rules for conversations and storytelling. These deficits in social communication are caused by functional limitations in effective communication, social participation, development of social relationships, academic achievement, and/or occupational performance. These deficits are not due to low abilities of structural language, or cognitive abilities. SPCD can be differentiated from ASD by the presence in ASD of restricted/repetitive patterns of behavior, interests, or activities, and their absence in SPCD. A diagnosis of SCPD is considered only if the developmental history fails to reveal any evidence of restricted/repetitive patterns of behavior, interests, or activities (American Psychiatric Association, 2013).

SCPD can be characterized by the following deficits in verbal and nonverbal language:

- Deficits in using communication for social purposes such as greeting and sharing information in a manner that is appropriate for the social context.
- Impairment in the ability to change communication to match context or the needs of the listener such as speaking differently in a classroom than on a playground, talking differently to a child than to an adult, and avoiding the use of overly formal language.
- Difficulties following rules for conversation and storytelling such as taking turns in conversation, rephrasing when misunderstood, and knowing how to use verbal and nonverbal signals to regulate interaction.
- Difficulties in understanding what is not explicitly stated (making inferences) and nonliteral or ambiguous meanings of language (e.g., idioms, humor, metaphors, multiple meanings that depend on the context for interpretation).

Approaches to SEL Interventions

Most individuals with ID, ASD, and SPCD will require Tier 3 intensive SEL interventions such as the ones described in Chapter 6. As discussed in Chapter 6, these interventions are intense in terms of time, "dosage," and response effort of treatment personnel. For these populations, these interventions must be highly individualized and targeted on the specific social skills deficits exhibited by these children. Children with ID, ASD, and SPCD will not respond adequately to Tier 1 universal or Tier 2 selected SEL interventions. As such, these children should be "fast-tracked" into a Tier 3 intensive intervention that will require a relatively long period of time to teach relatively few key social skills. These interventions should have the following characteristics:

- One-to-one direct instruction of social skills that includes discrete trial training.
- Sessions conducted twice a day, 5 days per week, lasting 30 minutes per session.
- Duration of 40 weeks.
- Professional responsible for supervising intervention sessions requires specialized training such as behavior analyst, psychologist, or behavior specialist.
- Progress monitoring is conducted 5 days per week for the duration of the intervention.

The instructional strategies of the SEL intervention include modeling, coaching, behavioral rehearsal, positive reinforcement of exhibited skills, and discrete trial training. Modeling, coaching, behavioral rehearsal, and positive reinforcement were described in Chapter 6 and will not be discussed here.

PIVOTAL RESPONSE TRAINING

Pivotal response training (PRT) is a method of systematically applying the principles of applied behavior analysis (ABA) to teach children with ASD functional social-communication and adaptive behavior skills within a naturalistic teaching format (Koegel & Koegel, 2006). Although PRT was initially developed exclusively for children with ASD, it can also be an effective means of teaching social skills to children with ID and SPCD. PRT builds on a child's initiative and interests and is particularly effective for developing communication, language, play, and social behaviors. PRT was developed to create a more efficient and effective intervention by enhancing four key pivotal learning variables: *motivation, responding to multiple cues, self-management,* and *self-initiations.* These skills are pivotal because they are the foundational skills upon which children can make widespread and generalized improvements in many other areas. Steps for implementing each of these four pivotal skills are described in this chapter.

It should be noted that PRT is viewed as a more effective alternative to *discrete trial training* (DTT) because it teaches skills in a more naturalistic social environment. DTT uses adult-directed, massed trial instruction and uses clear contingencies and repetition to teach new skills. DTT is a strong method for developing a new response to a stimulus. Its limitations, however, involve a lack of reinforcement of a child's spontaneity and difficulties in generalization of newly taught skills to other naturalistic environments.

Pivotal Behavior: Motivation

Seven steps are used in PRT to increase a child's motivation for learning new skills. Each of these seven steps is described below.

Step 1: Establish Learner Attention

- Teachers/therapists establish learner's attention before providing learning opportunities. For example, a therapist could tap the learner on the shoulder or make eye contact before providing instructions.
- Once the learner is attending, therapists can use brief and clear instructions with the learner.

Step 2: Use Shared Control

- In a shared control interaction, therapists decide which part of the routine they will complete for learners and which part learners will finish on their own. For example, if a child is learning how to put on his or her coat before going outside to play, the therapist could share control during the teaching interaction by (1) getting the coat from the child's cubby (therapist), (2) helping the child put on the coat (therapist), (3) starting to zip the zipper (therapist and child), and (4) having the child finish zipping the zipper before he or she can go outside (therapist and child).
- As children become more proficient at using target skills, therapists shift more control and responsibility to the child. Using the previous example, the therapist may now (1) get the coat from the child's cubby (therapist), (2) help the child get his or her coat on (therapist and child), and (3) have the child start the zipper and zip it completely up (child).
- Finally, the child would (1) get the coat by him- or herself (child), (2) put the coat on (child), and (3) zip the coat up without any assistance (child).
- By sharing control of the activity and material selection, therapists increase a child's motivation to participate and help them learn target behaviors and skills.

Step 3: Use Learner Choice

- Therapists observe learners when they have free access to materials to identify their preferences for items, activities, and toys. For example, a therapist may notice that a child plays with toy cars for most of free play. The cars could be used to increase motivation by allowing the child to play with the cars after completing a more difficult or less desirable task. Also, therapists could incorporate cars into classroom activities or during instruction (e.g., addition/subtraction with cars or writing letters that state the name of the car).
- Therapists arrange the environment with learner-preferred, age-appropriate objects and activities. For example, a therapist may provide multiple colored crayons for a child to complete a drawing task.
- Therapists allow learners to select materials, topics, and toys during teaching activities. Allowing learners to choose preferred objects or activities is particularly important when teaching new skills. Using toys, items, and activities that individual learners prefer increases their motivation to participate and therefore increases the likelihood that they will acquire target skills.
- Therapists incorporate choice-making opportunities into naturally occurring routines and activities throughout the day. For example, a ball, a clear box of blocks, a shape sorter, and a bottle of bubbles can all be

placed on a shelf in a classroom. When the learner points to the bottle of bubbles and says "Bubbles," the therapist says "Bubbles" while taking them down and starting to open them with the learner. The learner had the choice of several different objects, each providing an equal opportunity to practice requesting and communication.

Step 4: Vary Tasks and Responses

- Therapists vary tasks, materials, and activities to maintain learner interest and engagement.
- Therapists vary instructions and environmental conditions to facilitate learner response to a range of stimuli. Table 7.1 provides examples of behaviors that may indicate a need for a task variation.

Step 5: Intersperse Acquisition and Maintenance Tasks

- Therapists identify skills that are easy for individual learners (maintenance tasks) and ones that are more difficult (acquisition tasks).
- Therapists provide a mixture of easy and more difficult tasks so that learners can be successful at using a variety of skills.
- To facilitate maintenance of previously learned target skills, therapists provide (1) short requests that are easy and within current repertoire of skills to complete, followed by (2) one or two requests that are slightly more difficult for the learner to complete.

Reinforce Response Attempts

- Therapists reinforce all verbal attempts at responding that are clear, unambiguous, and goal-directed. For example, a nonverbal learner who is starting to make a goal-directed verbalization reaches for a book and says "Oh." Although this is not the targeted response ("Book"), the therapist immediately reinforces the attempt by saying "Book" while handing the book to the child, reinforcing attempted vocalization, and modeling the target skill.
- Therapists provide reinforcement immediately after a goal-directed attempt. For example, a therapist immediately reinforces a learner who lifts his or her hand a few inches off the desk in an attempt to raise his or her hand during class.

Use Natural and Direct Reinforcers

A natural reinforcer is a reinforcer that has a direct relationship to the learner's behavior. For example, a learner may be interested in blowing

TABLE 7.1. Examples of Behaviors Indicating Need for Task Variation

Behavior	Might indicate . . .	You may want to try . . .	Example
Signing or verbalizing "all done"	Boredom with task that is too easy	Interspersing newer, more challenging tasks with familiar ones	A learner who used to like playing football has a chance to play baseball or other outdoor activity
Vocally protesting	Frustration with task that is too difficult	Returning to familiar or mastered tasks before trying another new task	A therapist accepts a request for "turn" while teaching "turn the page"
Looking around, not focusing on the teaching materials	Distraction	Moving to a different location that may be less stimulating	Teaching is conducted in a quieter corner of the classroom or school (e.g., the library)
Getting up from seat or trying to leave the teaching area	Boredom with task because it is not interesting enough	Finding toys or materials that are more interesting to the learner and therefore more reinforcing	Providing a manipulative math activity with preferred objects rather than a math worksheet
Banging or throwing materials	Frustration or disinterest in item	Making sure that the teaching materials are not only interesting, but also are easy for the learner to access or use	A therapist provides a variety of books (factual, alphabet, story) within reach of a second grader during independent reading time

bubbles. When he or she blows the bubbles, the bubbles are in the natural environment for this behavior.

- Therapists identify materials and activities that can be used to address a learner's goal during a teaching opportunity. For example, a therapist could present a clear jar with a lid that contains highly motivating objects (e.g., bubbles, raisins, M&Ms). The learner will most likely try to open the jar and then look to the therapist for help. After the learner uses the target phrase (verbally or signing such as "Help me"), the therapist provides access to the reinforcer inside the jar.
- Therapists implement a learning task that is functionally and directly

related to the learner's goal. An example would be a learner whose target goal is to ask for a break instead of escaping task demands by screaming. In this case, when a learner indicates the request by saying or signing "break," the therapist immediately responds by allowing the learner to have a few minutes of free time while staying seated.

Pivotal Behavior: Responding to Multiple Cues

There are three steps in responding to multiple cues. These are described below.

Step 1: Vary Stimuli and Increase Cues

There are two ways to teach a learner to respond to multiple cues. Cues, also called properties or attributes, can be taught incrementally until learners respond to a more complex task.

- Therapists identify a variety of cues (properties or attributes) that are associated with the target skill and that can be used during a teaching activity. An example would be a therapist who selects cues such as colors, size, or shape to teach a receptive language task.
- Therapists provide at least two cues (e.g., overemphasizing feature of object, such as color, size, and shape of object, location of object) so that learners begin to use the target skill in response to more than one cue. For example, a therapist may ask the learner to identify the big blue car rather than just the blue car so the learner is responding to both "big" and "blue."
- Therapists gradually increase the number of cues associated with a particular object, material, or toy so that the learner can respond to a variety of stimuli. An example would be the therapist asking the learner for the big blue car that is outside the toy garage. As the learner responds appropriately, the tasks get more complex and involve more cues. The goal is for the learner to respond to a complex request such as "big blue car with white wheels."

Step 2: Schedule the Reinforcement

Therapists can also use different schedules of reinforcement to teach a learner to respond to multiple cues.

- Therapists identify numerous reinforcers that can be used to increase learners' motivation to employ the target skill. For instance, a therapist might notice that a learner enjoys playing games on the computer or reading comic books.

- Therapists provide reinforcement for every attempt to use the target skill successfully (continuous schedule of reinforcement). For example, the learner is allowed to look at a comic book every time he or she answers a question verbally or with signing.
- Therapists move from a continuous schedule of reinforcement (every response is reinforced) to a variable ratio schedule of reinforcement (e.g., one out of every three responses is reinforced).

Pivotal Behavior: Self-Management to Increase Positive Behaviors

The goal of self-management is to increase the independence of learners while decreasing their dependence on therapists. To promote self-management, learners are taught to discriminate their target behaviors and then to record or monitor the occurrence or absence of them. Self-management is a strategy that is designed to take place in the absence of therapists and provides learners with a set of procedures that promote autonomy and independence.

Step 1: Prepare the Self-Management System

- Therapists clearly define the target behavior in terms that are specific, observable, and measureable and include a specific criterion for receiving reinforcement. For instance, the learner receives a break after staying quiet for 2 minutes. The criterion of "staying quiet" is defined as remaining at his or her desk and looking at a book independently. Definitions of behaviors focus on what learners do, as opposed to what they should not do—for example, "Frank will complete 80% of the small-group and independent activities/tasks in math."
- Therapists collect frequency and duration data before the self-management system is implemented to establish a baseline or current performance of learners' behavior. A therapist might collect data on the number of times a learner gets out of his or her seat (frequency) or how long a temper tantrum lasts (duration). Figure 7.1 provides examples of frequency and duration data sheets that can be used to document a learner's level of problem behaviors.
- Therapists select items and activities that learners enjoy as rewards. If appropriate, learners help identify rewards that they would like to earn. Therapists should consider conducting a formal preference assessment at this point. For example, a learner might choose a Slinky from an array of sensory materials.
- Therapists determine how often (the interval) learners should record

Frequency Data Collection Sheet

Learner's Name: _____Frank_____

Interfering Behavior: _____Out of Seat_____

Date: _____9/22/2016_____

Learner's daily schedule	Number of times
A.M. recess	////
Math	//// //
Reading	
Gym	NA
Music	//// //// //
P.M. recess	
Daily Total	20

Duration Data Collection Sheet

Learner's Name: _____Frank_____

Date: _____9/22/2016_____

Activity/Location: Reading Class

Interfering behavior	No. of minutes/seconds
Tantrums	2 minutes
Tantrums	3 minutes
Tantrums	1 minute
Tantrums	2 minutes
Total Duration of Behavior	**8 minutes**

FIGURE 7.1. Frequency and duration tracking sheets.

their own behavior (e.g., every 7 minutes) based on the target behavior and ability of the learner to successfully monitor responses.

- Therapists determine what monitoring device or system will be used to record successful behavior.

Step 2: Teach Self-Management

When teaching self-management to individual learners, the first task it to teach learners how to discriminate between desirable and undesirable behaviors. This should be very specific and in a format that learners will understand. If learners do not understand what is and is not expected of them, they will not be able to manage their own behavior.

- Therapists teach learners how to discriminate between desirable and undesirable behavior in language that learners understand. For example, a therapist may ask a learner to demonstrate the desirable behavior in a trial session and reinforce the learner for demonstrating the desired behavior. If the therapist observes the learner using an undesirable behavior, the therapist can ask the learner to describe the behavior that he or she just exhibited. Once the learner responds, the therapist can ask the learner, "Was the behavior appropriate?" and can model the desirable behavior before having the learner demonstrate it again.
- Therapists provide learners with the specific reinforcer when the criterion has been reached. For example, a learner is allowed to walk around the school when he or she has 10 tokens.

Step 3: Create Independence

After teaching a learner how to respond to and record his or her own behavior, therapists then step back and provide support so that the learner begins to independently use the system.

- Therapists gradually increase the amount of time learners self-manage the target behavior by increasing the length of time between intervals. For instance, a learner who is reinforced after one class period would be reinforced after two class periods instead.
- Therapists fade the intensity and frequency of prompts as learners become more successful at managing their behavior. For example, a therapist might prompt the learner by pointing to a token instead of handing the token to him or her.
- Therapists increase the number of responses necessary for the reinforcer as learners become more successful at managing their behavior. The learner might have to respond appropriately three times before getting reinforced as opposed to getting reinforced for every appropriate response.
- Therapists gradually reduce their presence as learners become more successful at managing their behavior and/or administering their own reinforcer.
- Therapists teach learners self-management skills in additional settings and with other therapists and family members. The learner may need a break in gym class outside and may raise his or her hand, but the physical education teacher may not understand the behavior and may unintentionally ignore the request. In this case, the therapist should teach the

learner that he or she needs to approach the physical education teacher with a verbal or signed request.

Pivotal Behavior: Self-Management to Reduce Interfering Behaviors and Teaching Positive Replacement Behaviors

Self-management of competing problem behaviors (e.g., repetitive, stereotypical, disruptive behaviors) involves a second important phase after therapists have successfully implemented strategies that reduce and manage competing problem behaviors. To successfully decrease competing behaviors, however, learners must be involved in the process of developing a comprehensive intervention plan based on an FBA. An FBA was discussed extensively in Chapter 6.

Step 1: Define the Behavior

• Therapists conduct FBAs to identify, describe, and determine the function of competing problem behaviors for individual learners (see Chapter 6).

Step 2: Prepare the Self-Management System

After therapists have defined the competing problem behaviors, they identify potential replacement behaviors (prosocial alternatives) that can take the place of the competing problem behaviors (replacement behaviors).

• Therapists assess potential replacement behaviors by determining:
  • The behavior the learner will use to attract the therapist's attention (e.g., raising his or her hand, verbally requesting, or signing).
  • When the learner needs to exhibit the behavior (e.g., in what settings, situations, and with whom).
  • Whether the learner can independently use the behavior (can the learner physically complete the behavior?).
  • How the behavior will be measured (e.g., tokens, tally marks, free time minutes).
• Therapists clearly define the replacement behavior in terms that are specific, observable, and measureable—for example: "Frank will raise his hand until he is called on and ask 'Can I have a break, please?' and wait until the therapist gives him permission to take a break."
• Therapists identify meaningful rewards (some large and some small) for learners' use of the replacement behaviors (e.g., computer time, free time, access to activities).
• Therapists identify the overall goal and explain it to the learner in a developmentally and age-appropriate way.

- Therapists provide learners with many opportunities to experience success with using the replacement behaviors (e.g., throughout the day, in different classrooms, with different peers).

Step 3: Teach Self-Management

- Therapists teach learners how to discriminate between desirable and undesirable behavior in language that learners understand.
- Therapists teach learners to record whether their behavior was successful or unsuccessful across intervals.
- Therapists provide the learner with the specified reward when the criterion has been reached.

Step 4: Create Independence

- Therapists gradually increase the amount of time learners self-manage the target behavior by increasing the length of time between intervals. For example, progress monitoring data may indicate that the learner is able to tolerate two class periods or check off 20 boxes before needing a break, and therefore his or her self-management program is adjusted accordingly.
- Therapists gradually fade the intensity and frequency of prompts as learners become more successful at managing their behavior. For example, a therapist might use a light touch when prompting a learner rather than using hand-over-hand assistance.
- Therapists increase the number of responses necessary to receive the reinforcer as learners become more successful at managing their behavior.
- Therapists gradually reduce their presence as learners become more successful at managing their behavior and/or administering their own reinforcer.

Step 5: Generalize to Other Settings

- Therapists teach learners self-management skills in a variety of settings and with other individuals and family members.

Pivotal Behavior: Promoting Self-Initiations Using Peer-Mediated Strategies

Step 1: Implement Peer-Mediated Strategies

- Therapists select typically developing peers who are motivated to participate in peer-mediated activities.
- Therapists teach typically developing peers how to:
  - Secure the learner's attention before initiating a social exchange (e.g., saying "Hi").

- Provide the learner with choices among activities and materials.
- Vary materials according to the learner's preference.
- Provide frequent and varied models for appropriate play and social skills.
- Verbally reinforce learner attempts at social interactions and/or functional, appropriate play.
- Encourage conversation with the learner by withholding desired objects until an appropriate verbal response is given.
- Ask questions or encourage conversation that is relevant to the routine or activity.
- Take turns during play and other social interactions.
- Describe what they are doing during activities, including comments to share the social experience.
- Describe objects as clearly as they can during routines and activities and encourage learners to do the same.

Pivotal Behavior: Promoting Self-Initiations Using Learner-Initiated Strategies

Step 1: Teach Social Initiations

- Therapists teach learners:
  - Ways to initiate social interactions with others by sharing materials (e.g., "Can I play with you?" or "Can I have some blocks?").
  - How to organize play activities ("You build the road, I'll build the bridge").
  - How to take turns choosing activities.
  - How to be persistent when trying to initiate interactions with others.

Step 2: Teach Question Asking

- Therapists place highly preferred objects, items, and materials in an opaque bag.
- Therapists prompt the learner to ask, "What's that?"
- Therapists show learners what is inside the bag and give them immediate access to the item.
- Therapists gradually fade prompts as learners begin to spontaneously ask the question "What's that?"
- Therapists gradually replace preferred items in the bag with less preferred items.
- Therapists gradually fade the use of the opaque bag when learners spontaneously ask the question "What's that?"
- Therapists encourage generalization by placing items in other objects or locations.

Step 3: Teach Question

- Therapists select pop-up books that are related to learners' interests.
- Therapists prompt learners to either ask "What's happening?" or "What happened?" after they pull the tab for the pop-up pictures.
- Once learners ask questions, therapists model the correct verb ending (*dog is jumping* or *dog jumped*) and give learners a turn to pull the tab.

Step 4: Teach Language, Communication, and Social Skills Using Naturalistic Techniques

- Therapists imitate learners' actions during interactions, play, and other activities.
- Therapists provide the learner with the appropriate item after it is requested.
- Therapists provide a task demand, then wait for the learner to respond independently before providing a prompt.
- Therapists place preferred items out of reach to encourage independent requesting by the learner (e.g., preferred toys are kept on the top shelf so learners must verbally request them).

SEL INTERVENTIONS
FOR D/HOH YOUTH

Children and youth who are D/HOH vary widely in their intellectual, academic, and social abilities. Depending on the age of onset of hearing loss (congenital vs. acquired), type of interventions, response to intervention, and comorbidity with other disorders (e.g., ADHD, ID, ASD), these children differ significantly in language acquisition and thus social skills and abilities. A variety of SEL interventions have been shown to be successful with children and youth who are D/HOH. The key, however, to this success is based on providing communication access for the individual throughout the SEL intervention and activities.

Pragmatic Language and D/HOH

Pragmatic language involves using language in social situations for different purposes such as greeting, informing, demanding, requesting, and promising. It involves changing one's language to fit the situation such as by using a quieter voice indoors versus outside, speaking softly to a baby, and not interrupting or talking over someone else in a conversation. Pragmatic language involves following conversational rules such as knowing how to introduce new topics, understanding turn taking in conversation, using verbal and nonverbal cues, knowing how to end a conversation, and using appropriate body language and facial expressions during conversation.

Children with normal hearing have better inhibitory control, show more reciprocity, and display fewer competitive behaviors in cooperative dyadic interactions than children with poor inhibitory control. Research has shown that D/HOH children are less flexible, are less able to tolerate frustration, are socially immature, and are less accurate in identifying others' emotional states than children with normal hearing (Greenberg & Kusché, 1998). Reasons for this are due to having fewer opportunities to access social language, deficits in understanding affective vocabulary, poor advanced language and verbal reasoning skills, and poor understanding and use of conversational rules (i.e., communicative competence).

Children who are D/HOH have an absence of a fully accessible verbal communication mode from birth that creates a language delay in general syntax, pragmatics, and semantics that leads to poor communicative competence. D/HOH children miss opportunities for talking about things unseen including the past, imagined events, or absent objects. They have fewer prosocial exchanges that affect social conversation with peers over time. D/HOH children have incomplete acoustic access to social cues about a talker's mental and emotional state and mood. This creates difficulty in tasks that require simultaneous attention to the talker and a visual stimulus. They have difficulty in hearing in noisy listening environments that creates a barrier to incidental language learning.

Nearly one in five people experience some degree of hearing loss but D/HOH is considered a low-incidence disability. As such, very few professionals are trained to work with children and youth who are D/HOH. These professionals include educators, psychologists, physicians, social workers, and speech–language pathologists. Physicians and audiologists are often the first professionals encountered by parents and the medical resources they share will often consist of ways to "fix" the child to make him or her "hearing." As such, D/HOH children are seriously delayed in language development and are delayed in emotional understanding and social skills.

Delays in language and social skills development can be averted by early visual access to language even as auditory skills are being developed for HOH students. Direct instruction about social interactions, feelings, emotions, making choices, and taking turns is necessary to ensure that the child is aware of incidental details of his or her social environment. This access provides a *connection* to the child's social world. Providing early visual language such as sign language is often a challenge when parents of a D/HOH child have no idea of what to do to promote social development. This is because 90% or more of children who are D/HOH are born to hearing parents who do not know sign language and therefore cannot communicate effectively with their child. Having a child who is D/HOH can be socially isolating for both parents and the child. Seeking social interaction with other parents of children who are D/HOH not only provides support for parents, but also provides opportunities for peer social interaction with other D/HOH children.

Language delays and deficits can significantly impact a D/HOH child's social development. Language deficits impact a child's ability to effectively and positively interact with peers and adults. Similarly, limited hearing also affects one's opportunity for incidental learning. Many social skills are acquired through overhearing and observing how other people interact with one another. Although most children who are D/HOH have full cognitive capabilities, many of them do not have access via hearing to overhear social interactions and thus may lack insight and judgment regarding social interactions. It is important to understand that these social skills deficits are not related to limited cognitive ability, but rather they are due to lack of experience and a clear understanding of language, communication, social rules, and expectations. In fact, many individuals who are D/HOH often come off as blunt and rude due to their language and communication deficits. More often than not, these individuals do not understand that what they are doing is rude to the hearing world, but not to the D/HOH world.

SEL Intervention Recommendations

One system developed specifically to teach students who are D/HOH about social skills and language related to these skills is the Promoting Alternative Thinking Strategies (PATHS) intervention program. The PATHS program promotes peaceful conflict resolution, emotional regulation, empathy, and responsible decision making. Each lesson in the PATHS program is scripted beginning with an introduction that states background and goals, guidelines for implementation, suggestions for involving parents, supplementary activities, and family handouts. The PATHS program was implemented in a randomized control trial with D/HOH students (Greenberg & Kusché, 1998). Behavioral outcomes of this program include improved academic performance, increased positive social behavior, reduced conduct problems, and reduced emotional distress.

Another SEL intervention strategy is to simply read to children who are D/HOH if they can hear. Reading together is an excellent time to expand on pictures and incorporate discussions about feelings, emotions, and social interactions. Read stories over and over again and ask why a character is smiling, why a character is sad, and how they think the person in the story is feeling. It is important to be dramatic as you read and to overexaggerate facial expressions to make the feelings visual.

Often overlooked in working with students who are D/HOH is the importance of enlisting peers. Consider training other students in the class about deafness and how it impacts speech, hearing, and communication. Teach the class about what hearing aids and cochlear implants are and how they facilitate social interaction. This can be a critical strategy that is beneficial to social skill building of the student who is D/HOH as well as his or her peers. Students should be encouraged to write back and forth, gesture, learn ASL, or utilize technology such as texting on a shared classroom phone to share simple positive conversations and messages.

As more and more students who are D/HOH are placed in inclusion classrooms, it is important for the school climate to be one of acceptance and true inclusion. Very often, students who are D/HOH are unintentionally marginalized or left out of social experiences. These experiences are often one of the best developmental benefits of public school. Developing strategies among all students can help students who are D/HOH enjoy more opportunities for positive social interaction with hearing peers. It is important to remember that children who are D/HOH *want* to be included and connected. Accomplishing communication access is needed and very often requires a visual element in addition to any hearing element that may be used.

CHAPTER SUMMARY POINTS

- This chapter describes SEL interventions for special populations including those with ID, ASD, SCPD, and D/HOH.

- The diagnostic criteria for ID includes significantly subaverage intellectual functioning and deficits in conceptual, social, and practical adaptive behavior skills.

- Most individuals with mild ID have adaptive behavior deficits in the conceptual and social adaptive behavior domains. They have a limited understanding of risk in social situations, have limited social judgment, and are prone to being manipulated by others (gullibility).

- Individuals with severe and profound ID have extremely limited spoken language skills and have pervasive adaptive behavior deficits across conceptual, social, and practical domains.

- Individuals with ASD have limited communication and social interaction across multiple contexts. These deficits include (1) deficits in social–emotional reciprocity, (2) deficits in nonverbal communication (pragmatics), and (3) deficits in developing, adjusting, and maintaining behavior to suit social contexts; difficulties in sharing; and deficits in imaginative play.

- ASD have three levels of severity: (1) Level 3: "Requiring very substantial support," (2) Level 2: "Requiring substantial support," and (3) Level 1: "Requiring support."

- Individuals with SPCD have primary difficulties with pragmatics, or the social use of language. They differ from individuals with ASD in that they do not have restricted/repetitive patterns of behavior and interests or activities.

- SPCD is characterized by the following: (1) deficits in using communication for social purposes, (2) impairment in the ability to change communication to match the context or needs of the listener, (3) difficulties in following rules for conversation and storytelling, and (4) difficulties in making inferences or interpreting ambiguous meanings of language.

- Most individuals with ID, ASD, and SPCD will require Tier 3 intensive SEL interventions such as those described in Chapter 6. These interventions are more intensive in terms of "dosage," intensity, and response efforts of treatment personnel.

- These Tier 3 SEL interventions have the following characteristics: (1) one-to-one direct instruction of social skills that includes discrete trial training; (2) sessions conducted twice a day, 5 days per week, lasing 30 minutes per session for a duration of 40 weeks; (3) professionals responsible for supervising intervention sessions require specialized training such as behavior analyst, psychologist, or behavior specialist; and (4) progress monitoring should be conducted 5 days per week for the duration of the intervention.

- Instructional strategies include modeling, coaching, behavioral rehearsal, positive reinforcement, and discrete trial training.

- PRT is a method of systematically applying the principles of applied behavior analysis to teach children with ASD functional social-communication and adaptive behavior skills within a naturalistic teaching format.

- Although PRT was initially developed exclusively for children with ASD, it can also be an effective means of teaching social skills to children with ID and SPCD.

- PRT was developed to create a more efficient and effective intervention by enhancing four key pivotal learning variables: *motivation, responding to multiple cues, self-management,* and *self-initiations.*

- PRT is viewed as a more effective alternative to discrete trial training (DTT) because it teaches skills in a more naturalistic social environment.

- Children and youth who are D/HOH vary widely in their intellectual, academic, and social abilities.

- Research has shown that children who are D/HOH are less flexible, less able to tolerate frustration, are less socially mature, and less accurate in identifying others' emotional states than children with normal hearing.

▪ D/HOH children miss opportunities for talking about things unseen, including past events, imagined events, or absent objects.

▪ SEL interventions for children who are D/HOH should be based on direct instruction about social interactions, feelings, emotions, making choices, and taking turns.

▪ One system developed specifically to teach children who are D/HOH about social skills is the PATHS program that focuses on peaceful conflict resolution, emotional regulation, empathy, and responsible decision making.

▪ Another SEL intervention strategy is simply to read to children who are D/HOH. Reading together is an excellent time to expand on pictures and incorporate discussions about feelings, emotions, and social interactions.

IMPLICATIONS FOR PRACTICE

- Know that special populations such as children with ID, ASD, and D/HOH may require more specialized SEL interventions.

- Realize that these special populations will almost always require Tier 3 intensive SEL interventions.

- Consider the following guidelines in designing interventions for these special populations:

  ○ One-to-one direct instruction of social skills that includes discrete trial training.

  ○ Sessions conducted twice per day, 5 days per week, lasing 30 minutes per session.

  ○ Duration of 40 weeks.

  ○ Professional responsible for supervising intervention sessions requires specialized training such as a behavior analyst, school psychologist, or behavior specialist.

  ○ Progress monitoring is conducted 5 days per week for the duration of the intervention.

- Strongly consider PRT, which uses a child's initiative and interests to develop communication, language, play, and social behaviors.

CHAPTER EIGHT

Practical Considerations in Social–Emotional Learning Assessment and Intervention

This chapter provides a context for understanding and applying the material presented previously in this book. The chapter focuses on the social ecology and culture of schools as they relate to children and youth with social skills deficits and competing problem behaviors. This chapter describes procedural guidelines and key concepts governing the implementation of evidence-based SEL interventions.

This information will be helpful in making it more likely that best-practice, evidence-based SEL interventions will be delivered in a manner that will have a better chance of improving the social competencies of children and youth. The emphasis in this chapter is on school-based interventions. However, these children and youth often will require additional interventions that address issues and needs extending beyond the school setting, such as clinic-based and/or home-based programs.

THE SCHOOL'S ROLE IN SOCIALIZING CHILDREN

Policymakers and legislators view schools as the ultimate vehicle for accessing children and youth who need services, supports, and interventions that can impact their physical and mental health (e.g., sensory and medical screenings, vaccinations, and various kinds of interventions). Schools are also important settings for identifying children and youth who suffer from various forms of neglect and abuse at home. As families continue to abandon their parenting responsibilities on a broad scale, schools must increasingly assume the role of protector, socializing agent, and caregiver.

Several recent developments have seriously impacted the school's ability to socialize children and youth. Unfortunately, we continue to reduce our investment in public schools, ask schools to restructure and reform themselves to achieve higher academic standards, and are becoming more and more critical of school systems for their failure to compensate for our failures as a society. Numerous surveys show that we invest far less in our educational system and infrastructure than do other modern industrialized nations.

Differences among first-grade children in beginning reading literacy provide a good example of how many at-risk children are severely disadvantaged as they begin their school careers. A study by Juel (1988) showed that if a child was a good reader in grade 1, his or her probability of staying a good reader in grade 4 was .87. However, if a child was a poor reader in grade 1, the probability of continuing to be a poor reader in grade 4 was equally likely at .88. The good news is if you start school ready to learn and are a good reader, you will remain so; the bad news is that if you start school not ready to learn and you are a poor reader, you will remain so. These findings speak to the critical importance of school readiness skills, early literacy development, and the facilitation of academic achievement by teaching "academic enablers" (i.e., social skills).

There is an interesting parallel between reading success or failure in grade 1 and emerging patterns of competing problem behaviors. If challenging forms of behavior are not addressed effectively at the point of school entry, the behavior will most likely worsen as these students progress through school. Kazdin (1987) has shown, for example, that if children's antisocial behavior problems are not remediated by the end of grade 3, they were highly likely to continue this form of behavior throughout adolescence and adulthood.

THE IMPORTANCE
OF EVIDENCE-BASED INTERVENTIONS

The effectiveness of school-based interventions is a source of continuing debate among professionals and laypersons. These interventions have been described by some as a "silver bullet" that works every time, lasts indefinitely, and is easy to implement. Such interventions do not exist. Instead, some students will require powerful, multicomponent, multisetting interventions implemented over a relatively long period of time.

Frequently, interventions implemented in schools or clinic settings are not empirically based. Unfortunately, the most effective interventions are typically not those used most often by schools or clinics. Instead, interventions are selected that allow the implementer to address the problem and that appeal to him or her. Although no current intervention approach can claim to be a "cure" for particular behavior patterns, some practices are clearly more effective than others.

Recall from Chapter 2 the discussion of what constitutes *evidence* and basing intervention actions on how we define it. Some professionals accept what they consider evidence only if it fits into their preexisting belief systems and may reject any evidence that does not conform to these beliefs. For example, some teachers believe that the use of rewards to increase desirable behaviors is a form of bribery that should not be used in their classrooms. They maintain this belief despite overwhelming scientific evidence to the contrary.

Strategies for teaching beginning reading provide an illustration of this phenomenon. It seems prudent to use a teaching method that produces the lowest rate of reading failure among students. Based on years of accumulated empirical research, this strategy should involve instruction in phonics and phonemic awareness (National Reading Panel, 2000). In spite of this accumulated evidence, many schools continue to invest in less effective approaches to teaching beginning reading (e.g., whole-word approaches). As noted in Chapter 2, this is analogous to a heart surgeon who uses a treatment regimen because (1) he was trained in that particular treatment, (2) it is easier to perform, and (3) he simply likes it better. This surgical procedure may have a 20% mortality rate when an alternative procedure may have a 5% mortality rate. Such a practice by medical personnel would not be tolerated given the stakes, yet many educators use similar logic in teaching reading.

FACTORS AFFECTING THE MAGNITUDE OF TREATMENT OUTCOMES

A number of factors may affect the magnitude of treatment outcomes in SEL interventions. These include the treatment validity of assessment procedures, the strength of treatment, the treatment integrity, and the decision rules used to change tiers of intervention. These issues are discussed in the following sections.

Treatment Validity of Assessment

Treatment validity, sometimes referred to as treatment or instructional utility, is the degree to which any assessment procedure contributes to beneficial outcomes for individuals (Hayes, Nelson, & Jarrett, 1987). The treatment validity concept evolved from the behavioral assessment camp.

However, it shares several characteristics and concepts found in the traditional psychometric literature:

1. Treatment validity contains an aspect of the notion of *incremental validity* in that it requires an assessment procedure to improve prediction over and above existing procedures (Sechrest, 1963).
2. Treatment validity contains the ideas of *utility* and *cost–benefit analysis* that is common in the personnel selection literature (Wiggins, 1973).
3. Treatment validity is related to Messick's (1995) evidential basis for *test interpretation* and *use,* particularly as it relates to construct validity, relevance/utility, and social consequences. It is entirely possible for a particular assessment procedure to have construct validity, but to have little or no relevance or utility for a particular use of a test, such as recommending a particular treatment based on the assessment procedure.

A key distinguishing feature of SEL interventions, whether they emanate from social learning theory, cognitive-behavioral theory, or applied behavior analysis, is a clear relationship between the assessment data that are collected and treatment planning. For example, an applied behavior analyst conducting an FBA documenting that a problem behavior is maintained by social attention might select a treatment utilizing differential reinforcement of incompatible behavior (DRI) in teaching replacement behaviors. A professional operating out of a social learning framework might assess social self-efficacy to design a treatment using a combination of performance accomplishments and modeling to increase the frequency and enhance the quality of social skills performances. A cognitive-behavioral therapist treating a child's social anxiety might teach the child progressive relaxation exercises coupled with positive self-talk regarding social interactions with peers. In each of these cases, there is a direct link between assessment information and intervention strategies. What differs in each of the above cases is what is assessed and its relationship to the design of treatment (e.g., social attention, self-efficacy, or self-statements).

Treatment validity is a fundamental assumption in using evidence-based practices to guide intervention selection. For any assessment to have treatment validity, it must lead to the identification of target behaviors, result in more effective treatments, and be useful in evaluating treatment outcomes.

Strength of Treatment

As described earlier in this book, the strength of psychological and educational interventions is difficult to operationalize a priori because treatment strength may vary across individuals. Some treatments are strong for some people but not for others due to a variety of factors such as learning history, prior exposure to the treatment, and resistance to target behaviors to intervention (Gresham, 1991). The strength of most medical treatments is rather easy to quantify a priori—for example, medication dosage, number of radiation sessions, or degree of invasiveness of various surgical procedures. The strength of psychological and educational treatments can only really be known a posteriori (after the treatment has concluded) and is quantified by the magnitude of change in behavior. Although this is certainly the case, there are some features of treatments that can be used to quantify treatment strength a priori, including (1) intensity or "dose" of a treatment, (2) duration of treatment, and (3) comprehensiveness of treatment. These three features are discussed in the following sections.

Intensity/Dose of Treatment

The intensity or "dose" of a treatment can be conceptualized as how often an individual is exposed to a particular treatment. Relatively weak treatments may be implemented once per day and one time per week, whereas strong treatments may be implemented three times per day for 5 days per week. A good example of a strong treatment can be found in the autism treatment literature. Lovaas (1997) provided one group of children with autism with 40 or more hours of discrete trial training per week and another group of children the same treatment for only 10 hours per week. His results showed that the group receiving the "stronger" treatment (40 or more hours per week) improved much more than the group receiving the "weaker" treatment (10 hours per week).

It is unclear at this time, however, how to quantify the intensity or dose of various social skills treatments. Some strategies have greater behavior-change potential than other strategies but this issue has not been comprehensively investigated.

Duration of Treatment

Many behavioral problems are difficult to change and are often highly resistant to intervention. For example, children with ASD constitute a population that has severe social–emotional and communication difficulties that require a relatively long period of time to remediate. Many of these children remain in applied behavior analytic treatments for a period of 5 or more years. Other populations of children do not require such lengthy interventions. For example, typically developing children with social skills performance deficits may only require a replacement behavior intervention that takes place over a period of 1 month. The key in determining how long a treatment should last is to continuously progress-monitor how well or poorly a child is responding to that intervention and make a decision based on these data.

Comprehensiveness of Treatment

Some intervention strategies take place in only one setting (e.g., the school or the home), whereas other intervention strategies are implemented across multiple settings of home, school, and community environments. These more comprehensive interventions are conceptualized within an ecological framework and are based on the notion that certain types of behavior problems are multiply caused and maintained across a variety of social environments. Viewing behavior problems from this perspective allows for a broader conceptualization of behavioral ecologies that cause and maintain these types of behavior difficulties. Multicomponent interventions hypothesize that some behavior problems are initiated and maintained through the social interactions of a child with his or her environment.

Children and youth function in a context of environmental factors, including such things as interpersonal relations (e.g., peers, teachers, parents), social systems (home and school), and settings (e.g., community, neighborhood). Effective intervention must target most of these environmental contexts to lead to successful outcomes for children and youth. Also, several factors may moderate the development and maintenance of behavior problems such as socioeconomic disadvantage, high levels of stress, parental psychopathology, and marital discord. Unfortunately, we have little or no control over these moderator variables in terms of designing effective interventions.

Effective comprehensive treatments should include the family, teachers, and peers. These treatments, at a minimum, should incorporate the parents, siblings, and school and may involve seeing the parents separately, meeting with the entire family, and using teachers to assess and intervene at school. Contexts often change over the course of development. For example, with very young children it seems logical to involve parents extensively in treatment. For school-age children, it makes sense to involve teachers quite extensively in treatment. For adolescents, it would be prudent to involve peers to some extent in treatment, given their profound influence on youths' social behavior.

Treatment Integrity

The accuracy with which interventions are implemented as planned, intended, or programmed is known as treatment integrity or treatment fidelity (Peterson, Homer, & Wonderlich, 1982). The implementation of evidence-based intervention practices is predicated on the assumption that demonstrable changes in social behavior (the dependent variable) are due to systematic, manipulated changes in the environment (the independent variable) and not due to extraneous variables. The absence of objective and measured specification of an operationally defined independent variable (the treatment) and its subsequent measured application in a natural environment compromises any incontrovertible conclusions that might be drawn concerning a treatment of behavior change (Gresham, 1989; McIntyre, Gresham, DiGennaro, & Reed, 2007).

Establishing the accuracy of treatment implementation is a critical aspect of scientific investigation and of the practical application of behavior change strategies or instructional procedures. The ineffectiveness of many instructional or behavioral interventions is likely due to the low accuracy of implementation of these procedures rather than to the inert or weak nature of interventions in changing behavior.

Dimensions of Treatment Integrity

The treatment integrity construct is currently thought of as multidimensional, in contrast with its initial conceptualization as being unidimensional and consisting only of adherence to an established treatment protocol (Gresham, 1989; Peterson et al., 1982). *Treatment adherence* represents a quantitative dimension of treatment integrity because it can be measured in terms of the number or percentage of critical treatment components that are implemented over the course of a treatment. Treatment adherence can be conceptualized as the *accuracy* and *consistency* with which a treatment is implemented. In this view, there are two aspects of treatment adherence: (1) treatment component adherence and (2) session/daily adherence. Figure 5.1 depicts an example of how one might present data on these two dimensions of treatment adherence for an SEL intervention implemented twice per week. The figure shows (1) an overall component adherence of 64.3%, with three components being implemented half the time and one component never being implemented, and (2) that daily adherence to the treatment protocol was inconsistent (71.4% vs. 57.1%). Measuring these two aspects of treatment adherence allows one to assess which components are being inconsistently implemented on which days or sessions.

More recently, other dimensions of treatment integrity have evolved in the literature: *interventionist competence* and *treatment differentiation* (Perepletchikova, 2014). Interventionist competence refers to the skill and experience of an interventionist in delivering a treatment. "Competence" in this sense might be best conceptualized as a qualitative dimension of treatment integrity because it reflects judgments of how well a treatment is implemented. Interventionist competence varies across universal (Tier 1), selected (Tier 2), and intensive (Tier 3) SEL interventions. Universal interventions do not require a great deal of skill to be implemented with integrity and can be carried out by most classroom teachers. Selected interventions require more skill and usually are developed within a problem-solving context or by using a standard protocol approach. Intensive interventions require the highest level of skill and will need to be implemented by persons with a great deal of training and experience in delivering these interventions.

The relationship between treatment adherence and interventionist competence can sometimes be confusing because competence presupposes adherence but adherence does not presuppose competence. One may adhere to a particular treatment perfectly, yet do so in an incompetent manner. For example, a teacher might be instructed to deliver contingent praise for prosocial behavior and may do this task with perfect integrity. However, the quality of that praise may be stilted and insincere and thereby not be very reinforcing to the student. A breakdown in treatment integrity in this case would call for teacher training in implementing key components of a treatment plan.

Treatment differentiation refers to the theoretical distinctions between different aspects of two or more treatments. That is, treatment differentiation refers to the extent to which treatments differ on critical dimensions. For example, an applied behavior analytic approach to teaching prosocial behavior would manipulate the antecedents and consequences surrounding prosocial behavior to increase its frequency. A social learning approach to teaching prosocial behavior would use modeling, coaching, and performance feedback to teach prosocial behavior. Finally, a cognitive-behavioral therapy approach to teaching prosocial behavior would employ social cognitive strategies and emotional regulation skills to teach prosocial behavior and to decrease competing problem behaviors. These treatments vary greatly on what the controlling mechanism is for behavior change, although all might be equally effective.

A final dimension of treatment integrity is termed *treatment receipt* (Bellg et al., 2004). Treatment receipt is conceptualized by exposure/dose of the treatment, participant comprehension of the treatment, and participant responsiveness to the treatment. Exposure or dose of a treatment refers to the amount of treatment received by a participant. For example, the "dose" of a treatment might be the number of times per day or week the participant is exposed to the treatment. Exposure can also be conceptualized as the duration of a treatment regimen for a particular problem. Some problems might require only 3 weeks of exposure to a treatment, whereas other problems might require considerably longer time the solve a problem (e.g., 10–15 weeks). Note that these conceptualizations of treatment receipt are very similar to treatment strength, discussed earlier in this chapter.

Participant comprehension refers to the degree to which a participant understands or comprehends the content of the treatment. For example, a teacher's understanding of the difference between attention-maintained and escape-maintained behaviors would constitute participant comprehension. Participant responsiveness refers to the extent to which a participant is engaged in the treatment and finds it relevant.

Variables Influencing Treatment Integrity

The foundation of treatment integrity can be traced to Yeaton and Sechrest's (1981) seminal paper, which provided a clear conceptualization of treatment integrity, in which several key issues involved in its definition, measurement, and evaluation were outlined. Yeaton and Sechrest hypothesized reciprocal relationships among the strength, integrity, and effectiveness of treatments. In this view, the strength of treatments implemented with poor integrity decreased (i.e., active treatment ingredients are diluted) and the effectiveness of those treatments is therefore reduced. As such, treatment integrity is important for evaluating the strength and effectiveness of treatments for different behaviors, in different settings, for different individuals, and across different treatment implementers.

Gresham (1989), on the basis of a logical or intuitive analysis of the literature, identified several factors or variables that appear to be related to treatment integrity. These variables can be broadly classified into two categories: (1) variables related to the intervention (e.g., complexity, materials/resources, ease of implementation) and (2) variables related to the interventionist (e.g., motivation to implement, skill proficiency, self-efficacy).

Witt and Elliott (1985) suggested that treatments that are perceived to be more effective are likely to be more acceptable to practitioners, and therefore will be implemented with higher treatment integrity. Witt and Elliott's theoretical model of treatment acceptability stressed the interrelations among four elements of treatments: treatment acceptability, treatment use, treatment integrity, and treatment effectiveness (see Figure 8.1).

The hypothesized relationships among these four elements are viewed as sequential and reciprocal. Acceptability is the initial issue in the sequence of treatment selection and use. Once a treatment is viewed as acceptable, the probability of using the treatment rather than a less acceptable treatment is high. The key element linking use and effectiveness is integrity. If treatment integrity is high, the probability of that treatment leading to behavior change is enhanced, whereas if treatment integrity is low, the treatment is less likely to result in meaningful behavior change.

Interpretation of Treatment Integrity Data

It is important to remember that all components of an intervention are not equally important and thus rigid adherence to a treatment protocol may not necessarily be required or even desirable. There is probably a "ceiling effect" above which treatment integrity improvement may not be necessary

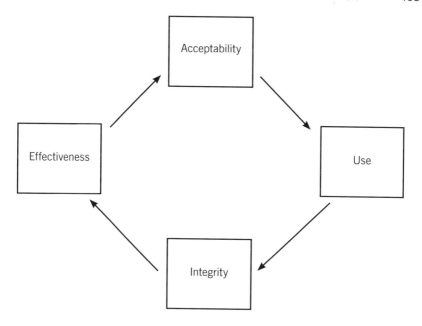

FIGURE 8.1. Witt and Elliott's intervention model.

or cost beneficial. The problem in this respect is that we do not know what level of integrity is necessary with which treatments to produce beneficial outcomes. We also do not know how far we might "drift" away from a treatment protocol and still have positive effects.

It may be the case that the level of adherence to treatment protocols depends on the type of research study being considered. It seems reasonable that rather stringent adherence to a treatment protocol would be required for *efficacy studies* because these studies seek to establish intervention effects under tightly controlled conditions (i.e., under conditions of high internal validity). It also seems reasonable to believe that less rigid adherence to treatment protocols would be required for *effectiveness studies* because these studies seek to establish intervention effects under less controlled conditions (i.e., under conditions of high external validity).

Currently, practitioners have no comprehensive database to guide them in deciding what the optimal levels of treatment integrity are for different treatments across different populations or individuals. Some problems might be effectively resolved with 75% treatment integrity, whereas other problems might require close to 100% treatment integrity to be effective. One potential avenue for future research and practice could be based in the notion of *treatment effect norms* (Yeaton, 1988). A "treatment effect norm" refers to the average outcomes of given treatments or a family of treatments whose goal is to alleviate a specific problem.

Practitioners could establish and catalog *treatment integrity effect norms* by quantifying what levels of treatment integrity, measured by what methods, with what interventions, produce what level of outcomes. For example, in using the SSIS-Intervention Guide, one might find that 80% treatment integrity measured by direct observations is required to produce socially valid increases in prosocial behavior for elementary school-age students. If might be the case that lower levels of treatment integrity using this intervention do not produce socially valid outcomes. Treatment integrity effect norms could be constructed across multiple tiers of intervention using different populations of children and youth.

Decision Rules in Changing Tiers of Intervention

An important task in using multiple tiers of intervention is the decision rule that should be used to change an individual to a more intense level of intervention. One useful way to guide one's thinking along these lines is to use single-case experimental design logic. Horner et al. (2005a) provided an instructive article regarding how single-case experimental designs can be used to support evidence-based practices. Single-case designs look at changes in *level, trend,* and *variability,* as well as at the immediacy of an effect, the proportion of data points in adjacent phases that overlap in level, the consistency of data patterns across multiple presentations of intervention and nonintervention conditions, and the magnitude of changes in behavior.

Changes in level refer to the average response an individual shows from baseline (pretreatment) to intervention (posttreatment) conditions. Changes in trend refer to the slope (increase or decrease) of behavior change over time. Variability refers to the variation in data points both within and across baseline and treatment conditions. Immediacy of effect refers to how long it takes a behavior to change from baseline to treatment phases of an intervention. The proportion of data points that overlap in level between baseline and treatment conditions represents a quantification of a treatment effect. The consistency of data patterns across multiple presentations of baseline and treatment conditions is another metric used to quantify effects in single-case designs. Finally, the magnitude of changes in behavior is used to quantify strong, moderate, or weak treatments. Single-case designs do not use tests of statistical significance, so the magnitude of effects can be rather subjective.

Single-case designs can and should be used as an aid in deciding when to change or intensify an intervention. Interventions that produce little or no change in level or slope should be changed or intensified based on this nonresponsiveness. In addition, interventions that do not produce an immediate effect should be changed as well. The decision of how long an intervention should be in place before changing it is a subjective judgment and depends on an individual case.

The Clinical Significance of Behavior Change

Clinical significance refers to the practical or applied value of an intervention and it determines whether an intervention made a real, genuine, practical, or noticeable difference in an individual's everyday functioning. It is entirely possible for an intervention to produce a reliable change in behavior, yet not be clinically significant. For example, an SEL intervention may move an individual from the 5th percentile to the 25th percentile on a social skills rating scale. This would be a reliable change but it would not be clinically significant because the individual's level of social skills is still exceeded by 75% of the population.

Several methods have been proposed to quantify or evaluate the clinical significance of change in interventions, including (1) comparison methods, (2) absolute change, (3) subjective evaluation, and (4) social impact (Kazdin, 2003b). *Comparison methods* involve the use of normative samples and evaluate the extent to which individuals fall within the normative range of performance. Demonstrating that after intervention individuals are indistinguishable from a normative sample would represent a clinically significant change. This method requires that the *measures employed must have adequate normative samples that can be used for comparison purposes.*

Absolute change refers to the amount of change an individual makes without comparison to a normative sample. This can be quantified by the amount of change from pretreatment to posttreatment (e.g., 2 standard deviations). It can also be quantified by an individual no longer meeting the criteria for a psychological disorder or the complete elimination of problem behaviors.

Subjective evaluation refers to impressions, judgments, or the opinions of significant others who interact with the child or youth. These could be quantified by ratings of current functioning, whether the original problem continues to be present, and/or whether the change produced by an intervention make a difference in the individual's functioning.

Social impact refers to changes on measures that are recognized or considered to be critically important in everyday life (i.e., the social importance of the effects of an intervention). These changes may be reflected on measures of truancy, ODRs, school suspensions/expulsions, and arrest rates.

CHAPTER SUMMARY POINTS

- Schools are the ultimate vehicle for accessing children and youth who need services, supports, and interventions that may impact their physical and mental health.

- Research has repeatedly shown the importance of school readiness skills, early literacy development, and the facilitation of academic achievement by teaching academic enablers or social skills.

- Research has shown that if children's antisocial behavior problems are not remediated by the end of grade 3, they are highly likely to continue this form of behavior throughout adolescence and into adulthood.

- Interventions often are implemented in schools or clinics that are chosen for convenience rather than based on empirical evidence.

- Treatment validity is the degree to which any assessment procedure contributes to beneficial outcomes and contains elements of incremental validity and cost–benefit analysis.

- SEL interventions based on applied behavior analysis, social learning theory, or cognitive-behavioral theory are all founded on a close relationship between assessment data collected and treatment planning.

- Treatment strength can be quantified by the intensity or "dose" of a treatment, the duration of a treatment, and the comprehensiveness of a treatment.

- The "dose" or intensity of a treatment can be conceptualized as how often an individual is exposed to a treatment.

- There is huge variability in the duration of treatments for certain populations (e.g., children with ASD vs. typically developing children).

- Some populations of children will require multicomponent interventions that take place in school, at home, and in community settings.

- Treatment integrity refers to the accuracy with which interventions are implanted as planned or intended and is also termed treatment adherence.

- Treatment adherence consists of two dimensions: (1) treatment component adherence and (2) session/daily adherence.

- Treatment integrity also includes interventionist competence, treatment differentiation, and treatment receipt.

- Treatments can be conceptualized as including treatment acceptability, treatment use, treatment integrity, and treatment effectiveness.

- Practitioners have no comprehensive database to guide them in deciding what the optimal levels of treatment integrity are for different treatments across different populations or individuals.

- Treatment integrity effect norms are a means of quantifying what levels of treatment, measured by what methods, with what interventions, produce what levels of outcomes.

- Single-case designs look at changes in level, trend, variability, and immediacy of effect to decide when to intensify or change a treatment.

- Clinical significance refers to the practical or applied value of an intervention and it determines whether an intervention made a real, genuine, practical, or noticeable difference in an individual's functioning.

- Treatment effects can be quantified by comparison methods, absolute change indices, subjective evaluation, or changes on social impact measures.

CHAPTER NINE

Summary, Conclusion, and Future Directions in Social–Emotional Learning

This book has emphasized the theory that poor peer relations in childhood are associated with substantial adjustment difficulties in adolescence and into adulthood. Based on these findings, researchers and practitioners developed preventive interventions designed to remediate social skills deficits that are associated with poor social adjustment. Over the past 10 years, there has been an intense interest in the development of SEL curricula to be implemented in schools as Tier 1, or universal, interventions. Over 500 evaluations have documented the effectiveness of universal school-based SEL curricula on a variety of outcomes (CASEL, 2012). This book has discussed SEL interventions for a number of populations ranging from typically developing children to individuals with specific mental health diagnoses such as ASD, ID, SPCD, and D/HOH.

CONCEPTUALIZATION OF SOCIAL COMPETENCE

Social competence was discussed from a number of theoretical perspectives. One conceptualization was described as the *sociometric conceptualization* of social competence in which indices of sociometric status are used to operationally define social competence. Sociometric status was described as the extent to which other individuals want to associate with a particular child, who wants to engage in certain social activities with a particular child, and who likes or dislikes a particular child. In this view, children who are rejected or neglected by peers are considered to be socially incompetent and children who are accepted or popular with peers are considered to be socially competent.

Although sociometric status is a relatively objective criterion, it often cannot identify the specific behaviors within specific situations that lead to peer rejection or acceptance. The behavioral correlates of outright peer rejection usually include such things as aggressive behavior, impulsivity, and negative social interactions with peers. The behavioral correlates of neglected sociometric status include such things as anxiety, social withdrawal, depression, and low rates of positive social interactions. The correlations between these behavioral correlates and sociometric status are relatively low and do not completely account for or explain an individual's sociometric status. Also, positive or negative sociometric status can occur for reasons that have nothing to do with an individual's social–behavioral strengths or weaknesses, such as physical attractiveness/unattractiveness, positive/negative reputational biases, critical negative behavioral events, and cross-sex nominations.

Three learning theories have been used to conceptualize the social skills construct. Social learning theory includes a number of variables that account for a person's social skills deficiencies and excesses in competing problem behaviors. Social learning theory identifies five major reasons that explain social skills deficiencies: (1) lack of knowledge, (2) lack of practice and feedback, (3) absence of or inattention to social cues, (4) lack of reinforcement, and (5) presence of competing problem behaviors. Social learning theory emphasizes cognitive–mediational processes to explain which environmental events are attended to, subsequently retained, and are performed when a person is exposed to modeling stimuli (i.e., vicarious learning). Social learning theory is based on the principle of reciprocal determinism that describes the effect an individual has on the environment and vice-versa.

Cognitive-behavioral theory is based on the assumption that a person's behavior in response to environmental events is mediated by cognitions or thoughts. SEL interventions based on cognitive-behavioral theory present individuals with social situations in which a variety of internal and external social cues are present. Based on past learning history, these cues are made more or less salient. Strategies such as self-monitoring, self-instruction, self-evaluation, and social problem solving are used in cognitive-behavioral SEL interventions.

Applied behavior analysis is based on the concept of the three-term contingency that describes the relationships among antecedent, behavior, and consequent events. In this view, behavior analysts identify the conditions that reinforce (positively or negatively) the occurrence of specific problem behaviors that need to be changed. Functional behavioral assessment (FBA) is paramount in the identification of environmental conditions that are functionally related to the occurrence of problem behaviors. Behavior analysts seek to replace competing problem behaviors with alternative prosocial behaviors (i.e., replacement behavior training).

Lastly, another way of conceptualizing social skills is based on the idea of social validity. In this view, social skills are behaviors exhibited within specific situations that predict important social outcomes for children and youth. Important social outcomes might be peer acceptance, friendships, consistent school attendance, and significant others' judgments of social competence. Included in a social validity conceptualization of social competence are the notions of the social significance of the behaviors targeted in SEL interventions and the social importance of the effects produced by a given SEL intervention. Social skills have also been shown to be academic enablers, which are the attitudes and behaviors that allow students to participate in and benefit from academic instruction in the classroom. Positive peer interactions promote competent forms of social behavior that in turn promote successful academic performance. Competing problem behaviors, particularly externalizing behaviors, interfere with or compete with the performance of social and academic skills. In this sense, these behaviors function as academic disablers in that they lead to decreases in academic performance.

IDENTIFICATION OF SOCIAL SKILLS STRENGTHS AND DEFICITS

There are four steps in identifying social skills strengths and deficits: (1) identifying social skills strengths, (2) identifying social skills acquisition deficits, (3) identifying social skills performance deficits, and (4) identifying competing problem behaviors. Social skills strengths are those behaviors that a child knows how to perform and are used consistently and appropriately. Social skills acquisition deficits are those social skills that the child does not know how to perform or to use appropriately. Social skills performance deficits are those social skills the child knows how to perform and use, but that he or she does not do consistently or frequently. Finally, competing problem behaviors are those behaviors that interfere with a child's acquisition or performance of a particular social skill.

CASEL is an organization devoted to evidence-based SEL interventions from preschool through high school. CASEL targets five interrelated sets of cognitive, affective, and behavioral competencies: (1) self-awareness, (2) self-management, (3) social awareness, (4) relationship skills, and (5) responsible decision making. A meta-analysis of 213 school-based universal SEL programs involving more than 270,000 students showed significant improvements in social and emotional skills, positive attitudes toward self and others, positive social behaviors, and reductions in conduct problems.

EVIDENCE-BASED TREATMENT AND PRACTICES

An evidence-based practice (EBP) is an approach to clinical or educational practice that originated in medicine around 1992 under the term *evidence-based medicine*. Since that time, many other fields have adopted EBPs unique to those fields (e.g., nursing, social work, audiology, speech and language pathology, and psychology). EBP involves making decisions about how to promote desirable outcomes by utilizing and integrating the best scientific evidence coupled with practitioner expertise and organizational resources. Researchers make a distinction between evidence-based treatments (EBTs) and evidence-based practices. EBTs are those treatments that have been shown to be efficacious through rigorous research methods having good internal validity. EBPs are grounded in scientific research that supports implementation of intervention approaches across groups, sites, investigators, and contexts and emphasize good external validity. EBTs are established via efficacy studies and EBPs are established via effectiveness studies.

TYPES OF RESEARCH EVIDENCE

Multiple types of research evidence that vary in quality and control are used to support EBPs, including (1) efficacy studies that are high in internal validity, (2) effectiveness studies that are high in external validity, (3) cost-effectiveness studies that estimate cost–benefit ratios, (4) longitudinal intervention outcome studies that consider the long-term benefits of interventions, and (5) epidemiological studies that are used to track the availability, utilization, and acceptance of various intervention procedures. A variety of research methods are used in these studies including (1) observation of individuals within target settings to generate hypotheses, (2) qualitative and mixed-methods research to evaluate the real-world experiences of persons undergoing interventions, (3) single-case experimental designs that are used to draw causal inferences about individuals in a controlled manner, (4) moderator–mediator studies used to identify the correlates and causes of intervention outcomes, (5) efficacy studies using randomized controlled trials, (6) effectiveness studies used to investigate the generalizability of intervention outcomes, and (7) meta-analyses that provide a quantitative index or metric of the synthesis of multiple studies.

Evaluation of evidence-based interventions is based on the validity of making inferences about phenomena under investigation. *Validity* can be defined as the truth of an inference or the degree to which evidence supports an inference being true or correct. In research methodology, there are four threats to the validity of inferences: (1) internal validity that reflects the degree to which one can attribute change in a dependent variable to systematic, manipulated changes in an independent variable (i.e., the treatment); (2) external validity that refers to the generalizability of the results of an investigation across populations, participants, therapists/teachers, settings, treatment variables, and measurement variables; (3) construct validity that establishes the basis for interpreting the causal relation between an independent and a dependent variable; and (4) statistical conclusion validity that refers to threats in drawing valid inferences that result from random error and inappropriate statistical analyses.

STANDARDS FOR EBTs

Several divisions within the American Psychological Association have proposed criteria for the levels of scientific evidence necessary for determining whether or not a treatment is evidence-based. Although there is some variation among these divisions' documents, all have agreed upon the criteria that should be in the classification of scientific evidence. These criteria are described below:

- *Criterion 1:* Well-established treatment based on two good group experimental design experiments conducted in at least two independent research settings, and by independent research teams demonstrating efficacy by showing the intervention to be (1) statistically superior to a pill or psychological placebo or another treatment, or (2) equivalent to an already established treatment in experiments with sufficient statistical power to detect moderate differences, and (3) treatment manuals or their logical equivalent were used in treatment implementation.
- *Criterion 2:* Probably efficacious treatment based on at least two good experiments showing that the treatment is superior to a wait-list control group or one or more good experiments meeting the criteria for well-established treatments with one exception of having been conducted in two independent research settings and by different investigatory teams.
- *Criterion 3:* Possibly efficacious treatment based on at least one good study showing the treatment to be efficacious in the absence of conflicting evidence.
- *Criterion 4:* Experimental treatment in which the treatment has not been tested in trials meeting established criteria for methodology.

ASSESSMENT OF SOCIAL SKILLS

The main purpose of social skills assessment is to collect information that will lead to correct decisions about individuals. Five types of decisions are usually made in this assessment process: (1) screening decisions, (2) identification and classification decisions, (3) intervention decisions, (4) progress-monitoring decisions, and (5) evaluation of intervention outcomes decisions. A useful way of thinking about these types of decisions is to think of them as different types of "tests." A screening test looks for indicators of the specific problem and uses reliable and valid cutoff scores to correctly identify children and youth who do have (sensitivity) and who do not have social skills deficits (specificity). A diagnostic test looks for the presence of some problem such as the use of norm-referenced multi-informant social skills behavior rating scales to identify social skills deficits. A treatment decision test is designed to guide intervention decisions and yields information regarding "why" a problem is occurring (e.g., FBA). A monitoring test tracks the progress of a behavior in an intervention using systematic direct observations, direct behavior ratings, brief behavior ratings, and/or ODRs.

Sociometric assessment has a long history in the study of peer relationships in children and youth. Longitudinal studies have shown that children who are rejected by their peers have much higher rates of externalizing and internalizing behavior patterns. Two methods have been used frequently in the sociometric assessment literature: (1) peer ratings and (2) peer nominations. These methods have been used to calculate social preference and social impact scores that, in turn, are used to classify children into different sociometric status groups (popular, rejected, neglected, controversial, and average). The problem with sociometric assessments is that they are insensitive in detecting short-term treatment effects and they show relatively weak correlations and specific prosocial behaviors measured by other methods (e.g., teacher ratings, direct observations, self-ratings). Given these problems with sociometric assessment, it is not a recommended assessment strategy to make screening, classification, intervention, or progress-monitoring decisions.

MULTI-TIERED SEL INTERVENTIONS

SEL interventions, depending on the severity of the social skills deficit, vary in terms of intensity and duration because not all individuals will require the same "dose" of an intervention. One way of classifying SEL interventions is to group them into three levels of intensity: primary prevention, secondary prevention, and tertiary prevention. Primary prevention interventions seek to keep problems from emerging, with the goal being to prevent harm. Secondary prevention interventions are those that seek to reverse harm. Tertiary prevention interventions are targeted for the most at-risk children and youth and whose purpose is to reduce already existing harm.

This three-level classification system served as the basis for what is now known as response to intervention (RTI). RTI is based on the idea of determining whether an adequate or inadequate change in behavior has been observed through the implementation of an intervention. Professionals make decisions using the RTI approach to select, change, or titrate interventions depending on how individuals respond to those interventions. RTI assumes that if an individual shows an inadequate response to the best intervention available that is implemented with integrity, then that individual can and should receive a more intensive intervention.

Universal, or Tier 1, interventions are those designed to impact all students in the same manner under the same conditions. Each student receives the intervention at the same "dosage" level and it is delivered in a common format and is repeated on a daily or weekly basis. These interventions are appropriate for classwide or schoolwide applications. It is expected that about 80% of students will respond adequately to these universal interventions.

Selected, or Tier 2, interventions are used for an identified or individually tailored intervention that is fine-tuned to meet the needs of a particular student. Examples of selected interventions might include individualized programs designed to remediate oppositional–defiant behaviors or small-group SEL interventions for students who share similar social skills deficits. About 15% of students will respond adequately to these selected or Tier 2 interventions.

A very small percentage of students (approximately 5%) will require the most intense level of intervention, which are called intensive, or Tier 3, interventions. These interventions are very intense, expensive, and time-consuming and should be reserved for the most severe at-risk students. Examples of intensive interventions are function-based SEL interventions that require an FBA to design and implement the intervention.

It is important to remember that two sets of descriptors help in understanding the multi-tier model of intervention. First, the notion of *most, some,* and *few* related to the commonly cited percentages of students (80%, 15%, and 5%) should be thought of as a general concept rather than as specific numbers. Tier 1, or universal, interventions should meet the needs of most students. Despite this desired goal, even with effective universal interventions, some students will require Tier 2 intervention. However, there will still be a few students who need intensive, or Tier 3, interventions.

Second, the notion of *least, more,* and *most* is a way of thinking about the intensity of interventions. Tier 1 interventions are the least intensive and should be scientifically based with the goal of promoting positive development and preventing problems. Tier 2 interventions should be customized to the individual child and represent more intensive interventions. Tier 3 interventions are highly intense and represent the most intensive intervention.

Two basic approaches are used to deliver Tier 2 selected and Tier 3 intensive interventions: (1) problem-solving approaches and (2) standard protocol approaches. Problem-solving approaches are based on the behavioral consultation model that takes place in a sequence of four steps: (1) problem identification, (2) problem analysis, (3) plan implementation, and (4) problem evaluation. This sequence of steps answers four basic questions: What is the problem? Why is it occurring? What should we do about it? Did we solve the problem? The goal in problem solving is to define the problem in clear, unambiguous, and operational terms; to identify environment conditions related to the problem (antecedents and consequences); to design and implement an intervention plan; and to evaluate the effectiveness of the intervention plan. In a problem-solving approach, a problem is defined as a discrepancy between current and desired levels of performance: the larger this discrepancy, the larger the problem.

An important distinction to be made in problem solving is to determine why the problem is occurring. At this juncture, the distinction between the "can't do" and "won't do" problem is important. Can't do problems, or acquisition deficits, occur because the person does not have the skill or behavior in his or her repertoire. These deficits must be remediated by directly teaching the individual the deficit social skill. Won't do problems are considered performance deficits, meaning that the person knows how to perform the behavior or skill, but does not do so at an acceptable level. Performance deficits can result from the absence of opportunities to perform the skill or the lack of or low rate of reinforcement for performing the skill. In this case, interventions should involve providing multiple opportunities to perform the behavior and increasing the rate of reinforcement for engaging in the behavior.

Standard protocol approaches involve the use of manualized, scripted treatments in which the components of the intervention are written in explicit detail. In SEL interventions, these scripted programs typically specify procedures for using modeling, coaching, behavioral rehearsal, and generalization programming to teach social skills. A good example of a Tier 2 standard protocol SEL intervention is the SSIS-IG, designed for those students who demonstrate social skills deficits and who fail to respond to a Tier 1 universal SEL intervention program.

Tier 3 intensive interventions have several characteristics that differentiate them from Tier 2 selected interventions. These interventions are more intense in terms of time, "dosage," and response effort on the part of interventionists. They are highly individualized and tailored to the specific needs of an individual. They are based on an FBA that reveals the function of problem behavior and replaces them with a functionally equivalent socially skilled behavior that serves the same function (replacement behavior training). These interventions take place over a considerably longer period of time than Tier 2 selected interventions. Several factors are related to a behavior's lack of response to Tier 2 interventions; they include (1) severity of behavior, (2) chronicity of behavior, (3) generalizability of behavior change, (4) treatment strength, (5) treatment integrity, and (6) treatment effectiveness.

SEL INTERVENTIONS WITH SPECIFIC POPULATIONS

SEL intervention strategies have been shown to be effective with children and youth with developmental disorders (ID, ASD, and SPCD) and D/HOH individuals. SEL interventions for children and youth with ID and ASD are similar in terms of teaching strategies and target behaviors. Approximately 75% of children diagnosed with ASD have IQs in the range of persons with ID. Comorbid diagnosis of ID and ASD is based on social communication abilities being below those expected for the child's general developmental level.

Most persons diagnosed with ID have adaptive behavior deficits primarily in the conceptual and social domains. When compared to their typically developing peers, these individuals are immature in their social interactions and have difficulties in perceiving peers' social cues. Communication, conversation, and language skills are more concrete than expected for their age. They have a limited understanding of risk in social situations, their social judgment is immature, and they are prone to be manipulated by others because of gullibility.

Individuals diagnosed with ASD demonstrate persistent deficits in social communication and social interaction across multiple contexts. These persons show deficits in social–emotional reciprocity, limitations in reciprocal conversation skills, deficits in nonverbal or pragmatic skills, and deficiencies in developing, maintaining, and understanding social relationships.

SPCD is characterized by a central difficulty with pragmatics, or the social use of language and communication. These persons have deficits in understanding and following social rules of verbal and nonverbal communication in naturalistic settings, altering their language to meet the needs of the listener or situation, and following rules for conversations. These deficits are not due to low abilities of structural language or cognitive abilities and can be differentiated from ASD by the presence in ASD of restricted/repetitive patterns of behavior, interests, or activities, and their absence in SPCD.

Most individuals with ID, ASD, and SPCD will require Tier 3 intensive

SEL interventions such as the ones described in Chapter 6. Children with these disorders will not respond adequately to Tier 1 or Tier 2 SEL interventions. SEL interventions for these populations must be highly individualized and targeted to the specific social skills deficits exhibited by these children and youth. These interventions should have the following characteristics: (1) one-to-one direct instruction of social skills; (2) sessions conducted at least twice a day, 5 days per week, lasting at least 30 minutes per session; (3) duration of at least 40 weeks; (4) professional responsible for supervising intervention sessions requires specialized training; and (5) progress monitoring is conducted 5 days per week for the duration of the intervention.

An extremely effective SEL intervention for these individuals is pivotal response training (PRT), a method of systematically applying the principles of applied behavior analysis to teach children with ASD functional social-communication and adaptive behavior skills within a naturalistic teaching format. It was originally developed for children with ASD, but it can also be effective with children with ID and SPCD. PRT is based on four key pivotal learning variables: (1) motivation, (2) responding to multiple cues, (3) self-management, and (4) self-initiations. These skills are pivotal because they are the foundational skills upon which children can make widespread and generalized improvements in many other areas.

PRT is considered to be a more effective alternative to discrete trial training (DTT) because it teaches social skills in a more naturalistic social environment. DTT uses adult-directed, massed trial instruction and uses clear contingencies and repetition to teach new skills. DTT is a strong method for developing a new response to a stimulus, but it is limited because it does not reinforce a child's spontaneity and has difficulty in the generalization of new skills to other naturalistic environments.

FACTORS AFFECTING THE MAGNITUDE OF TREATMENT OUTCOMES

One factor affecting the magnitude of treatment outcomes is treatment validity, which refers to the degree to which any assessment procedure contributes to beneficial treatment outcomes. Treatment validity shares at least three characteristics found in the traditional psychometric literature: (1) incremental validity that requires an assessment procedure to improve prediction over and above existing procedures, (2) utility and cost–benefit analysis that is common in the personnel selection literature, and (3) evidential basis for test interpretation and use. It is possible for an assessment procedure to have construct validity, but to have little or no relevance for recommending a particular treatment based on an assessment procedure. SEL intervention procedures, whether they are based on social learning theory, cognitive-behavioral theory, or applied behavior analysis, all have a clear relationship between assessment data collected and treatment planning.

A second factor affecting the magnitude of treatment outcomes is the strength of treatment. Treatment strength involves three characteristics: (1) dose or intensity of treatment, (2) duration of treatment, and (3) comprehensiveness of treatment. The dose or intensity of a treatment can be conceptualized as how often an individual is exposed to a treatment. Weak treatments may be implemented once per day and once per week for 2 weeks, whereas strong treatments may be implemented three times per day for 5 days per week for 6 weeks. The duration of a treatment also relates to treatment strength, with some treatments lasting only several weeks and other treatments for some problems lasting 5 or more years. Finally, some interventions only take place in one setting (e.g., school), whereas other treatments are implemented across multiple settings of home, school, and community environments.

A third factor affecting the magnitude of treatment outcomes is treatment integrity, which reflects the accuracy with which interventions are implemented as planned or intended. Treatment integrity is a multidimensional concept and includes (1) treatment adherence, or the accuracy and consistency with which a treatment is implemented over time; (2) interventionist competence, or the degree of skill and experience of an interventionist in implementing a particular treatment; (3) treatment differentiation, or the theoretical distinctions between different aspects of two or more treatments; and (4) treatment receipt, or a participant's understanding and responsiveness to a given treatment.

DECISION RULES IN
CHANGING TIERS OF INTERVENTION

An important challenge in using multiple tiers of intervention is the decision rule that should be used to change an individual to a more intensive level of intervention. A useful way to guide one's thinking in this regard is to use single-case experimental design logic. Single-case designs look at changes in level, trend, and variability as well as at the immediacy of effect, the proportion of data points in adjacent phases that overlay in level, the consistency of data patterns across multiple presentations of intervention and nonintervention conditions, and the magnitude of behavior change. Single-case designs can and should be used as an aid in deciding when to change or intensify an intervention. Interventions that produce little or no change in level or slope should be changed or intensified based on nonresponsiveness to an intervention. Also, interventions that do not produce an immediate effect should be changed or intensified as well.

Practitioners should also establish the clinical significance of behavior change, which refers to the practical or applied value of an intervention that determines the genuine, practical, and noticeable difference in an individual's everyday functioning. Four methods have been recommended for establishing the clinical significance of behavior change: (1) comparison methods that involve the use of normative samples; (2) absolute change that refers to the amount of change an individual makes without comparison to a normative sample; (3) subjective evaluation that refers to impressions, judgments, or opinions of significant others; and (4) social impact that refers to changes on measures that are considered to be critically important in everyday life.

CHAPTER TEN

Case Studies in Social–Emotional Learning Assessment and Intervention

Rachel M. Olinger Steeves, Kelsey Hartman, and Sarah Metallo

Given the complexity and nuanced nature of social behaviors and the knowledge that not all individuals require the same intensity of intervention, applying an RTI framework to social skills assessment and intervention has clear benefits. The logic behind RTI emphasizes the idea that when interventions are systematically selected based upon need, schools are more effective in reaching all students. Data-based decision making, using student responsiveness to determine the focus and intensity of interventions, is encouraged. Implementing interventions at the universal, targeted, and individual levels provides an opportunity for early identification and intervention with at-risk students, prevention of more severe social behavior problems, and a feasible method for differentiating social skills instruction.

This chapter includes a series of case studies for the purpose of illustrating evidence-based social skills assessment and intervention strategies

Rachel M. Olinger Steeves, MA, Kelsey Hartman, MA, and Sarah Metallo, MA, are graduate students in the Department of Psychology at Louisiana State University.

across a multi-tiered system of support. Each case study is meant to provide guidance to professionals considering the development and implementation of interventions aimed at improving social behavior. Ideal circumstances for doing so within an RTI framework, including strategies for assessing the nature of the social concern, intervening in a systematic fashion, and monitoring progress, are presented.

Case studies address a variety of social behaviors across a diverse group of students and interventions. First, three interrelated case examples are presented, each progressing sequentially through the three tiers. A universal intervention designed to address classwide social behavior is followed by a targeted peer intervention for a small group of students. Finally, one nonresponsive student receives an individualized intervention based on the function of his or her behavior. Next, two additional primary approaches to intervening at the classwide level are presented, each representing a different approach to universal intervention and progress monitoring. Case studies six and seven present two targeted interventions, one with a small group of students demonstrating partial acquisition social skill deficits, and the other a targeted intervention for an individual student. Finally, two Tier 3 interventions for individuals from specialized populations are presented to demonstrate adaptations beneficial for these populations.

CASE STUDY 1:
TIER 1 UNIVERSAL SEL CURRICULUM

Teacher Name: Mr. Paul Roberts
Class/Subject: General education, English language arts
Grade: 5
Student Ages: 10–12

Background Information

Mr. Roberts, a fifth-grade general education teacher at a public elementary school, contacted the school psychologist for assistance. He reported difficulty with disruptive behavior in his homeroom, particularly with significant problems in interpersonal interactions between students. Mr. Roberts reported that a significant number of his students demonstrated difficulty understanding each other's emotions and coping with their own frustrations. As a result, verbal arguments and physical fights occurred more frequently, disrupting the classroom learning environment and resulting in students regularly being sent out of the classroom. Students often yelled at each other and would lash out in anger over seemingly trivial disagreements. He and his colleagues saw these behaviors more prominently in his homeroom than in the other fifth-grade classes and believed that the students would greatly benefit from learning to better regulate their own emotions and to understand each other's as well. Mr. Roberts sought out the school psychologist's expertise in selecting a curriculum he could implement with ease in his current schedule and that they could reinforce across all other fifth-grade classrooms.

Assessment

Classroom Observations

To further assess Mr. Roberts's concerns, the school psychologist conducted a series of classroom observations. Observations revealed a pattern of negative peer interactions across a significant percentage of students. During instruction, students were observed knocking each other's belongings off their desks, kicking each other under their tables, and calling each other names. On four separate occasions, different students reacted inappropriately to these interactions, either by yelling at each other, becoming visibly angry and refusing to complete their work, or having to be removed from the classroom for escalating behavior. When students were sent out of the classroom, the instructional environment was visibly impacted, resulting in restlessness and difficulty concentrating for many of the remaining students. Classroom conduct grades and office discipline referrals were also collected and reviewed by the school psychologist to provide additional evidence of the nature of the problem and to establish a baseline for monitoring progress once an intervention was implemented.

Classroom Conduct Grades

Mr. Roberts and his colleagues developed a daily conduct report corresponding to classroom behavioral expectations and discipline procedures at the start of the school year. These conduct grades were designed as a method for parents to monitor their children's behavior throughout the week. Each day, teachers kept a tally of rule violations for each of the behavioral expectations and sent home the reports to students' parents to review and return. The behaviors monitored with weekly conduct grades included (1) followed directions the first time given; (2) kept hands, feet, and objects to self; (3) used kind words; (4) completed and turned in classwork; and (5) took responsibility for their own actions. At the end of each week, overall conduct letter grades were assigned to each student based on the total number of behavioral infractions.

Conduct grades were collected for all students the week prior to the implementation of the universal intervention, halfway through implementation, and again at the end of the intervention to monitor progress and assess for changes in classwide behavior problems. The number of students receiving lower conduct grades varied each week. However, data collected during the week immediately before beginning the SEL curriculum revealed that 20% of students had A conduct grades, 15% had B's, 35% had C's, and 30% had D's and F's, demonstrating that a majority of students were exhibiting difficulty following the classroom expectations.

Office Discipline Referrals

Teachers and school administrators also routinely collected and reviewed ODRs in order to identify the most common types of infractions to then target with intervention. Prior to initiating the universal intervention, the majority of ODRs in fifth-grade classrooms included infractions such as disrespect, inappropriate language, disturbing others (e.g., pushing, pulling, shoving), and name calling or bullying. These documented behavior problems provided further support for Mr. Roberts's reported concerns and identified a need for targeting self-regulation and interpersonal skills with explicit teaching of skills to all students in the classroom. Collecting the number of ODRs for each student in the class also served as a method for monitoring classwide response to intervention and identifying any students in need of further support at the conclusion of the universal intervention.

Intervention

Universal Strong Kids SEL Curriculum

Given the nature of the challenges faced by Mr. Roberts and his students, and the overwhelming majority of students in his class displaying similar problems, a universal classwide intervention was selected with an explicit focus on teaching social and emotional skills. The curriculum selected was the Strong Kids SEL curriculum, designed with the purpose of prevention and intervention by teaching an understanding of emotions, promoting resilience, strengthening assets and skills for getting along with others, and increasing coping skills in children and early adolescents.

The Strong Kids, Grades 3–5 curriculum (Merrell, Carrizales, Feuerborn, Gueldner, & Tran, 2007) includes 12 distinct lessons covering a broad range of social and emotional skills, which are each outlined in further detail in Table 10.1. Lessons in the curriculum are designed to last 45–55 minutes and to be integrated into daily classroom practices. Mr. Roberts implemented the Strong Kids curriculum 3 days per week with his homeroom for a period of 45 minutes per session. Monday and Wednesday's sessions provided the lessons as written in the curriculum in a sequential fashion. Friday's session involved review of the prior week's lessons, a review of the homework assignments and supplemental activities, and an

TABLE 10.1. Strong Kids Lesson Outlines

Lesson title	Skills taught/purpose
1. About Strong Kids: Emotional Strength Training	Introduction to Strong Kids curriculum
2. Understanding Your Feelings 1	Introduction to types of feelings, increases emotional vocabulary
3. Understanding Your Feelings 2	Appropriate ways to express feelings
4. Dealing with Anger	Understanding and handling anger
5. Understanding Other People's Feelings	Empathy skills and ability to identify other's feelings
6. Clear Thinking 1	Strategies to identify thinking errors and negative patterns of thinking
7. Clear Thinking 2	Strategies for replacing maladaptive thinking with realistic and helpful thoughts
8. The Power of Positive Thinking	Optimistic thinking for addressing problems and ways to offset negative thinking
9. Solving People Problems	Skills for solving interpersonal problems and conflict-resolution without violence
10. Letting Go of Stress	Identifying stressors, ways to handle stress, and managing anxiety and worry
11. Behavior Change: Setting Goals and Staying Active	Setting realistic goals, strategies for being successful, and increasing positive actions
12. Finishing UP!	Review of all major concepts from Strong Kids curriculum
13. Strong Kids Booster: Putting It All Together	Optional booster session designed to revisit key lessons several weeks after finishing the curriculum

opportunity for students to practice the skills of the week. Strong Kids lessons were implemented over the course of 6 weeks.

All three fifth-grade teachers decided to implement the curriculum with their homeroom students to ensure consistency and improve the skills of all students in the fifth grade. In order to generalize the skills taught during the sessions, teachers worked together to reinforce the topics throughout the day. Teachers used Strong Kids terminology whenever possible during their instruction, tying in the skills to the academic curriculum. Terminology was applied most frequently outside the Strong Kids sessions when redirecting disruptive students or prompting students to use their coping skills. Students who actively engaged in Strong Kids skills themselves or who encouraged their peers to practice the skills were praised and rewarded by their teachers. Parents were also informed of the content of the lessons through weekly letters sent home with students. In these letters, the skills being taught for the week were described in detail, and parents were encouraged to support practice of the skills at home.

Outcomes

Following implementation of the full curriculum, Mr. Roberts reported a substantial change in the types of behaviors engaged in by his students. Students, overall, appeared more aware of their own emotions and engaged in more adaptive ways of handling their anger, such as asking to take a break or removing themselves from situations that provoked negative emotions. Students also reportedly expressed more concern with each other's success and less frequently yelled or fought with one another. Data collected over the course of implementation showed an increase in the number of A and B weekly conduct grades and a reduction in the overall number of students earning C's, D's, and F's each week. Specifically, Mr. Roberts reported a decrease in the overall number of violations for failing to keep hands, feet, and objects to self, use kind words, and take responsibility for own actions. Weekly classroom conduct grade data are displayed further in Figure 10.1.

At the conclusion of the curriculum, ODRs were reviewed again to

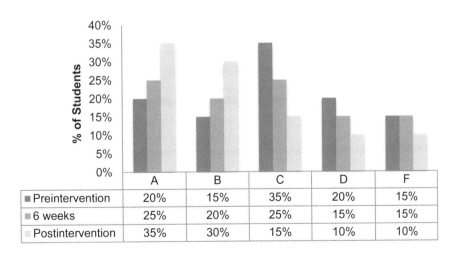

	A	B	C	D	F
Preintervention	20%	15%	35%	20%	15%
6 weeks	25%	20%	25%	15%	15%
Postintervention	35%	30%	15%	10%	10%

FIGURE 10.1. Classroom conduct grades.

determine any changes in the types of violations being reported. Overall, the total number of classwide ODRs had decreased since the Strong Kids intervention was initiated (see Table 10.2).

However, four students continued to receive referrals to the principal's office for use of inappropriate language with their peers, fighting, and peer conflict. All four students were identified as those continuing to receive lower grades (C's, D's, and F's) in weekly classroom conduct. As a result, Mr. Roberts, the administrative staff, and the school psychologist determined that they had not responded adequately to the universal intervention and would require additional targeted interventions.

CASE STUDY 2: TIER 2 POSITIVE PEER REPORTING INTERVENTION

Student Names: Alex Johnson, Tracy Jones, Heidi Williams, and Ryan Davis
Grade: 5
Ages: 11–12
Race/Ethnicity: African American and Caucasian
Sex: Male and female

Background Information

Following the implementation of a universal SEL curriculum in Mr. Roberts's fifth-grade classroom, Alex Johnson, Tracy Jones, Heidi Williams, and Ryan Davis were identified as in need of further support. Alex was an 11-year-old Caucasian boy with a history of impulsive behavior, but no formal diagnosis or history of receiving behavioral interventions. He engaged in repeated outbursts toward his peers, frequently imitating the behavior of other students in the class and behaving aggressively. Tracy was an 11-year-old African American girl with no history of academic or behavioral problems in previous years, but who struggled to work well with others in class, often name calling and bullying students into following her lead. Heidi was a 12-year-old Caucasian girl, previously retained in the first grade for

TABLE 10.2. ODR Data for Mr. Roberts's Class during the Universal SEL Intervention

	Prior to implementation	Implementation to conclusion
Class total number of ODRs	21	10
Range of individual ODRs	0–5	0–4

academic concerns related to a specific learning disability special education eligibility in reading. Since retention, her peer relationships suffered and she was often isolated, engaging in maladaptive behaviors to seek peer attention. Finally, Ryan was an 11-year-old African American boy, previously diagnosed with ADHD and ODD by his pediatrician. Mr. Roberts reported that Tracy and Ryan had a history of teasing and picking on one another during previous years in class together.

Data collected following the universal intervention revealed that each of the four students continued to display significant difficulty engaging in positive peer interactions and in regulating their own emotions. These challenges often led to increased conflict, including verbal and physical aggression, and noncompliant behavior in the classroom. As a result, Mr. Roberts, the administrative staff, and the school psychologist determined that they had not responded adequately to the universal intervention and would require additional targeted interventions. These four students were therefore nominated for an additional SEL intervention, a Tier 2 selected intervention to foster prosocial behavior, to promote cooperation, and to motivate the students to act appropriately with their peers.

Assessment

Review of Previous Data

Prior to implementing an intervention for the group of students, the school psychologist reviewed the data from the classwide intervention administered in Mr. Roberts's class. Alex, Tracy, Heidi, and Ryan were identified as having the most frequent referrals to school administrators for disruptive and aggressive behavior. Additionally, classroom conduct grades for each of these students remained lower than most other students' grades from week to week. At the conclusion of the universal intervention, all four of them averaged C's, D's, or F's in weekly conduct. According to Mr. Roberts, when including minor disagreements that did not result in a referral to the principal's office, Alex, Tracy, Heidi, and Ryan each had an average of three incidents of inappropriate peer interactions per day.

Each student's individual behavior varied during the course of the universal SEL instruction and intermittent individual progress was demonstrated; therefore, it was hypothesized that the behaviors in question were performance deficits, not acquisition deficits, for the four target students. Each student had received explicit teaching of social and emotional skills and participated in activities to practice these skills throughout the year. However, given the nuanced nature and complexity of enhancing the performance of social skills, school staff believed the selected intervention would be most effective if it incorporated strategies to both foster motivation and to further teach prosocial behaviors.

School Social Behavior Scales–2

Mr. Roberts completed the SSBS-2 on each of the four students prior to the implementation of the Tier 2 intervention to further identify risk areas and to establish a baseline for social and problem behaviors. The SSBS-2 has two composite scales: Social Competence (measuring adaptive prosocial behaviors) and Antisocial Behaviors (measuring socially relevant problem behaviors). Data from Mr. Roberts's initial completion of the SSBS-2 revealed all four students were at high risk in the Social Competence domains of Peer Relations and Self-Management/Compliance and in the Antisocial Behaviors domain of Defiant/Disruptive behavior. Additionally, Tracy and Ryan's scores also indicated high risk on both the Hostile/Irritable and Antisocial/Aggressive domains. Heidi's scores revealed additional risk on the Academic Behavior domain. At the conclusion of the Tier 2 intervention, Mr. Roberts completed the SSBS-2 on each student to assess progress and identify students potentially needing further support. Data from the follow-up SSBS-2 are presented for each student below.

Progress Monitoring

Throughout the course of the positive peer reporting (PPR) intervention, Mr. Roberts collected data on the frequency and negative interactions among Alex, Tracy, Heidi, and Ryan and their classmates throughout the week. Throughout each day, Mr. Roberts carried a Post-it note or chart on his clipboard and tallied instances of negative peer interactions, as these were most salient and directly related to the built-in method for assigning classroom conduct grades each week. This information served as further progress-monitoring data used to determine individual responsiveness to the PPR intervention.

Intervention: Positive Peer Reporting

PPR is designed to address the behavior of poorly accepted children or children who disrupt the classroom environment by engaging in negative attention-seeking behaviors. Students generally learn from an early age to report instances of inappropriate peer behavior to their teachers. The aim of PPR, alternatively, is to encourage students to report on the *positive* behaviors of their peers. Targeted students are students who often intentionally irritate their classmates in an attempt to be noticed or students who find themselves socially isolated due to a history of disruptive and oppositional behaviors. Classmates in the PPR intervention are trained to allocate attention to their peers for exhibiting appropriate and prosocial behaviors rather than negative and disruptive attention-seeking behaviors. PPR was chosen as the targeted intervention strategy for Alex, Tracy, Heidi, and Ryan.

Following a training session in which all students in the class were taught how to praise each other, Mr. Roberts implemented the PPR intervention daily in his classroom. He put posters of examples of praise on the wall of his classroom and explained to students that they would have the ability to earn group rewards by using PPR. Every day, Mr. Roberts selected two of the four target students to be "Student of the Day" to receive praise from their classmates. Alex, Tracy, Heidi, and Ryan alternated turns being the "Student of the Day." Throughout the day, the rest of the students in the class earned points every time they successfully praised one of the two target students. Mr. Roberts kept a tally on the white board of the number of praises and when the class earned a collective total meeting their goal, they were rewarded with a group prize (e.g., 10 extra minutes of recess, small candy bars, 10 minutes of free time before dismissal).

Outcomes

After 4 weeks of implementing the PPR intervention, Mr. Roberts reported that he observed a significant change in the behavior of three out of the four students: Alex, Tracy, and Heidi. Scores on the SSBS-2 reflected these changes, demonstrating that Alex's scores were no longer elevated on any of the Social Competence or Antisocial Behaviors scales. Heidi's high-risk scores on the Peer Relations and Self-Management/Compliance subscales decreased and resulted in functioning at a seemingly average level. Additionally, Heidi's Academic Behavior scores also improved; while still listed as at risk, Mr. Roberts expressed assurance that her progress would continue to improve. Tracy's Hostile/Irritable and Aggressive behaviors also significantly improved.

Figure 10.2 is a graphical representation of the number of peer praises tallied each week during the intervention. Initially, as students were still navigating the procedures and learning to acknowledge the positive behavior of their peers, the number of peer-reported praises was lower, with each target student receiving an average of approximately one to three praises per day. With time, however, the frequency with which students were reporting praises for the target students more than doubled, eventually earning the target students an average of three to five praises per day. Tracy and Heidi received the most praises from their peers, followed by Alex and then finally Ryan.

Additional data collected for each of the target students revealed an overall decrease in negative interactions (see Figure 10.3). Alex's negative peer interactions over the course of a week decreased from 12 at baseline to four at the conclusion of the PPR intervention. Similarly, Tracy's negative interactions decreased from 14 to three and Heidi's decreased from 13 to two. All three students reported that they felt more involved in the class and were more likely to praise each other on days they were the target students.

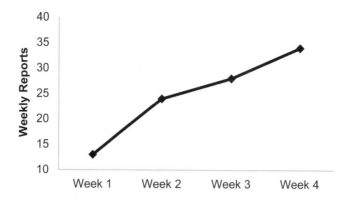

FIGURE 10.2. Total positive reports.

According to Mr. Roberts's report, the frequency of helping behaviors during group assignments also increased. For Alex, Tracy, and Heidi, the intervention was deemed a success. Mr. Roberts continued to monitor their behaviors and provide praise and reminders for appropriate behavior, but it was decided that a formal intervention plan was no longer necessary.

While Ryan's overall total of negative peer interactions did decrease from 16 to eight by the end of the 4-week intervention (see Figure 10.3), his data was more variable when compared to Alex, Tracy, and Heidi. Ryan's scores on the SSBS-2 also reflected less progress than the other three

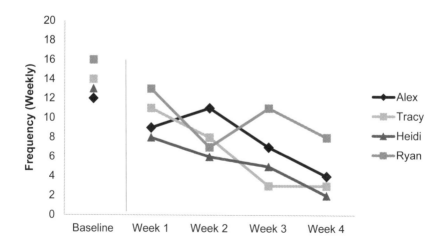

FIGURE 10.3. Negative peer interactions.

students. While his scores on the Hostile/Irritable subscale and the Anti-social/Aggressive domains improved to the average range, his scores on the Peer Relations, Self-Management/Compliance, and Defiant/Disruptive behavior scales remained at risk or in the high-risk range of functioning.

Additionally, Ryan was still sent out of the classroom approximately twice per week for swearing at other students or refusing to comply with the teacher's instructions when angry. Mr. Roberts felt that the PPR intervention was not enough to meet his needs and the data collected confirmed that he was not making sufficient progress. Therefore, he was referred for additional support from the school psychologist.

CASE STUDY 3: TIER 3 INDIVIDUALIZED SEL INTERVENTION

Student Name: Ryan Davis
Grade: 5
Age: 11
Race/Ethnicity: African American
Sex: Male

Background Information

Ryan Davis, an 11-year-old African American student in Mr. Roberts's fifth-grade class, was referred to the school psychologist for an individualized SEL intervention to address his oppositional and impulsive behavior in the classroom. Ryan was diagnosed in fourth grade with ODD and ADHD by his pediatrician, but was not prescribed any medication at the time of the referral to the school psychologist. Further review of his records revealed a pattern of noncompliant behavior and conflict with peers in school. He had never been retained or received supplemental academic interventions, as his academic skills were not an area of concern. Mr. Roberts reported that since the beginning of the school year, Ryan was viewed by his peers as a "bully" and engaged in many argumentative behaviors throughout the school day. Many of these behaviors led to Ryan being sent to the principal's office or out of the classroom to take a break and calm down. During class, he often required frequent redirections to focus on his work and leave his classmates alone. This frequent redirection often resulted in Ryan arguing with his teacher and not completing his work.

Prior to the referral, Mr. Roberts had implemented a series of interventions in his classroom to teach interpersonal skills and self-regulation. All of the fifth-grade teachers implemented the Strong Kids SEL curriculum with their students during the fall semester, leading to a decrease in disruptive behavior and peer conflict across the grade level. Ryan was among a small group of students who did not respond sufficiently to the universal intervention, and were subsequently the targets of a selected PPR intervention. Although Ryan mostly participated in the Strong Kids lessons and even demonstrated some progress during the PPR intervention, he continued to display difficulty implementing the skills throughout the school day. Mr. Roberts mentioned Ryan's particular difficulty in blurting out inappropriate comments toward his peers during instruction (e.g., swearing and calling students names) and in picking fights with the other students. Mr. Roberts and the school psychologist agreed that Ryan would likely benefit from a more intensive and individualized intervention to address these behaviors.

Assessment

Functional Behavioral Assessment

In order to enhance the effectiveness of an individualized intervention for Ryan, the school psychologist conducted an FBA with the intent of identifying the purpose behind Ryan's negative behavior and then using the resulting information to match his intervention to the identified function of his behavior. The FBA included interviews with Ryan's teachers, a series of behavioral observations, and direct behavior ratings from Ryan's teachers.

Teacher Interview

The school psychologist first conducted a detailed interview with Ryan's teachers during a grade-level team meeting. According to his teachers, Ryan's disruptive behavior did not appear to occur during any specific subject or at any specific time of day. Instead, his teachers found that he was most likely to engage in disruptive behavior during whole-group instruction and independent work. During these times, Ryan would wander through the classroom, talking to his peers about unrelated subjects and avoiding his work. When redirected, Ryan would often lash out at his teachers in anger, calling them inappropriate names or refusing to follow directions. With his classmates, Ryan also frequently called them names and provoked arguments.

Systematic Direct Observations

Following an interview with his teachers, the school psychologist conducted three systematic direct observations of Ryan's behavior in the classroom. During the initial observation, Ryan was on-task 13% of the time, inattentive 20% of the time, and disruptive 67% of the time. He engaged in attention-seeking behaviors by talking out, wandering around the classroom disrupting other students' work, and walking up to the teacher's desk when he was supposed to be completing his assignments. During the second observation, Ryan was on-task 58% of the time, inattentive 9%, and disruptive 33%. Most disruptive behavior involved calling out. However, on three separate occasions during this observation, Ryan called another student in the class a name or made fun of him or her for doing his or her work. During the final observation, Ryan was on-task 67%, inattentive 12%, and disruptive 21% of the time. Toward the end of the observation, he approached another student and whispered something in her ear, leading her to ask the teacher to switch her seat. When the teacher prompted Ryan to take a break for a minute in the hallway, Ryan swore at the teacher and then was sent to the principal's office.

School Social Behavior Scales–2

Before and after the implementation of the PPR intervention, Mr. Roberts completed the SSBS-2 to assess Ryan's progress related to social competence and antisocial behaviors. Following the PPR intervention, Ryan's scores remained elevated on the Peer Relations, Self-Management/Compliance, and Defiant/Disruptive behavior scales. Mr. Roberts completed the SSBS-2 again 4 weeks after implementing Ryan's Tier 3 behavioral intervention to further assess for progress.

Functional Hypothesis

Ryan's noncompliance, work avoidance, and disruptive behaviors were often preceded by nonpreferred tasks or whole-group lectures, or by a sustained period of time without attention from peers or teachers. Additionally, Ryan's behaviors were often followed by either teacher attention (e.g., reprimanding or acknowledging him), attention from peers, or attention from school staff outside the classroom when sent to the office. Based on the data collected in the FBA, it was hypothesized that Ryan's disruptive behavior was maintained by peer and teacher attention.

Intervention

Ryan's treatment plan involved a series of components, which, when implemented together, provided him with the individualized intervention necessary to address the intensity of his problem behavior. Each component is outlined in detail below.

Differential Reinforcement of Incompatible Behavior

The primary intervention strategy for Ryan was directly targeted at the function of his behavior. The FBA revealed that Ryan's behavior was maintained by attention from his peers and teachers. Therefore, an intervention plan was designed to encourage appropriate behaviors that would gain him attention from his teacher and peers. DRI behavior interventions are aimed specifically at reinforcing a behavior that cannot occur simultaneously with the competing problem behavior, while also at the same time withholding reinforcement following occurrences of problem behavior. For Ryan, this included providing reinforcement and attention for staying calm, for using kind words and engaging in prosocial behaviors, for following directions, and for completing his own classwork. This also involved then withdrawing attention and praise for the negative attention-seeking behaviors he had previously engaged in. The components of the DRI intervention included specific praise, planned ignoring, reinforcement of replacement behaviors through a behavior chart intervention, and individual sessions to reteach and review appropriate alternative behaviors.

Specific Praise

Ryan's teachers observed his behavior throughout the school day and provided specific praise as often as possible for any instances of appropriate or prosocial behavior (e.g., following directions, completing work, staying calm, helping peers, working together). Praise was delivered for both academic behaviors and social behaviors. Since Ryan's classmates were also well equipped to provide praise following the PPR intervention, they were encouraged to continue to provide Ryan with attention and praise through high-fives and positive comments for appropriate behavior.

Planned Ignoring

Although the natural instinct for Ryan's teachers and classmates was to respond to him when he insulted them or called out inappropriately, these behaviors were being partially reinforced by the negative attention Ryan received in these situations. To alter this contingency, Ryan's teachers and classmates decided not to acknowledge his minor inappropriate behavior. His peers were coached to ignore Ryan's comments and assured that his teachers were aware of the inappropriate comments he made. Other than briefly and directly reminding Ryan to engage in the appropriate alternative behavior, Mr. Roberts and the other fifth-grade teachers also ignored his negative attention-seeking behaviors.

Conduct Grades Behavior Chart

Since Mr. Roberts already had in place a system for tracking and reporting Ryan's behavior in the form of classroom conduct grades, the form used by his teacher was tweaked to work as an intervention. The Daily Behavior Chart was a supplemental component to the intervention aimed at ensuring

Ryan received feedback about his behavioral performance throughout the day. At the beginning of every day, Mr. Roberts reviewed Ryan's behavior from the previous day with him, reminding him of his goals and what he would need to do to earn a prize at the end of the week. Throughout the day, Ryan's teachers tallied his rule violations as they would normally, but instead of waiting until the end of the day to provide feedback, the teachers gave Ryan explicit feedback at the end of each class period. He was told how many checks he'd earned and what he had done well during that class period, along with reminders for what to do differently next time. At the end of the day, Ryan took his conduct grade home with him to review with his parents.

Explicit Teaching of Coping Skills and Prosocial Behaviors

Ryan also received weekly individual sessions with the school psychologist. The purpose of these meetings was to ensure that Ryan had "tools" to respond appropriately when faced with difficult or frustrating social situations. The school psychologist reviewed the material from previous lessons with Ryan and supplemented these lessons where necessary to teach him alternative strategies for coping, relaxation, self-awareness, and prosocial behavior.

Outcomes

Results of the Tier 3 function-based individualized intervention for Ryan revealed a steady change in behavior over the course of 4 weeks. DBR data presented in Figure 10.4 show that Ryan's use of coping strategies to remain calm when angry increased along with the frequency with which he used kind words, followed teacher directions, and completed classwork. As a result, the incompatible behaviors he was engaging in previously (i.e., disrupting peers, noncompliance, and inappropriate language) decreased substantially. Ryan was less frequently calling his peers names and was much less likely to lash out at his teachers for reprimanding his negative behaviors.

Additionally, Ryan's ratings on the SSBS-2 changed drastically from the initial levels of elevation when assessed prior to implementing the PPR intervention. Data showing the change in elevation on the scales and subscales from the beginning of the PPR intervention to the conclusion of the 4-week Tier 3 individualized intervention is displayed in Table 10.3.

Following the 4 weeks of the individualized intervention, Ryan's performance improved across all target behaviors. However, reports from Mr. Roberts revealed that Ryan still had particular difficulty raising his hand before speaking in class and remaining calm when reprimanded. He also occasionally reverted to using inappropriate language with his peers and

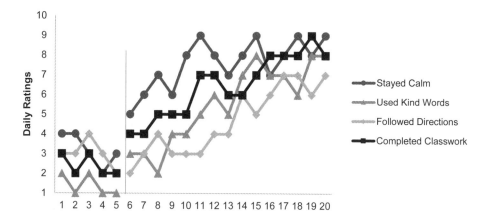

FIGURE 10.4. Ryan's daily behavior ratings.

needed reminders to follow directions from his teachers on the first try. Given Ryan's progress and the need for continual support, Mr. Roberts and the school psychologist agreed to slowly fade out the components of his intervention.

Mr. Roberts and the other fifth-grade teachers began by fading out the behavior chart component of his intervention, only providing Ryan feedback on his conduct grades at the end of each day rather than after each class. His teachers continued the DRI components with Ryan, as they were helpful in maintaining the progress he had made and were easily applied in the classroom setting. The school psychologist also gradually decreased the

TABLE 10.3. Ryan's SSBS-2 Social Functioning Levels

Scales	Pre-PPR	Post-PPR	Post-Tier 3
Social Competence			
Peer Relations	High risk	At risk	Average
Self-Management/Compliance	High risk	High risk	At risk
Academic Behavior	Average	Average	Average
Antisocial Behaviors			
Hostile/Irritable	High risk	Average	Average
Antisocial/Aggressive	High risk	Average	Average
Defiant/Disruptive	High risk	High risk	At risk

frequency of her individual meetings with Ryan, eventually only providing sessions on an as-needed basis.

CASE STUDY 4: TIER 1 INCREDIBLE YEARS CHILD TRAINING PROGRAM WITH GROUP CONTINGENCY

Teacher Name: Ms. Anne Miller
Class/Subject: Special education
Grades: K–2
Student Ages: 5–8

Background Information

Early elementary students exhibiting significant emotional and behavioral difficulties were placed in a special education classroom taught by Ms. Miller in one of the elementary schools in a suburban school district. Students in Ms. Miller's class typically qualified for special education services under "emotional disturbance or other health impairment" for ADHD. In addition to time devoted to the core academic subjects, time was also built in for a social behavior class in the daily schedule. Social behavior class consisted of lessons lasting approximately 30 to 45 minutes and included instruction, discussion, and practice of social skills in order to address the students' emotional and behavioral difficulties. Altogether, 10 students in grades K–12 (ages 5–8) participated in the social behavior class, including several students who qualified under different special education categories, such as a learning disability with co-occurring emotional and behavioral problems.

Common concerns regarding the students' behavior included negative peer interactions (e.g., arguing and fighting), verbal aggression toward the teacher (e.g., inappropriate language and disrespectful tone), and difficulty managing emotions, especially frustration and anger. The school administrator determined that implementing an SEL curriculum to target social skills and emotional and behavioral regulation during the social behavior class would be beneficial for all of the students. The school purchased The Incredible Years Child Training Program (Webster–Stratton, 2011), and the Classroom Dinosaur School Curriculum for Ms. Miller to implement with all students in her social behavior class. The administrator chose Dinosaur School for implementation because of the curriculum's focus on developing skills to understand and recognize feelings, solve problems, manage anger, and develop and maintain friendships.

Assessment

Needs Assessment

Upon receiving the curriculum, Ms. Miller and the school administrator met on several occasions to determine the needs of the classroom and which of the approximately 60 available lessons within the seven targeted units in Dinosaur School would best address those needs. Ms. Miller reported that she was most concerned about peer conflict, specifically in providing opportunities for students to learn how to manage frustration in peer interactions and to solve social problems. In fact, office discipline referrals (ODRs) were most frequently assigned for verbal and physical aggression among peers. Ms. Miller and the school administrator therefore determined that these behaviors would be targeted first by implementing the Dinosaur School lessons addressing these concerns immediately, with the the remaining lessons to be conducted throughout the school year.

Once the needs of the class were established, the teacher and the administrator continued to review the curriculum to determine which lessons were developmentally appropriate out of the multiple levels available in the curriculum, which activities would be feasible in terms of materials needed and time to prepare the activities, and how the lessons would fit with the strengths and abilities of her students. Since Ms. Miller's students enjoyed activities involving movement, she made a greater effort to include activities in each lesson where students would have the opportunity to interact with one another, move around the room, or complete hands-on activities. Doing so also provided more opportunities for students to practice skills and receive feedback from the teacher while engaging in peer interactions.

Assessing Progress

After selecting the lessons and activities, Ms. Miller and the administrator discussed how they would determine whether the program was effective for the students. They decided to monitor ODRs and the students' daily conduct grades as assigned by the teacher during the fall. Students who received more than one ODR and/or earned an average daily conduct grade of a D or lower would be considered nonresponsive to the program. They set a date in early winter to meet again to review and discuss the data and determine whether any students needed more intensive supports.

Intervention

Dinosaur School

Ms. Miller delivered lessons from the Dinosaur School Curriculum for approximately 30–45 minutes two times per week throughout the school year. Each lesson consisted of 20-minutes of classroom circle time during which Ms. Miller taught the new skill, followed by small- or large-group activities designed for students to practice the skills taught during the lesson. Activities and materials used by Ms. Miller included DVD brief vignettes and discussion regarding examples of appropriate or inappropriate use of social skills, puppets, cue cards and other visual aids, games, and songs. Throughout the remainder of the school day after the lesson, she prompted students to use new skills when appropriate in other situations in the classroom. In order to further encourage skill development, Ms. Miller also sent a letter home to parents describing skills taught each week, thereby providing an opportunity for them to reinforce the skills at home. In addition, parents were given a homework assignment to complete with their child at home.

Interdependent Group Contingency

To encourage her students to practice and utilize the skills learned during the Dinosaur School lessons throughout the school day, Ms. Miller developed and implemented a classwide contingency for appropriate social behavior, with the assistance of the behavior interventionist at her school. Because she recognized that many of her students already seemed to have some knowledge of the skills but failed to use them in everyday interactions (i.e., performance rather than skill deficits), Ms. Miller knew that they would likely require some extra motivation to use the skills. Following each lesson, Ms. Miller observed the students who remained in her classroom. When a student exhibited the social behavior targeted during the lesson of the day (e.g., expressing feelings appropriately by naming emotions), she put a tally mark on the board. If her students earned a set number of tally marks as a class by the end of the day, they could either select a reward from the treasure box or spend 10 minutes of free time on the computer or playing a game quietly. If the students did not meet their goal as a class, then they did not earn a reward. Based on Ms. Miller's desired behavioral goals for her classroom, this contingency was implemented to increase her students' appropriate social behaviors and to decrease competing problem behaviors.

Outcomes

When Ms. Miller and the administrator met in early winter to discuss the students' progress in the social behavior class with the use of the Dinosaur School Curriculum, the administrator asked Ms. Miller to describe her general impressions regarding the acceptability, feasibility, and effectiveness of the program. Ms. Miller reported seeing improvements in behavior for most of her students. She explained that the outcomes of the program outweighed the time constraints and effort required when planning for implementation. Her students appeared mostly engaged in the lessons and seemed to be learning the skills. Ms. Miller reported that when students were prompted to identify a strategy to manage their feelings, each student was able to provide at least one accurate response. She also noticed that students seemed to be engaging in more positive interactions with one another. Ms. Miller reported that she would be interested in continuing the program throughout the school year. However, she expressed some concerns about continued behavior problems with several students.

The administrator collected and presented the data on ODRs and conduct grades earned over the fall semester. The average conduct grade for the class in the fall was a B and the average number of ODRs was 2.10 (range 0–7, total 21). Data comparing the beginning and end of the fall semester are presented in Table 10.4. Review of the October ODR data revealed that students earned these for noncompliance and verbal aggression with both peers and adults. Based on the review of the data, Ms. Miller and the school administrator determined that three students met criteria to receive additional intervention by earning more than two ODRs or having an average conduct grade of a D or lower.

Given the success of the Dinosaur School program, Ms. Miller continued to implement the curriculum during social behavior class for the remainder of the school year. Several students also received Tier 2 and Tier 3 interventions targeting social and emotional skills in small groups or as individuals. The teacher and the school administrator continued to monitor the number of ODRs in her class and the types of behaviors that resulted in ODRs. Although the data did not show a change in average conduct grades, Ms. Miller subjectively reported a decrease in negative peer interactions. The primary goal was to improve peer relationships by developing skills to manage negative emotions and solve social problems, and Ms. Miller noted that her students were making progress on these skills with the use of Dinosaur School and a classwide behavior contingency. A combination of the two interventions was effective in addressing her students' skill and performance deficits. Ms. Miller continued to teach new skills and review the skills taught previously throughout the year. She also altered the classwide contingency regularly to target the skills her students seemed to be using the least or having the most difficulty applying.

TABLE 10.4. Ms. Miller's Classwide ODRs and Conduct Grades

	August	October
Total number of ODRs	10	6
Average conduct grade	B	B

CASE STUDY 5:
TIER 1 UNIVERSAL TOOTLING INTERVENTION

Teacher Name: Ms. Elizabeth Phillips
Class/Subject: General education, English language arts, and social studies
Grade: 7
Student Ages: 12–13

Background Information

Ms. Phillips, a seventh-grade general education teacher at a public middle school, contacted the school psychologist for assistance with managing problem behavior in her classroom. She was in her second year of teaching and was interested in learning additional classroom management strategies. Ms. Phillips was primarily concerned with the behavior of students in her homeroom, as she also taught them during the first and last periods of the school day. Ms. Phillips reported that the class engaged in disruptive behaviors and verbal and relational aggression on a frequent basis. She felt that she spent an excessive amount of time reprimanding the class, which was taking valuable time away from instruction. Additionally, some students privately reported instances of bullying occurring in unsupervised settings including during recess and in the bathroom. Broadly defined, the disruptive behavior included students talking at inappropriate times or leaving their assigned seat without receiving permission. Negative peer interactions primarily involved exclusion from conversations and verbal altercations between peers, often including inappropriate comments and making threatening remarks.

Assessment

Classroom Observations

In order to obtain additional information regarding the nature of the behavior and social concerns in Ms. Phillips' classroom, and to assess her classroom management strategies, the school psychologist conducted a sequence of observations. Three, 10-minute observations of classroom management were conducted using the Classroom Check-Up observation method (Reinke, Herman, & Sprick, 2011) prior to beginning the intervention with the class. The Classroom Check-Up observation form is a 10-minute recording system to collect the frequency of the most commonly endorsed effective classroom management strategies, including providing numerous opportunities to respond, delivery of praise, and delivery of reprimands. During the observations, Ms. Phillips used frequent and variable methods of opportunities to respond. However, she responded to student disruptive behavior with negative feedback and a harsh, critical tone. Less frequently, she was observed giving general praise toward appropriate academic responses. On average, she engaged in three instances of negative feedback for every one form of praise.

The Classroom Check-Up system also allows the observer to collect information regarding the accuracy of student responding and the frequency of disruptions. Across all of the baseline observations, students engaged in an average of four disruptions per minute. Disruptive behavior most frequently involved students engaging in verbal altercations with their peers during group instruction or independent work. Students threatened one another or made negative comments about another classmate, in both a direct and an indirect manner. Relational aggression was also observed within a particular group of girls in the class when students made sarcastic comments about each other's performance or rolled their eyes when speaking. More than 75% of the students participated in the verbal aggression or otherwise disruptive behavior during the initial baseline observations. Following the initial three baseline observations, the school psychologist continued to conduct observations twice per week during both morning and afternoon classes and recorded the rate of disruptive behavior in order to measure the level of student response to the intervention.

Prosocial Behavior

To establish a baseline level of positive behaviors, Ms. Phillips recorded the frequency of student prosocial behaviors during both the morning and afternoon class periods. Prosocial behaviors were defined as students engaging in helpful behaviors toward peers, providing positive compliments to their classmates regarding academic or other student characteristics, and any other nice or respectful act directed toward another student. Across 3 days of tallying for both periods, the class engaged in an average of 10 prosocial behaviors per day. Ms. Phillips reported that each student demonstrated appropriate behavior on occasion, indicating that the students likely had the skills necessary to engage appropriately with each other, but were not doing so on their own. Ms. Phillips continued to record the amount of prosocial behaviors observed in the morning and afternoon period throughout the course of the intervention implementation in order to measure progress.

Intervention

Given that inappropriate behavior was observed in more than 75% of the students in the class, the school psychologist concluded an intervention targeting the whole classroom was the most appropriate strategy to reduce disruptive behavior and increase positive interactions between peers.

Tootling

The school psychologist trained Ms. Phillips to implement a classwide intervention termed "tootling." Tootling (Skinner, Skinner, & Cashwell, 1998) encourages positive peer reporting, where students are prompted to "tattle" on their classmate's appropriate classroom and prosocial behavior and are reinforced for doing so. Procedures used by Ms. Phillips with her class were modified from Skinner, Cashwell, and Skinner's (2000) original intervention. Once trained herself, Ms. Phillips introduced the intervention to her classroom and trained the students using the teach–show–practice approach, the procedure for tootling on their peers. Tootling was described to them as telling on a peer for following the classroom rules, including things such as raising a hand to speak or to participate in the lesson. Additionally, tootling was described as telling on a peer for helping or saying nice things to another student or staff member in the school. To account for the developmental level of the class, the teacher introduced the intervention as "bragging" instead of tootling. No other modifications to the procedure were made. Students demonstrated criteria for understanding the concept of tootling after they each recorded two appropriate tootles on their notecards.

After training the students on the process of the tootling intervention, and practicing tootling for a period of time, Ms. Phillips implemented the intervention daily. Implementation included the following components: (1) review the rules of the intervention during homeroom each morning, (2) remind and prompt students to tootle throughout the day, and (3) provide the classroom reward if students reached the criteria for reinforcement. After the first morning bell, students were allowed to begin tootling. Students documented their tootles by recording the details on Post-it notes or index cards at the time they observed appropriate or prosocial behavior in a classmate. The name of the student observed, a brief description of the prosocial or appropriate behavior, and their own name were written on the note. A "tootle box" (modified as a "brag box" in Ms. Phillips's class) was placed by the teacher's desk, where students placed their cards at specific times throughout the day. Tootles were reported on any classmate for any positive behaviors observed during the school day.

To reach their goal as a class, students were informed they had to record and turn in 30 appropriate tootles before receiving a reward each afternoon. To prevent inappropriate tootles, Ms. Phillips informed students that she would subtract one tootle for every inappropriate comment placed in her box. Before students were dismissed, Ms. Phillips counted the number of tootles and provided a reward to all students in the class if they had earned enough points. Rewards were based on the preferences of the students and included items such as eating vending machine snacks in class, homework passes, 10 minutes of extra recess, and PBIS bucks. The class-wide intervention was implemented daily over a period of 1 month.

Classroom Management Strategies

Based on her classroom management during the preassessment observations, Ms. Phillips received feedback and coaching related to additional positive classroom management strategies that complemented the tootling procedures. She was encouraged to review her classroom rules and behavioral expectations before transitions and to provide consistent reprimands and consequences for rule violations. Ms. Phillips also increased the amount of praise she delivered to students in her class by providing specific feedback for positive behavior.

Outcomes

Before the tootling intervention was implemented, observations during the regular classroom routine revealed that students engaged in disruptive behavior throughout an average of 37% of the observations, often talking without permission and in a verbally aggressive manner. After implementation of the tootling procedure, the rate of classroom disruptions dramatically decreased to an average of 11% of the observations, down to an average of one disruption per minute. Percentage of time during the observations that included disruptive behavior throughout the month of intervention is

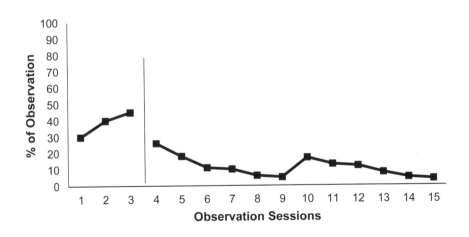

FIGURE 10.5. Rate of disruptive behavior.

displayed in Figure 10.5. Besides a slight spike on the 10th day of observation (during the third week of intervention), the data revealed a steady
and consistent decrease in disruptive behavior throughout the course of the
intervention.

Additional data collected by Ms. Phillips showed that the amount of
prosocial behaviors the students engaged in increased substantially during
the month in which the intervention was implemented (see Figure 10.6).
According to Ms. Phillips's reports, the average amount of daily prosocial
behaviors increased from 10 to 32 instances by the end of the intervention.

After the intervention concluded, the school psychologist followed
up with Ms. Phillips to gauge her perceptions of the acceptability, effectiveness, and feasibility of the tootling intervention. Ms. Phillips reported
the intervention was easy to implement consistently and that she liked it
because it also aligned with her school's behavioral expectations. She also
felt as though having the students report on each other's positive behavior
also helped her to more readily notice and praise the positive things students did throughout each day. Furthermore, Ms. Phillips reported interest
in continuing the intervention and increasing the goals for reward.

Finally, each student was administered an acceptability rating measure to capture his or her perceptions of the intervention. Students reported
tootling was an appropriate and effective intervention that did not include
negative unfair strategies. Of note, three students anonymously reported
they no longer felt targeted by their peers and had established more positive relationships with fellow classmates. Assessment and interview data
revealed that tootling was an acceptable and effective intervention strategy
for reducing disruptions while also encouraging prosocial skills.

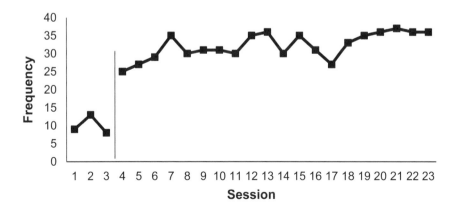

FIGURE 10.6. Prosocial behavior.

CASE STUDY 6: TIER 2 SMALL-GROUP
SEL INTERVENTION

Student Names: Andrew Fields, Darius Matthews, and Joseph Torres
Grade: Kindergarten
Ages: 5–6
Race/Ethnicity: Caucasian, African American, and Hispanic
Sex: Male

Background Information

Andrew Fields, Darius Matthews, and Joseph Torres were referred to the guidance counselor by their kindergarten teacher, Mr. Greene, for social skills concerns. At the time of the referral, Andrew was a 5-year-old boy who was evaluated by the school district and received special education services under the exceptionality of developmental delay. Darius was a 6-year-old boy who had been retained the previous year for not meeting kindergarten social and academic benchmarks, each of which were criteria for promotion, as outlined in school policy. Joseph was a 5-year-old boy who was diagnosed by his primary pediatrician with pervasive developmental disorder (PDD) and epilepsy and received .02 mg of Epitril daily for his seizures. Mr. Greene reported some side effects of hyperactivity due to the medication. All three boys were receiving supplemental support services in school at the time of the referral. Andrew and Joseph received weekly school-based speech therapy services to address articulation errors and establish appropriate verbal communication. Darius received reading intervention services weekly in an attempt to improve his academic achievement in reading. Darius was enrolled in Mr. Greene's general education classroom in which Andrew and Joseph would attend the first 3 hours of the school day for inclusion.

Mr. Greene reported all three students had difficulty responding appropriately in social situations. They often interrupted other's conversations with irrelevant topics, cried out and pinched other students when they were not given access to preferred items, or yelled and cried when presented with a difficult independent task. Andrew, Darius, and Joseph also displayed significant difficulty taking turns in conversations, saying "please" and "thank you," asking for help, and respecting social boundaries. These behaviors occurred during both instructional and unstructured play activities. Additionally, other students reported Andrew and Darius took other's personal belongings without returning them and the parents of these students had expressed these concerns to the school administrators. Given the pervasive nature of these concerns, the school administrators and Mr. Greene sought help from the guidance counselor in providing evidence-based interventions to these students with the intention of fostering positive peer interactions and appropriate classroom behaviors.

Assessment

Social Skills Improvement System—Performance Screening Guide

All kindergarten teachers completed the SSIS-PSG in an effort to identify any students at risk for behavior concerns. Each teacher completed the screener using a 5-point Likert scale with ratings from 1 (very poor, limited skills in this area) to 5 (excellent, and highly developed skills in this area) for all the students in their classes. Students were identified as "moderate risk" if they had ratings of 1, 2, or 3 on the Prosocial Behavior scale, indicating that they rarely engaged in the listed prosocial behaviors. Scores on the SSIS-PSG identified Andrew, Darius, and Joseph to be at moderate risk on the Prosocial Behavior scale, indicating they would likely benefit from targeted interventions to improve appropriate social behaviors.

Social Skills Improvement System—Rating Scales

Once his students were identified by the screener, Mr. Greene completed the SSIS-RS for each at-risk student to further assess for specific positive social behaviors. Mr. Greene's responses for Andrew, Darius, and Joseph revealed significant deficits on the Social Skills scale along with elevations on the Problem Behaviors scale. In particular, consistent themes emerged for all three boys, showing elevations on the Communication, Cooperation, and Engagement subscales. Furthermore, Mr. Greene's responses suggested that Andrew, Darius, and Joseph likely demonstrated deficits in the acquisition of these social skills, rather than just difficulty in performing the skills appropriately.

The SSIS manualized intervention is often used to teach and promote social skills in a group format. As the SSIS-RS is directly linked to units within the SSIS, it is especially useful in assessing a child's responsiveness to the components of the intervention. To determine the amount of progress each child made after receiving the intervention, Mr. Greene completed the SSIS-RS again after the conclusion of the intervention and after a 3-week follow-up period in order to determine maintenance of skills.

Intervention

Social Skills Improvement System—Intervention Guide

Based on the data reported by Mr. Greene and the rating scales, the SSIS-IG was chosen to target the students' deficits through the explicit teaching and reinforcement of the social behaviors. The school's guidance counselor implemented the social skills training in a small-group format twice weekly, for 45-minute durations, using strategies and lessons from the SSIS manual. Units were introduced during the first lesson of the week and were exhaustively practiced during the second lesson of the week. Given Mr. Greene's concerns regarding Andrew, Darius, and Joseph's behavior, the following skills were targeted in explicit units: taking turns in conversations, saying "please" and "thank you," expressing feelings, asking for help, and respecting other people's things. The students were introduced to one unit each week. The final week included a review of all sessions and a graduation of each student from the program.

During the lessons, the counselor applied the recommended instructional sequence: tell, show, do, practice, monitor progress, and generalize. Specifically, students were taught the skills of each unit, and then observed while the counselor model the skill. Students were then asked to practice the skill themselves and were given corrective feedback from the counselor while doing so. In an effort to promote generalization of the skills, teachers and parents were provided brief descriptions of the lessons after they were completed and were asked to prompt students to use the skills. They also provided praise to students when they were observed using the skills outside of the group format. Following the conclusion of the curriculum, Andrew, Darius, and Joseph's parents and teacher continued to encourage and praise positive behavior and social interactions.

To enhance engagement and decrease disruptions, the guidance counselor employed differential reinforcement of low rates of disruptive behavior (DRL) during the sessions as a behavior management strategy. Students received tallies for talking out without permission, getting out of seat without permission, and saying mean comments to peers. Each student had the opportunity to earn a prize after each session if he had five or less tallies.

Implementation Integrity

Throughout the implementation of the curriculum, the guidance counselor received assistance from an administrator who observed the intervention for integrity and provided feedback using the Intervention Integrity Scale, an intervention component checklist provided in the SSIS-IG. The assistant principal observed the counselor for 40% of the sessions and recorded the degree to which each of the components of the instructional approach was implemented. A percentage of components that were implemented fully served as the measure of treatment integrity. Based on the observations, the average number of components utilized with integrity was 100%.

Outcomes

The SSIS-RS was administered before and after implementation of the social skills training and again 3 weeks after the termination of the intervention to assess for maintenance. Before the intervention, Mr. Greene's ratings of Andrew revealed a Social Skills score of 72 and ratings of Joseph indicated a score of 74, placing both within the Below Average range of functioning. Darius's scores resulted in a Social Skills score of 61, placing him in the Well-Below Average range of social functioning. These scores suggested that the students did not exhibit social skills as frequently as other children their age. Immediately following the intervention, Mr. Greene's ratings of Andrew, Darius, and Joseph's Social Skills each improved, placing them in the Average, Average, and Above Average ranges, respectively. Three weeks after the intervention concluded, ratings of the boys' social skills remained in the Average and Above Average ranges, suggesting that the skills learned during instruction with the guidance counselor were maintained inside the classroom. Scores for the SSIS-RS Social Skills ratings are shown in Table 10.5.

Before implementation of the SSIS intervention, Mr. Greene's ratings of Andrew, Darius, and Joseph on the Problem Behavior scale fell in the Above Average range, indicating that these behaviors were observed more often in these three boys than in their peers. Following the SEL intervention, scores on the Problem Behavior scale improved, placing all three within the Average range. After 3 weeks, Andrew and Joseph scores maintained their postimplementation performance. However, ratings of Darius revealed that his Problem Behavior scale returned to the Above Average range of functioning, suggesting that he may benefit from additional lessons and a targeted intervention inside the classroom promoting more generalization of these skills. Scores for the SSIS-RS Problem Behavior ratings are shown in Table 10.6.

The guidance counselor reported that the intervention was easy and enjoyable to implement, as the manual provided explicit steps for each lesson. This simplicity likely contributed to the high levels of treatment integrity during observations. Additionally, parents of all students expressed satisfaction with the skills their children learned and appreciated receiving information about the steps of each lesson to generalize at home.

TABLE 10.5. SSIS-RS Social Skills Ratings

Student	Preassessment	Postassessment	3-week follow-up
Andrew	72 (below average)	112 (average)	105 (average)
Darius	61 (well below average)	93 (average)	86 (average)
Joseph	74 (below average)	125 (above average)	116 (above average)

TABLE 10.6. SSIS-RS Problem Behavior Ratings

Student	Preassessment	Postassessment	3-week follow-up
Andrew	125 (above average)	110 (average)	90 (average)
Darius	127 (above average)	114 (average)	116 (above average)
Joseph	116 (above average)	90 (average)	95 (average)

CASE STUDY 7: TIER 2 TARGETED CHECK-IN/CHECK-OUT WITH POSITIVE PRACTICE

Student Name: Max Underwood
Grade: 3
Age: 8
Race/Ethnicity: Caucasian
Sex: Male

Background Information

Max was an 8-year-old, third-grade student in Mr. Eugene's class. At Max's school, all teachers implemented the PATHS program in order to encourage peaceful conflict resolution, emotion regulation, empathy, and responsible decision making in all students. Mr. Eugene noted that most of the students in his class appeared to demonstrate increased knowledge and use of the social–emotional skills targeted by the PATHS curriculum. Although Max was engaged in the majority of the lessons, and even provided appropriate responses during PATHS discussion and activities, he continued to display difficulty implementing the skills throughout the school day. Mr. Eugene mentioned his concerns to the school psychologist, who agreed that Max likely needed more intensive intervention to address his behavior. Based on Max's knowledge of the skills, paired with his lack of skill performance, it was determined that Max would benefit from CICO to improve his social behavior at school.

Assessment

Teacher Interview

The school psychologist met with Mr. Eugene to obtain more information on the nature of Max's behavior problems. Mr. Eugene indicated that he was primarily concerned with Max's inability to deal with frustration and anger. When he became upset, he struggled to manage his emotions and stay calm. Max had a tendency to feel angry when Mr. Eugene provided corrective feedback or a consequence, when other students disagreed with him, or when his teacher denied his request. When angry, Max yelled in a disrespectful tone and used inappropriate language (e.g., name calling, profanity). Mr. Eugene estimated that these behaviors occurred approximately two to three times per day. He typically responded to Max's verbal aggression by reminding him of the classroom rules, recording a checkmark by his name on a class chart of rule violations, and/or writing up an ODR if behaviors were severe enough to warrant one. The number of checkmarks given throughout the day corresponded to a conduct grade that was sent home to Max's parents. The conduct grade served to identify students in Mr. Eugene's class for reinforcement at the end of the week. For example, students with A's and B's during the week were able to choose from a treasure box with candy, small toys, and school supplies. Unfortunately, even though Max earned a B on average, he also usually earned at least one C or lower during the week and therefore was unable to choose a reward from the treasure box.

Based on the information provided by Mr. Eugene, the school psychologist identified two target behaviors for intervention. First, Max would stay calm when upset, as shown by keeping his voice at a normal level and using appropriate language (no profanity, name-calling, or disrespectful words or comments). Second, he would use problem-solving skills when disagreeing, as demonstrated by communicating his feelings to others appropriately and talking to others to resolve a problem at an acceptable time and place.

Daily Progress Report

Mr. Eugene completed a DPR by rating Max's performance on the selected skills at the end of each subject during the day. Max earned 2 points for exhibiting the appropriate behavior for most of the class period, 1 point for exhibiting the behavior sometimes, and 0 points for failing to engage in the behavior. To assess Max's current use of the identified skills, the school psychologist requested that Mr. Eugene complete a DPR for 3 days without providing feedback or reinforcement to Max. The percentage of total possible points Max earned on his DPR were tracked daily to measure his progress. Data were graphed and visually analyzed to assess changes in level and trend of behavior. As the ultimate purpose was fort Max to engage in more appropriate social behaviors over time, the immediate goal was for Max to consistently earn 80% of the total possible points on his DPR.

Intervention

Check-In/Check-Out

The school counselor, Ms. Bernard, and Max's teacher, Mr. Eugene, co-implemented CICO with Max. When Max arrived at school each morning, he immediately went to the school counselor's office to check in with Ms. Bernard. She gave Max a DPR sheet with a goal for points for the day (beginning with 60% of the total possible points and increasing to 80% of possible points), reviewed the target behaviors, and provided encouragement. Upon arriving to class, Max handed his DPR to the teacher. At the end of each subject, Max's teacher circled a rating on the DPR and provided feedback related to the expected behaviors. Mr. Eugene would praise Max for staying calm in situations where another student took his worksheet off his desk, or he felt unfairly criticized, but he also reminded Max to attempt to solve problems by asking the student nicely to return the worksheet, asking the teacher to intervene, or voicing his frustration in a respectful manner.

At the end of the day, Max returned to the counselor's office and gave her the completed DPR. Ms. Bernard reviewed Max's performance by addressing low ratings, adding up his points, and providing praise for appropriate behaviors. If Max reached his goal, he received reinforcement, such as extra computer time, lunch with the teacher the next day, or a reward from the treasure box. If he did not reach his goal, Ms. Bernard encouraged him to try again the next day. Max's DPR was sent home to his parents in order to maintain home–school communication and allow his parents to provide reinforcement for success. His parents were also asked to sign the form and send it back to school the next day with Max. Additionally, the DPR was collected as a measure of treatment integrity. The permanent product provided information regarding whether or not specific components of the intervention were implemented, including rating Max's behavior and providing reinforcement, if applicable.

Positive Practice

When Max earned a zero on either target behavior during the school day, his mentor, the school counselor, addressed the behavior at check-out. She asked Max to describe the problem behavior and the appropriate replacement behavior for the situation. For example, if Max yelled and cursed at another student who was humming during class, Ms. Bernard asked him to identify an appropriate response (e.g., ask the student nicely to stop humming). Then she required him to suggest several nice things he could say to the student the next day. Ms. Bernard spoke with Mr. Eugene and Max the next day to inquire whether Max had practiced saying nice things to his peer.

Outcomes

With implementation of CICO with the DPR, Max's performance of appropriate social skills (e.g., staying calm when upset and using problem-solving skills in social situations) improved. During baseline, Max received an aver-age of 27.7% of the total possible points. Following the CICO procedures, Max's behavior immediately improved, and he earned an average of 80% of the possible points throughout the intervention phase. Data on Max's CICO performance is shown in Figure 10.7. There were several days he did not reach his goal and therefore did not earn a reward. On those days and other days when he earned zero points during a subject, Ms. Bernard engaged Max in a discussion of the appropriate alternative behaviors and urged him to practice these positive behaviors the following day.

Max also showed improvement in his daily conduct grades. He contin-ued to have some days when he earned a C letter grade, but he was able to choose from the treasure box on Fridays more often due to more frequent A's and B's and fewer C's, D's, and F's. Additionally, Mr. Eugene reported a decrease in ODRs, although Max still had some days with verbal aggres-sion and subsequent ODRs.

Mr. Eugene and the school counselor, Ms. Bernard, agreed that the increase in Max's use of the targeted social skills and the consequent decrease in verbal aggression were both significant. They found CICO to be effective, acceptable, and feasible to implement. In fact, Ms. Bernard began implementing it with several other students in the school. Mrs. Bernard continued to have some concerns about Max's occasional verbal aggres-sion but she felt satisfied with his overall improvement. They determined that it would be beneficial to continue implementation of CICO with Max until he consistently earned at least 80% of his points for approximately 6 weeks. Ms. Bernard also agreed to monitor Max's ODRs and conduct grades and to check in with Mr. Eugene throughout the school year.

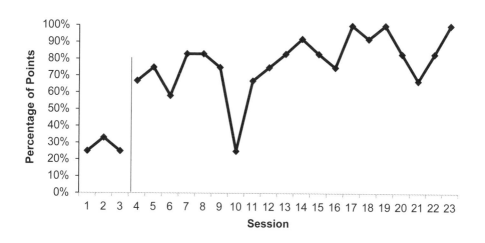

FIGURE 10.7. CICO points earned on DPR.

CASE STUDY 8: TIER 3 INDIVIDUALIZED
PIVOTAL RESPONSE TRAINING INTERVENTION

Student Name: Emma Gehlar
Age: 8
Grade: 2
Race/Ethnicity: Caucasian
Sex: Female

Background Information

Emma Gehlar was an 8-year-old girl attending second grade at a specialized school for children with developmental disabilities. She was identified by her primary teacher, Mr. Hall, as needing additional support due to concerns about her inappropriate peer interactions. Emma received an outside psychological evaluation from a local psychologist and was diagnosed with ASD without accompanying intellectual impairment. Additionally, she received an evaluation from the school district and qualified for special education services under the exceptionality of autism. Emma achieved her developmental milestones on time, with the exception of speech. At the time of the referral, she received school-based speech therapy services and occupational therapy two times a week for 30 minutes to target her goals described in her IEP. In addition to her speech and occupational therapy services at school, Emma received support from a guided aide during 4 hours of the school day. Emma was currently prescribed .20 mg of Risperidone, which was administered at home to alleviate Emma's reactions when overstimulated.

Mr. Hall was primarily concerned with Emma's absence of engaging in social interaction. When prompted, she refused to interact with her classmates during play times, often playing with items alone and becoming increasingly isolated from her peers. Although she spoke to her family at home, she had difficulty initiating conversations and making verbal requests for items in school. Mr. Hall reported that Emma takes items without asking, resulting in some peer rejection. With assistance from her assigned paraprofessional, Mrs. Gouvier, Emma had no academic concerns and was maintaining average to above-average grades. Emma was described as a student motivated to learn but detached from other's feelings and behaviors. Mr. Hall expressed that while Emma rarely engaged in disruptive behavior, taking items from her classmates had resulted in disturbances in academic instruction. During these incidents, Mr. Hall addressed these disruptions by facilitating appropriate problem solving between students, often interrupting academic instruction.

Assessment

Parent Interview

A parent interview was conducted with Mr. and Mrs. Gehler, who reported similar but less frequent behavior patterns. At home, Emma engaged in social play with familiar family members, but Mr. Gehler reported needing to prompt Emma to engage in conversations with others. Emma also frequently took items from others at home without permission, just as she reportedly did at school. When asked about Emma's friendships, Mr. and Mrs. Gehler were not able to identify any close friends, aside from occasional play dates with her cousins, and reported that Emma had never been invited to social gatherings outside of school. No behavioral problems at home were reported.

Direct Behavior Ratings

Mr. Hall completed DBRs, assessing the frequency of Emma's positive peer interactions. The frequency was recorded on a 7-point Likert scale with 1 indicating the behavior "never" occurred and 7 suggesting the behavior "always" occurred. The rating scales were completed by Mr. Hall for 4 days to establish a baseline prior to intervention implementation and confirmed reports that Emma was rarely engaging in positive peer interactions. Given the potential long-term consequences of Emma's isolation and social skills deficits, the behavior strategist determined Emma would likely benefit from pivotal response training as an intervention. To monitor progress, Mr. Hall continued completing DBRs.

Systematic Direct Observations

A series of observations was conducted by the behavior strategist as an additional method for assessing Emma's progress. Target behaviors observed across a 15-minute observation included the frequency with which Emma (1) initiated conversations with peers, (2) made verbal requests, and (3) engaged in 5 seconds of social play. According to baseline data, Emma made zero verbal requests for preferred items, often grabbing for them and only occasionally making vocalizations. She made zero attempts to initiate conversation with peers or engage in social play for more than 5 seconds. Of note, she was observed making frequent attempts to engage in social play with her paraprofessional but rarely attempted to engage in social play with peers. Observations were conducted during the pivotal response training and for 1 week after the training. To assess for maintenance of skills, an additional observation was conducted after 2 weeks from the previous observation.

Intervention: Pivotal Response Training

The behavior strategist trained Mrs. Gouvier on the pivotal response training (PRT) technique, including explicit instruction, modeling, and performance feedback until she was able to complete all the components of the procedure without assistance. PRT aims to enhance a child's foundational skills so he or she is able to make generalizations to improvements in other areas of functioning by building on the child's natural interests and initiations. PRT with Emma involved the following procedures.

To start, a preference assessment was conducted to determine what items in the natural setting Emma preferred most and was most likely to engage with herself. Once preferred items were established, the natural classroom setting was enriched with those various items. When Emma reached out for one item, Mrs. Gouvier held the item out of reach from her and prompted her to make a verbal request (e.g., "May I use that?"), initiate a conversation (e.g., "How are you?"), or engage in play with a nearby peer. When Emma complied with the request or made a successful attempt to complete the action, she was praised and given access to the preferred item for 1 minute. Mrs. Gouvier then retrieved the item and began the procedure again.

Mrs. Gouvier conducted the PRT during unstructured free time throughout the school day. If Emma made an attempt to grab a peer's pencil or other school item during academic instruction, Mrs. Gouvier intervened with the PRT procedure. The intervention continued for 2 weeks, with the types of prompts varied throughout (i.e., verbal request, initiate conversation, or engage in play with a peer). Following the second week of the training, the paraprofessional began fading verbal prompts to eventually provide the least amount of instruction possible (e.g., "Ask" or "Play"). The intervention then continued for two additional weeks. Intermittently throughout the intervention, the behavior strategist observed for treatment fidelity, identifying the percentage of components fully completed by Mrs. Gouvier. The average percentage of components she implemented with integrity was 81%.

Outcomes

Daily observations revealed Emma did not engage in any of the target behaviors before PRT was implemented. Upon implementation of the intervention, Emma's performance of the three target behaviors increased immediately, as shown in Figure 10.8. This positive progress was mostly consistent throughout the month with the exception of two specific days. During these days, Mrs. Gouvier noticed that Emma appeared disinterested with her preferred items. To assess if this was the case, an additional preference assessment was conducted and the resulting preferred items were introduced the following day. Although Emma engaged in social play less frequently than the other target behaviors throughout PRT, the rate at which she engaged in all three increased.

Initially, the paraprofessional reported her hesitance about implementing the intervention independently. Two weeks after implementation, and with feedback from the behavior strategist, she reported feeling confident in her ability to implement the PRT and also acknowledged the efficacy of the intervention itself. Furthermore, Mr. and Mrs. Gehlar stated that the amount of verbal requests Emma used at home had also increased. She also reportedly initiated conversations with unfamiliar peers on the neighborhood playground, providing further support that the skills Emma gained through the PRT at school also generalized to other settings.

Mr. Hall's ratings on the DBRs revealed that Emma engaged in positive peer interactions very often to always at the conclusion of the PRT intervention (see Figure 10.9). Specifically, students expressed interest in Emma's activities and she engaged appropriately with peers during playtime. Additionally, Mr. Hall found that he was able to spend more time on classroom instruction following the intervention, given the reduction in disruptions. Furthermore, he reported Emma engaged in appropriate behaviors in the absence of the paraprofessional, suggesting the behaviors were generalized to other trainers as well.

Overall, the data collected demonstrated that PRT had a positive effect on Emma's social skills, which maintained when assessed 2 weeks following the conclusion of the intervention. In an effort to generalize these skills across settings and in the presence of other adults, and to further enhance Emma's social play and peer acceptance, Mr. Hall selected strong peers in the classroom and incorporated a peer-mediated PRT component. The

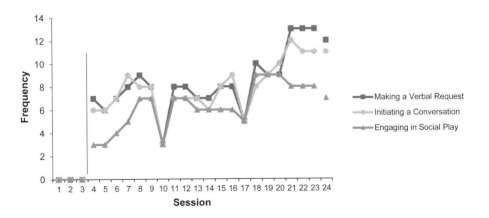

FIGURE 10.8. Frequency of positive social behaviors.

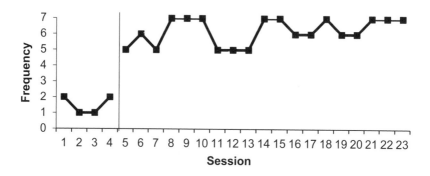

FIGURE 10.9. Positive peer interactions.

behavior strategist followed up with Mr. Hall after implementation of the peer-mediated PRT. He reported that Emma's social skills continued to improve; specifically, she continued to demonstrate increased social play.

CASE STUDY 9: TIER 3 INDIVIDUALIZED INTERVENTION FOR A D/HOH STUDENT

Student Name: Jessica Hayes
Grade: 6
Age: 12
Race/Ethnicity: African American
Sex: Female

Background Information

Jessica Hayes was an 11-year-old, sixth-grade student, who was deaf and communicated solely using ASL at the beginning of the school year. She qualified for special education services under the category of Hearing Impairment. During the summer before her sixth-grade year, she underwent a procedure to receive a cochlear implant. She was in the process of adapting to hearing and speaking and received instruction in the general education setting with assistance from a paraprofessional and interpreter. It was Jessica's first year at the school, as she had previously attended a school for D/HOH students. She had difficulty communicating with her peers, resulting in limited peer interactions and trouble making friends. Jessica's paraprofessional and her teacher, Mrs. Talbot, spoke with the school psychologist seeking skills and strategies to help enhance Jessica's pragmatic language and social skills in the classroom.

Assessment

Teacher and Paraprofessional Interview

The school psychologist met with Mrs. Talbot and the paraprofessional to gain more information about Jessica's current social skills. They reported that Jessica had difficulty understanding conversational rules. She tended to interrupt conversations, overly contribute, and struggle with the "give-and-take" nature of conversations. In addition, when peers were upset, she did not appear to fully understand social cues or respond appropriately. That is, Jessica often did not identify a need for giving classmates space or providing them with comfort. Instead, she often avoided social interactions or stood near her peers and watched their interactions. Finally, Jessica had trouble making friends, and specifically with joining groups, initiating conversation or activities, and maintaining mutual conversations. Her teachers indicated that there was one peer with whom Jessica interacted with sometimes and sat with during lunch. However, their friendship appeared one-sided and Jessica did not initiate interactions with other peers.

Direct Observation

To get a better understanding of the frequency and quality of interactions between Jessica and her peers, the school psychologist conducted several observations in Jessica's classroom and during less-structured activities, such as lunch and gym class. She recorded the frequency of the number of times Jessica initiated social interactions with peers across all observations. Observation data revealed that Jessica initiated very few interactions, at most initiating peer contact once during each observation. The school psychologist also took anecdotal notes about the quality and sequence of the interactions, including conversation skills and responsiveness to social cues. It was noted that Jessica frequently interrupted conversations and abruptly joined peer groups. Her peers often ignored her or provided limited responses, such as a smile, but little conversation.

DBR and Frequency Count

Jessica's paraprofessional was asked to complete a DBR at the end of each day with an emphasis on observations at times when peer interactions were possible, such as gym, group work, or other less-structured activities. The behavior rated was the quality of peer interactions, which was defined as using appropriate conversational rules, initiating interactions in acceptable ways, and responding to interactions appropriately. That is, the paraprofessional was asked to rate the percentage of time that Jessica used appropriate social skills for peer interactions during the day. In addition, the paraprofessional was asked to keep a frequency count of the number of instances in which Jessica initiated an interaction with peers throughout the day. Baseline data was collected during the week before implementing the individualized SEL intervention with the school psychologist. Later collection of the ratings would allow for progress monitoring of both frequency and quality of Jessica's interactions with her peers.

Intervention

Strategies used with Jessica are similar to those outlined in Chapter 8. Many of the strategies included in that chapter for D/HOH students were employed with Jessica. (For citations and resources for these intervention strategies, refer to Chapter 8.)

Direct Instruction

The school psychologist met with Jessica individually three times per week for 30 minutes to provide direct instruction on social skills for initiating and maintaining peer relationships. As Jessica was still adjusting to her cochlear implant, the school psychologist delivered lessons in both ASL and English. Lessons focused on topics such as conversation skills (e.g., taking turns, initiating at appropriate times), understanding social cues from others (e.g., feelings and nonverbal cues), and joining groups or inviting others to join her activity. These skills were targeted to increase her awareness of the social environment, improve her social skills, and increase the quality of her peer interactions and relationships. The school psychologist structured the lessons using a tell–show–do approach. First, the school psychologist defined the social skill, discussed its importance, and presented the steps for performing the social behavior. Next the school psychologist used pictures, videos, and *in vivo* modeling to show positive and negative examples or models of the social behavior being taught. The school psychologist then reviewed the social skill definition, discussed its importance, and reviewed the skill step components. Once Jessica understood the components of each skill, she engaged in role-play activities where she acted-out a situation using the skill and the school psychologist provided prompts and feedback on her performance as she did so. Mrs. Talbot was provided with a description of the skills taught in individual sessions in order to ensure that she was able to praise Jessica for practicing those skills throughout the day.

Behavioral Contract

In order to encourage Jessica to practice the social skills she learned with the school psychologist in other settings, such as in the classroom and at home, the school psychologist developed a behavioral contract with Jessica and her teachers. The contract outlined a contingency between the demonstration of social behaviors that Jessica needed to practice and access to reinforcement provided by Mrs. Talbot and her teachers. The school psychologist included a description of the target behaviors, behavioral goal, and reinforcement contingency in the contract. The contract specified that Jessica would be responsible for increasing the number of self-initiated peer interactions per day from none/one to five interactions per day, as reported by her teacher. At the end of the day, Jessica could choose a reward from a menu of options, including computer time, gum, or leaving class several minutes early. If Jessica did not meet her goal, her consequence was losing the opportunity to earn a reward. Jessica and her teachers signed the contract (see below).

> "I, Jessica Hayes, agree to begin at least five conversations or other interactions with my peers during the day. If I do this, with a rating by my paraprofessional of 70% quality of interactions for the day, I will earn a reward of my choice from the menu to be provided by my teacher at the end of the day."

Peer Involvement

The school psychologist and Jessica's teachers also identified one of Jessica's peers whom she interacted with most frequently. This peer was trained and encouraged to promote practice of the social skills Jessica learned with the school psychologist. Following the lesson on conversational skills, for example, the peer was encouraged to engage Jessica in conversation and allow her to practice not interrupting and the give-and-take in a conversation.

Outcomes

Progress-monitoring data collected by Jessica's paraprofessional over 6 weeks of intervention showed that with direct instruction and the addition of the behavioral contract, the frequency and quality of Jessica's interactions with her peers improved. In comparing baseline data during Week 1 to the data collected during the intervention phase in Weeks 2–6, Jessica's performance of the targeted social skills showed an increasing trend, as indicated by the average frequency of her self-initiated interactions per week (see Figure 10.10) and the outcomes for the DBR of the quality of her interactions each week (see Figure 10.11).

Jessica's paraprofessional and Mrs. Talbot observed steady progress in Jessica's social skills. She began initiating more peer interactions and increased the amount of time engaged in high-quality interactions. Although they noted that the behavioral contract was fairly easy to implement and

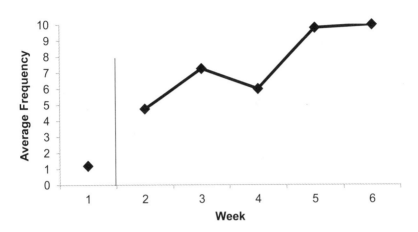

FIGURE 10.10. Self-initiated peer interactions.

had been effective in incentivizing Jessica to interact with her peers, Jessica's teachers discontinued use of the behavioral contract to reduce the amount of data collection, including frequency counts and DBRs. The natural reinforcement from her peers for her improved social skills would likely be sufficient to maintain her social skills. The school psychologist continued with another 3 weeks of SEL intervention with Jessica to address any difficulties with previously taught skills that were noticed by teacher observation.

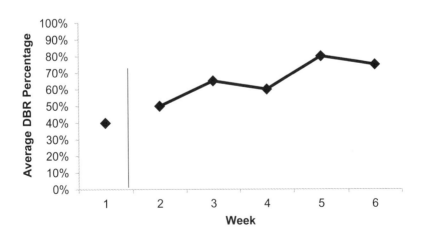

FIGURE 10.11. Direct behavior rating of quality of social interactions.

References

Aber, J., Brown, J., & Jones, S. (2003). Developmental trajectories toward violence in middle childhood: Course, demographic differences, and response to school-based intervention. *Developmental Psychology, 39,* 324–348.

Aber, J., Jones, S., Brown, J., Chaudry, N., & Samples, F. (1998). Resolving conflict creatively: Evaluating the developmental effect of a school-based violence prevention program in neighborhood and classroom context. *Development and Psychopathology, 10,* 187–213.

Achenbach, T., & Rescorla, L. (2001a). *Manual for the ASEBA School-Age Forms and Profiles.* Burlington: University of Vermont Research Center for Children, Youth, and Families.

Achenbach, T., & Rescorla, L. (2001b). *Teacher Rating Form, Child Behavior Checklist, Youth Self-Report.* Burlington: University of Vermont Research Center for Children, Youth, and Families.

American Association on Intellectual and Developmental Disabilities. (2010). *Intellectual disability: Definition, classification, and systems of supports* (11th ed.). Washington, DC: Author.

American Psychiatric Association. (2013). *Diagnostic and statistical manual of mental disorders* (5th ed.). Arlington, VA: Author.

Asher, S., & McDonald, K. (2009). The behavioral basis of acceptance, rejection, and perceived popularity. In K. Rubin, W. Bukowski, & B. Laursen (Eds.), *Handbook of peer interactions, relationships, and groups* (pp. 232–248). New York: Guilford Press.

Bandura, A. (1977). *Social learning theory.* Englewood Cliffs, NJ: Prentice-Hall.

Bandura, A. (1986). *Social foundations of thought and action: A social cognitive theory.* Englewood Cliffs, NJ: Prentice-Hall.

Baron, R., & Kenny, D. (1986). The moderator–mediator variable distinction in social psychology research. *Journal of Personality and Social Psychology, 51,* 1173–1182.

Battistich, V. (2000). Effects of a school-based program to enhance development on children's peer relations and social adjustment. *Journal of Research in Character Education, 1,* 1–17.

Battistich, V., Schaps, E., Watson, M., & Solomon, D. (1996). Prevention effects of the Child Development Project: Early findings from an ongoing multisite trial. *Journal of Adolescent Research, 11,* 12–35.

Battistich, V., Schaps, E., Watson, M., Solomon, D., & Lewis, C. (2000). Effects of the Child Development Project on students' drug use and other problem behaviors. *Journal of Primary Prevention, 21,* 75–99.

Battistich, V., Solomon, D., Watson, M., Solomon, J., & Schaps, E. (1989). Effects of an elementary school program to enhance prosocial behavior on children's cognitive–social problem-solving skills and strategies. *Journal of Applied Developmental Psychology, 10,* 147–169.

Beelman, A., Pfingsten, U., & Losel, F. (1994). Effects of training social competence in children: A meta-analysis of recent evaluation studies. *Journal of Clinical Child Psychology, 23,* 260–271.

Beets, M., Flay, B., Vuchinich, S., Snyder, F., Acock, A., Burns, K., et al. (2009). Use of a social and character development program to prevent substance use, violent behaviors, and sexual activity among elementary-school students in Hawaii. *American Journal of Public Health, 99,* 1438–1445.

Bellg, A., Borrelli B., Resnick, B., Hecht, J., Minicucci, D., Ory, M., et al. (2004). Enhancing treatment fidelity in health behavior change studies: Best practices and recommendations from the NIH Behavior Change Consortium. *Health Psychology, 23,* 443–451.

Benson, P. (2006). *All kids are our kids: What communities must do to raise responsible and caring children and adolescents.* San Francisco: Jossey-Bass.

Bergan, J. (1977). *Behavioral consultation.* Columbus, OH: Merrill.

Bergan, J., & Kratochwill, T. (1990). *Behavioral consultation and therapy.* New York: Plenum Press.

Bierman, K. L. (2004). *Peer rejection: Developmental processes and intervention strategies.* New York: Guilford Press.

Bierman, K. L., & Greenberg, M. (1996). Social skills training in the Fast Track program. In R. Peters & R. McMahon (Eds.), *Preventing childhood disorders, substance abuse, and delinquency* (pp. 65–89). Thousand Oaks, CA: SAGE.

Bierman, K. L., & Powers, C. J. (2009). Social skills training to improve peer relations. In K. Rubin, W. Bukowski, & B. Laursen (Eds.), *Handbook of peer interactions, relationships, and groups* (pp. 603–621). New York: Guilford Press.

Brown, E., Low, S., Smith, B., & Haggerty, K. (2011). Outcomes from a school-randomized controlled trial of Steps to Respect bullying prevention program. *School Psychology Review, 40,* 423–443.

Brown, J., Jones, S., LaRusso, M., & Aber, J. (2010). Improving classroom quality: Teacher influences and experimental impacts of the 4Rs program. *Journal of Educational Psychology, 102,* 153–167.

Caprara, G., Barbaranelli, C., Pastorelli, C., Bandura, A., & Zimbardo, P. (2000). Prosocial foundations of children's academic achievement. *Psychological Science, 11,* 302–305.

Chafouleas, S., McDougal, J., Riley-Tilman, C., Panahon, C., & Hilt, A. (2005). What do daily behavior report cards (DBRCs) measure?: An initial comparison of DBRCs with direct observation for off-task behavior. *Psychology in the Schools, 42,* 669–676.

Chafouleas, S., Riley-Tilman, C., & McDougal, J. (2002). Good, bad, or in-between: How does the daily behavior report card rate? *Psychology in the Schools, 39,* 157–167.

Coie, J., Dodge, K., & Coppotelli, H. (1982). Dimensions and types of social status: A cross-age perspective. *Developmental Psychology, 18,* 557–570.

Coie, J., Dodge, K., & Kupersmidt, J. (1990). Peer group behavior and social status. In S. Asher & J. Coie (Eds.), *Peer rejection in childhood* (pp. 17–59). New York: Cambridge University Press.

Coie, J., & Jacobs, M. (1993). The role of social context in the prevention of conduct disorder [Special Issue]. *Development and Psychopathology, 5,* 26–27.

Coie, J., Lochman, J., Terry, R., & Hyman, C. (1992). Predicting early adolescent disorder from childhood aggression and peer rejection. *Journal of Consulting and Clinical Psychology, 60,* 697–714.

Collaborative for Academic, Social, and Emotional Learning (CASEL). (2012). *CASEL guide: Effective social and emotional learning programs—Preschool and elementary school edition.* Chicago: Author.

Collaborative for Academic, Social, and Emotional Learning (CASEL). (2013). *CASEL guide: Effective social and emotional learning programs-preschool and elementary school edition.* Chicago: Author.

Collaborative for Academic, Social, and Emotional Learning (CASEL). (2015). *District guide to systemic social and emotional learning.* Chicago: Author.

Conduct Problems Prevention Research Group. (1992). A developmental and clinical model for the prevention of conduct disorders: The Fast Track Program. *Development and Psychopathology, 4,* 505–527.

Conduct Problems Prevention Research Group. (1999a). Initial impact of the Fast Track Prevention Trial for Conduct Problems: I. The high-risk sample. *Journal of Consulting and Clinical Psychology, 67,* 631–647.

Conduct Problems Prevention Research Group. (1999b). Initial impact of the Fast Track Prevention Trial for Conduct Problems: II. Classroom effects. *Journal of Consulting and Clinical Psychology, 67,* 648–657.

Conduct Problems Prevention Research Group. (2010). The effects of a multiyear universal social–emotional learning program: The role of student and school characteristics. *Journal of Consulting and Clinical Psychology, 78,* 156–168.

Conners, C. K. (1997). *Conners Rating Scales—Revised: Technical manual.* Toronto: Multi-Health Systems.

Connolly, J., & Johnson, A. (1996). Adolescents' romantic relationships and the structure and quality of their close interpersonal ties. *Personal Relationships, 3,* 185–195.

Cook, C. R., Browning-Wright, D., Gresham, F. M., & Burns, M. (2010). *Transforming school psychology in a RTI era: A guide for administrators and school psychologists.* Palm Beach, FL: LRP Publications.

Cook, C. R., Volpe, R., & Delport, J. (2014). Systematic progress monitoring of students with emotional and behavioral disorders. In H. M. Walker & F. M.

Gresham (Eds.), *Handbook of evidence-based practices for emotional and behavioral disorders: Applications in schools* (pp. 211–228). New York: Guilford Press.

Cooper, J., Heron, T., & Heward, W. (2007). *Applied behavior analysis* (2nd ed.). Upper Saddle River, NJ: Prentice-Hall.

Cowen, E., Pedersen, A., Babigian, H., Izzo, I., & Trost, M. (1973). Long-term follow-up of early detected vulnerable children. *Journal of Consulting and Clinical Psychology, 41,* 438–446.

Crone, D., Hawken, L., & Horner, R. (2010). *Responding to problem behavior in schools: The Behavior Education program.* New York: Guilford Press.

Crowe, L., Beauchamp, M., Catroppa, C., & Anderson, V. (2011). Social function assessment tools for children and adolescents: A systematic review from 1988 to 2010. *Clinical Psychology Review, 31,* 767–785.

DiPerma, J., & Elliott, S. N. (2000). *Academic Competence Evaluation Scale.* Minneapolis: Pearson Assessments.

DiPerma, J., & Elliott, S. N. (2002). Promoting academic enablers to improve student achievement: An introduction to the miniseries. *School Psychology Review, 31,* 293–297.

DiPerma, J., Lei, P., Bellinger, J., & Cheng, W. (2015). Efficacy of the Social Skills Improvement System Classwide Intervention Program (SSIS-CIP) Primary Version. *School Psychology Quarterly, 30,* 123–141.

Dodge, K. (1986). A social information processing model of social competence in children. In M. Perlmutter (Ed.), *Minnesota symposium on child psychology* (Vol. 18, pp. 77–125). Hillsdale, NJ: Erlbaum.

Dodge, K., Dishion, T., & Lansford, J. (Eds.). (2006). *Deviant peer influences in programs for youth: Problems and solutions.* New York: Guilford Press.

Domitrovich, C., Cortes, R., & Greenberg, M. (2007). Improving young children's social and emotional competence: A randomized trial of the preschool PATHS curriculum. *Journal of Primary Prevention, 28,* 67–91.

Durlak, J., Weissberg, R., Dymnicki, A. B., Taylor, R., & Schellinger, K. (2011). The impact of enhancing students' social and emotional learning: A meta-analysis of school-based universal interventions. *Child Development, 82,* 474–501.

Eddy, J., Reid, J., & Curry, V. (2002). The etiology of youth antisocial behavior, delinquency, and violence in a public health approach to prevention. In M. Shinn, H. Walker, & G. Stoner (Eds.), *Interventions for academic and behavior problems: II. Preventive and remedial approaches* (pp. 27–51). Bethesda, MD: National Association of School Psychologists.

Elliott, S. N., & Gresham, F. M. (2007). *Social Skills Improvement System: Classwide intervention program teacher's guide.* Minneapolis, MN: Pearson.

Elliott, S. N., & Gresham, F. M. (2008). *Social Skills Improvement System: Intervention guide.* Minneapolis, MN: Pearson.

Fawcett, S. (1991). Social validity: A note on methodology. *Journal of Applied Behavior Analysis, 24,* 235–239.

Feis, C., & Simmons, C. (1985). Training preschool children in interpersonal cognitive problem-solving skills: A replication. *Prevention in Human Services, 3,* 71–85.

Flay, B., & Allred, C. (2003). Long-term effects of the Positive Action program. *American Journal of Health Behavior, 27*(Suppl. 1), S6–S21.

Flay, B., Allred, C., & Ordway, N. (2001). Effects of the Positive Action program on achievement and discipline: Two matched-control comparisons. *Prevention Science, 2,* 71–89.

Frey, K., Hirschstein, M., Snell, J., Van Scholack, L., MacKenzie, E., & Broderick, C. (2009). Reducing playground bullying and supporting beliefs: An experimental trial of the Steps to Respect program. *Developmental Psychology, 41,* 479–491.

Frey, K., Nolen, S., Edstrom, L., & Hirschstein, M. (2005). Effects of a school-based social–emotional competence program: Linking children's goals, attributions, and behavior. *Journal of Applied Developmental Psychology, 26,* 171–200.

Gersten, R., Fuchs, L., Compton, D., Coyne, M., Greenwood, C., & Innocenti, M. (2005). Quality indicators for group experimental and quasi-experimental research in special education. *Exceptional Children, 71,* 149–164.

Glass, G., McGaw, B., & Smith, M. (1981). *Meta-analysis in social research.* Beverly Hills, CA: SAGE.

Greenberg, M., & Kusché, C. (1998). Preventive intervention for school-age deaf children: The PATHS curriculum. *Journal of Deaf Studies and Deaf Education, 5,* 49–63.

Greenspan, S. (2006). Functional concepts in mental retardation: Finding the natural essence of an artificial category. *Exceptionality, 14,* 205–224.

Gresham, F. M. (1989). Assessment of treatment integrity in school consultation and pre-referral intervention. *School Psychology Review, 18,* 37–50.

Gresham, F. M. (1991). Conceptualizing behavior disorders in terms of resistance to intervention. *School Psychology Review, 20,* 23–36.

Gresham, F. M. (1999). Noncategorical approaches to K–12 emotional and behavioral difficulties. In D. Reschly, W. D. Tilly, & J. Grimes (Eds.), *Functional and noncategorical special education* (pp. 107–137). Longmont, CO: Sopris West.

Gresham, F. M. (2002). Teaching social skills to high-risk children and youth: Preventive and remedial strategies. In M. Shinn, H. Walker, & G. Stoner (Eds.), *Interventions for academic and behavior problems: Preventive and remedial approaches* (2nd ed., pp. 403–432). Bethesda, MD: National Association of School Psychologists.

Gresham, F. M. (2007). Evolution of the response-to-intervention concept: Empirical foundations and recent development. In S. Jimmerson, M. Burns, & A. VanDerHeyden (Eds.), *Handbook of response to intervention: The science and practice of assessment and intervention* (pp. 10–24). New York: Springer.

Gresham, F. M. (2010). Evidence-based social skills interventions: Empirical foundations for instructional approaches. In M. Shinn & H. Walker (Eds.), *Interventions for achievement and behavior problems in a three-tier model including RTI* (pp. 337–362). Bethesda, MD: National Association of School Psychologists.

Gresham, F. M. (2014). Measuring and analyzing treatment integrity data in research. In L. Sanetti & T. Kratochwill (Eds.), *Treatment integrity: A foundation for evidence-based practice in applied psychology* (pp. 109–130). Washington, DC: American Psychological Association.

Gresham, F. M., Cook, C. R., Collins, T., Dart, E., Rasetshwane, K., Truelson, E., et al. (2010). Developing a change-sensitive brief behavior rating scale as a progress monitoring tool for social behavior: An example using the Social Skills Rating System–Teacher form. *School Psychology Review, 39,* 364–379.

Gresham, F. M., & Elliott, S. N. (1990). *Social Skills Rating System.* Minneapolis, MN: Pearson.

Gresham, F. M., & Elliott, S. N. (2008). *Social Skills Improvement System: Rating scales manual.* Minneapolis, MN: Pearson.

Gresham, F. M., & Elliott, S. N. (2014). Social skills assessment and training in emotional and behavioral disorders. In H. Walker & F. M. Gresham (Eds.), *Handbook of evidence-based practices for emotional and behavioral disorders: Applications in schools* (pp. 152–172). New York: Guilford Press.

Gresham, F. M., & Elliott, S. N. (2017). *Social Skills Improvement System Social Emotional Learning Edition Rating Forms.* Minneapolis, MN: Pearson Assessments.

Gresham, F. M., McIntyre, L. L., Olson-Tinker, H., Dolstra, L., McLaughlin, V., & Van, M. (2004). Relevance of functional behavioral assessment research for school-based interventions and positive behavior support. *Research in Developmental Disabilities, 25,* 19–37.

Gresham, F. M., Van, M., & Cook, C. R. (2006). Social skills training for teaching replacement behaviors: Remediation of acquisition deficits for at-risk children. *Behavioral Disorders, 30,* 32–46.

Gresham, F. M., Watson, T. S., & Skinner, C. H. (2001). Functional behavioral assessment: Principles, procedures, and future directions. *School Psychology Review, 30,* 156–172.

Grossman, D., Neckerman, H., Koepsell, T., Liu, P., Asher, K., Beland, K., et al. (1997). Effectiveness of a violence prevention curriculum among children in elementary school: A randomized controlled trial. *Journal of the American Medical Association, 277,* 1605–1611.

Hartup, W. (2009). Critical issues and theoretical viewpoints. In K. Rubin, W. Bukowski, & B. Laursen (Eds.), *Handbook of peer interactions, relationships, and groups* (pp. 3–19). New York: Guilford Press.

Hawkins, R. (1991). Is social validity what we are interested in?: Argument for a functional approach. *Journal of Applied Behavior Analysis, 24,* 205–213.

Hayes, S., Nelson, R., & Jarrett, R. (1987). The treatment utility of assessment: A functional approach to evaluating assessment quality. *American Psychologist, 42,* 963–974.

Hedges, L., & Olkin, I. (1985). *Statistical methods for meta-analysis.* Orlando, FL: Academic Press.

Herrnstein, R. J. (1961). Relative and absolute strength of response as a function of frequency of reinforcement. *Journal of the Experimental Analysis of Behavior, 4,* 267–272.

Herrnstein, R. J. (1970). On the law of effect. *Journal of the Experimental Analysis of Behavior, 13,* 243–266.

Hinshaw, S. (1992). Externalizing behavior problems and academic underachievement in childhood and adolescence: Causal relationships and underlying mechanisms. *Psychological Bulletin, 111,* 127–155.

Holsen, I., Iversen, A., & Smith, B. (2008). Universal social competence promotion program in school: Does it work for children with low socio-economic background? *Advances in School Mental Health Promotion, 2,* 51–60.

Holsen, I., Smith, B., & Frey, K. (2008). Outcomes of the social competence program Second Step in Norwegian elementary schools. *School Psychology International, 29,* 71–88.

Horner, R. H., Carr, E., Halle, J., McGee, G., Odom, S., & Wolery, M. (2005). The use of single-case research to identify evidence-based practice in special education. *Exceptional Children, 71,* 165–179.

Hoza, B., Molina, B., Bukowski, W., & Sippola, L. (1995). Aggression, withdrawal, and measures of popularity and friendship as predictors of internalizing and externalizing problems during adolescence. *Development and Psychopathology, 7,* 787–802.

Humphrey, N., Kalambouka, A., Wigelsworth, M., Lendrum, A., Deighton, J., & Wolpert, M. (2011). Measures of social and emotional skills for children and young people: A systematic review. *Educational and Psychological Measurement, 71,* 617–637.

Issacson, W. (2007). *Einstein: His life and universe.* New York: Simon & Schuster.

Jiang, X., & Cillessen, A. (2005). Stability of continuous measures of sociometric status: A meta-analysis. *Developmental Review, 25,* 1–25.

Jones, S., Brown, J., & Aber, J. (2011). Two-year impacts of a universal school-based social–emotional and literacy intervention: An experiment in translational developmental research. *Child Development, 82,* 533–554.

Juel, C. (1988). *Learning to read and write: A longitudinal study of 54 children from first through fourth grade.* Paper presented at the annual conference of the American Educational Research Association, New Orleans, LA.

Kam, C., Greenberg, M., & Kusché, C. (2004). Sustained effects of the PATHS curriculum on the social and psychological adjustment of children in special education. *Journal of Emotional and Behavioral Disorders, 12,* 66–78.

Kamphaus, R., & Reynolds, C. (2015). *BASC-3 Behavioral and Emotional Screening System.* Minneapolis, MN: Pearson.

Kauffman, J. (2014). On following the scientific evidence. In H. Walker & F. M. Gresham (Eds.), *Handbook of evidence-based practices for emotional and behavioral disorders: Applications in schools* (pp. 1–5). New York: Guilford Press.

Kazdin, A. E. (1987). Treatment of antisocial behavior in childhood: Current status and future directions. *Psychological Bulletin, 102,* 187–203.

Kazdin, A. E. (2003a). Problem-solving skills training and parent management for conduct disorder. In A. E. Kazdin & J. Weisz (Eds.), *Evidence-based psychotherapies for children and adolescents* (pp. 241–262). New York: Guilford Press.

Kazdin, A. E. (2003b). Clinical significance: Measuring whether interventions make a difference. In A. E. Kazdin (Ed.), *Methodological issues and strategies in clinical research* (3rd ed., pp. 691–710). Washington, DC: American Psychological Association.

Kazdin, A. E. (2004). Evidence-based treatments: Challenges and priorities for practice and research. *Child and Adolescent Psychiatry Clinics of North America, 13,* 923–940.

Kazdin, A. E., & Weisz, J. R. (2003). Context and background of evidence-based psychotherapies for children and adolescents. In A. E. Kazdin & J. R. Weisz (Eds.), *Evidence-based psychotherapies for children and adolescents* (pp. 3–20). New York: Guilford Press.

Koegel, R. L., & Koegel, L. K. (2006). *Pivotal response treatments for autism: Communication, social, and academic development.* Baltimore, MD: Brookes.

Kohler, F., & Strain, P. (1990). Peer-assisted interventions: Early promises, notable achievements, and future aspirations. *Clinical Psychology Review, 10,* 441–452.

Kratochwill, T., Hitchcock, T., Horner, R., Levin, J., Odom, S., Rindskopf, D., et al. (2010). Single-case design technical documentation. Retrieved from *http//ies.ed.gov/ncee/wwc_scd.pdf.*

Kupersmidt, J., Coie, J., & Dodge, K. (1990). The role of peer relationships in the development of disorder. In S. Asher & J. Coie (Eds.), *Peer rejection in childhood* (pp. 274–308). New York: Cambridge University Press.

La Greca, A. M. (1993). Social skills training with children: Where do we go from here? *Journal of Clinical Child Psychology, 22,* 288–298.

Landau, S., & Milich, R. (1990). Assessment of children's social status and peer relations. In A. La Greca (Ed.), *Through the eyes of the child* (pp. 259–291). Boston: Allyn & Bacon.

Lane, K., Oakes, W., Menzies, H., & Germer, K. (2014). Screening and identification approaches for detecting students at risk. In H. M. Walker & F. M. Gresham (Eds.), *Handbook of evidence-based practices for emotional and behavior disorders: Applications in schools* (pp. 129–151). New York: Guilford Press.

Li, K., Washburn, I., DuBois, D., Vuchinich, S., Ji, P., Brechling, V., et al. (2011). Effects of the Positive Action Programme on problem behaviors in elementary school students: A matched-pair randomized control trial in Chicago. *Psychology and Health, 3,* 187–204.

Lochman, J. (2002). The Coping Power Program at the middle school transition: Universal and indicated prevention efforts. *Psychology of Addictive Behaviors, 34,* 540–554.

Lochman, J., Barry, T., & Pardini, D. (2003). Anger control training for aggressive youth. In A. E. Kazdin & J. R. Weisz (Eds.), *Evidence-based psychotherapies for children and adolescents* (pp. 263–281). New York: Guilford Press.

Lochman, J., & Gresham, F. M. (2009). Intervention development, assessment, planning, and adaptation: The importance of developmental models. In M. Mayer, R. Van Acker, J. Lochman, & F. M. Gresham (Eds.), *Cognitive-behavioral interventions for emotional and behavioral disorders* (pp. 29–57). New York: Guilford Press.

Lovaas, O. I. (1997). Behavioral treatment and normal educational and intellectual functioning in young autistic children. *Journal of Consulting and Clinical Psychology, 55,* 3–9.

Maag, J. W. (2005). Social skills training for youth with emotional and behavioral disorders and learning disabilities: Problems, conclusions, and suggestions. *Exceptionality, 13,* 155–172.

Maag, J. W. (2006). Social skills training for students with emotional and behavioral disorders: A review of reviews. *Behavioral Disorders, 32,* 5–17.

Malecki, C. M., & Elliott, S. N. (2002). Children's social behaviors as predictors of academic achievement: A longitudinal analysis. *School Psychology Quarterly, 17,* 1–23.

Martens, B. K. (1992). Contingency and choice: The implications of matching theory for classroom instruction. *Journal of Behavioral Education, 2,* 121–137.

Martens, B. K., & Houk, J. L. (1989). The application of Herrnstein's Law of Effect to disruptive and on-task behavior of a retarded adolescent girl. *Journal of the Experimental Analysis of Behavior, 51,* 17–27.

Martens, B. K., Lochner, D. G., & Kelly, S. Q. (1992). The effects of variable-interval reinforcement on academic engagement: A demonstration of matching theory. *Journal of Applied Behavior Analysis, 25,* 143–151.

Mastropieri, M., & Scruggs, T. (1985–1986). Early intervention for socially withdrawn children. *Journal of Special Education, 19,* 429–441.

Mayer, M., Van Acker, R., Lochman, J., & Gresham, F. M. (Eds.). (2009). *Cognitive-behavioral interventions for emotional and behavioral disorders.* New York: Guilford Press.

McIntosh, K., Frank, J., & Spaulding, S. (2010). Establishing research-based trajectories of office discipline referrals for individual students. *School Psychology Review, 39,* 380–394.

McIntyre, L. L., Gresham, F. M., DiGennaro, F. D., & Reed, D. D. (2007). Treatment integrity of school-based interventions with children in *Journal of Applied Behavior Analysis* from 1991–2005. *Journal of Applied Behavior Analysis, 40,* 659–672.

Merrell, K. W. (1993). *School Social Behavior Scales.* Austin, TX: Pro-Ed.

Merrell, K. W. (1994). *Preschool and Kindergarten Behavior Scales.* Austin, TX: Pro-Ed.

Merrell, K. W. (1999). *Behavioral, social, and emotional assessment of children and adolescents.* Mahwah, NJ: Erlbaum.

Merrell, K. W. (2002). *Preschool and Kindergarten Behavior Scales.* Austin, TX: PRO-ED.

Merrell, K. W. (2003). *Preschool and Kindergarten Behavior Scales–2.* Brandon, VT: Clinical Psychology.

Merrell, K. W., & Candarella, P. (2008). *School Social Behavior Scales–2.* Baltimore, MD: Brookes.

Merrell, K. W., Carrizales, D., Feuerborn, L., Gueldner, B. A., & Tran, O. K. (2007). *Strong Kids: A social and emotional learning curriculum for students in grades 3–5.* Baltimore, MD: Brookes.

Messick, S. (1995). Validity of psychological assessment: Validation of inferences from persons' responses and performances as scientific inquiry into score meaning. *American Psychologist, 50,* 741–749.

Nathan, P., & Gorman, J. (2002). *A guide to treatments that work* (2nd ed.). New York: Oxford University Press.

Nathan, P., Stuart, S., & Dolan, S. (2000). Research on psychotherapy efficacy and effectiveness: Between Scylla and Charybdis? In A. E. Kazdin (Ed.), *Methodological issues and strategies in clinical research* (3rd ed., pp. 505–546). Washington, DC: American Psychological Association.

National Reading Panel. (2000). Teaching children to read: An evidence-based assessment of the scientific research literature on reading and its implication for reading instruction. Retrieved from *www.nichd.nih.gov/publications/ pubskey.fm?from=nrp.*

Nelson, S., & Dishion, T. (2004). From boys to men: Predicting adult adaptation from middle childhood sociometric status. *Development and Psychopathology, 16,* 441–459.

Nevin, J. (1988). Behavioral momentum and the partial reinforcement effect. *Psychological Bulletin, 103,* 44–56.

Newcomb, A., Bukowski, W., & Pattee, L. (1993). Children's peer relations: A meta-analytic review of popular, rejected, neglected, controversial, and average sociometric status. *Psychological Bulletin, 113,* 306–347.

Northrup, J., Fusilier, I., Swanson, V., Roane, H., & Borrero, J. (1997). An evaluation of methylphenidate as a potential establishing operation for some common classroom reinforcers. *Journal of Applied Behavior Analysis, 29,* 615–625.

Nunnally, J., & Kotsche, W. (1983). Studies of individual subjects: Logic and methods of analysis. *Journal of Clinical Psychology, 22,* 83–93.

Oden, S. L., & Asher, S. R. (1977). Coaching children in social skills for friendship making. *Child Development, 48,* 495–506.

Offord, D., Boyle, M., & Racine, Y. (1989). Ontario Child Health Study: Correlates of disorder. *Journal of the American Academy of Child and Adolescent Psychiatry, 28,* 856–860.

Parker, J., & Asher, S. (1987). Peer relations and later personal adjustment: Are low-accepted children at risk? *Psychological Bulletin, 102,* 357–389.

Peery, J. (1979). Popular, amiable, isolated, rejected: A reconceptualization of sociometric status in preschool children. *Child Development, 50,* 1231–1234.

Pereplechikova, F. (2014). Assessment of treatment integrity. In L. Hagermoser Sanetti & T. Kratochwill (Eds.), *Treatment integrity: A foundation for evidence-based practice in applied psychology* (pp. 131–158). Washington, DC: American Psychological Association.

Peterson, L., Homer, A., & Wonderlich, S. (1982). The integrity of independent variables in behavior analysis. *Journal of Applied Behavior Analysis, 15,* 477–492.

Prinstein, M., Rancourt, D., Guerry, J., & Browne, C. (2009). Peer reputations and psychological adjustment. In K. Rubin, W. Bukowski, & B. Laursen (Eds.), *Handbook of peer interactions, relationships, and groups* (pp. 548–567). New York: Guilford Press.

Reinke, W. M., Herman, K. C., & Sprick, R. (2011). *Motivational Interviewing for effective classroom management: The Classroom Check-Up.* New York: Guilford Press.

Rogers, E. (2003). *Diffusion of innovations* (5th ed.). New York: Free Press.

Rosenthal, R. (1984). *Meta-analytic procedures for social research.* Beverly Hills, CA: SAGE.

Rosenthal, R., & Rubin, D. B. (1978). Interpersonal expectancy effects: The first 345 studies. *Behavioral and Brain Sciences, 3,* 377–386.

Rosenthal, R., & Rubin, D. B. (1982). A general purpose display of magnitude of experimental effect. *Journal of Educational Psychology, 74,* 166–169.

Rubin, K., Bukowski, W., & Laursen, B. (Eds.). (2009). *Handbook of peer interactions, relationships, and groups.* New York: Guilford Press.

Sabornie, E., & Weiss, S. (2014). Qualitative and mixed design research in emotional and behavioral disorders. In H. Walker & F. M. Gresham (Eds.), *Handbook of evidence-based practices for emotional and behavioral disorders: Applications in schools* (pp. 537–551). New York: Guilford Press.

Schmidt, F., & Hunter, J. (1977). Development of a general solution to the problem of validity generalization. *Journal of Applied Psychology, 62*, 529–540.

Schneider, B. (1992). Didactic methods for enhancing children's peer relations: A quantitative review. *Clinical Psychology Review, 12*, 363–382.

Sechrest, L. (1963). Incremental validity: A recommendation. *Educational and Psychological Measurement, 23*, 153–159.

Sechrest, L., McKnight, P., & McKnight, K. (1996). Calibration of measures for psychotherapy outcome studies. *American Psychologist, 51*, 1065–1071.

Shadish, W., Cook, T., & Campbell, D. (2002). *Experimental and quasi-experimental designs for generalized causal inference*. Boston: Houghton-Mifflin.

Shure, M., & Spivack, G. (1979). Interpersonal and cognitive problem-solving and primary prevention: Programming for preschool and kindergarten children. *Journal of Clinical Child Psychology, 2*, 89–94.

Shure, M., & Spivack, G. (1980). Interpersonal problem-solving as a mediator of behavioral adjustment in preschool and kindergarten children. *Journal of Applied Developmental Psychology, 1*, 29–44.

Shure, M., & Spivack, G. (1982). Interpersonal problem-solving in young children: A cognitive approach to prevention. *American Journal of Community Psychology, 10*, 341–356.

Skinner, B. F. (1953). *Science and human behavior*. New York: Macmillan.

Skinner, C. H., Cashwell, T. H., & Skinner, A. L. (2000). Increasing tootling: The effects of a peer-monitored group contingency program on students' reports of peers' prosocial behaviors. *Psychology in the Schools, 37*(3), 263–270.

Skinner, C. H., Skinner, A. L., & Cashwell, T. H. (1998). *Tootling, not tattling*. Paper presented at the 26th annual meeting of the Mid-South Educational Research Association, New Orleans, LA.

Smith, M., & Glass, G. (1977). Meta-analysis of psychotherapy outcome studies. *American Psychologist, 32*, 752–760.

Smith, R. G., & Iwata, B. A. (1997). Antecedent influences on behavior disorders. *Journal of Applied Behavior Analysis, 30*, 343–375.

Snyder, J., & Stoolmiller, M. (2002). Reinforcement and coercion mechanisms in the development of antisocial behavior: The family. In J. Reid, G. Patterson, & J. Snyder (Eds.), *Antisocial behavior in children and adolescents: A developmental analysis and model for intervention* (pp. 65–100). Washington, DC: American Psychological Association.

Sprague, J., Cook, C., Browning-Wright, D., & Sadler, C. (2008). *RTI and behavior: A guide to integrating behavioral and academic supports*. Horsham, PA: LRP.

Stokes, T., & Baer, D. (1977). An implicit technology of generalization. *Journal of Applied Behavior Analysis, 10*, 349–367.

Stokes, T., & Osnes, P. (1982). Programming the generalization of children's social behavior. In P. Strain, M. Guralnick, & H. Walker (Eds.), *Children's social behavior: Development, assessment and modification* (pp. 407–443). Orlando, FL: Academic Press.

Stokes, T., & Osnes, P. (1989). An operant pursuit of generalization. *Behavior Therapy, 20*, 337–355.

Strain, P., Kohler, F., & Gresham, F. M. (1998). Problems in logic and interpretation with quantitative syntheses of single-case research: Mathur and colleagues (1998) as a case in point. *Behavioral Disorders, 24*, 74–85.

Sugai, G., Horner, R., & Gresham, F. M. (2002). Behaviorally effective school environments. In M. Shinn, H. Walker, & G. Stoner (Eds.), *Interventions for academic and behavior problems: II. Preventive and remedial approaches* (pp. 313–350). Bethesda, MD: National Association of School Psychologists.

VanDerHeyden, A., & Witt, J. (2008). Best practices in can't do/won't do assessment. In A. Thomas & J. Grimes (Eds.), *Best practices in school psychology* (Vol. 5, pp. 131–139). Bethesda, MD: National Association of School Psychologists.

Vidair, H., Sauro, D., Blocher, J., Scudellari, L., & Hoagwood, K. (2014). Empirically supported school-based mental health programs targeting academic and mental health functioning: An update. In H. Walker & F. M. Gresham (Eds.), *Handbook of evidence-based practices for emotional and behavioral disorders: Applications in schools* (pp. 15–53). New York: Guilford Press.

Walker, H. M., Irvin, L., Noell, J. & Singer, G. (1992). A construct score approach to the assessment of social competence: Rational, technological considerations, and anticipated outcomes. *Behavior Modification, 16*, 448–474.

Walker, H. M., & McConnell, S. (1995). *Walker–McConnell Scale of Social Competence and School Adjustment.* Florence, KY: Thomson.

Walker, H. M., Ramsey, E., & Gresham, F. M. (2004). *Antisocial behavior in school: Evidence-based practices* (2nd ed.). Belmont, CA: Thomson.

Walker, H. M., Seeley, J., Small, J., Severson, H., Graham, B., Feil, E., et al. (2009). A randomized controlled trial of First Step to Success early intervention: Demonstration of program efficacy in a diverse urban school district. *Journal of Emotional and Behavioral Disorders, 17*, 197–212.

Webster-Stratton, C., Reid, M., & Hammond, M. (2001). Preventing conduct problems, promoting social competence: A parent and teacher training partnership in Head Start. *Journal of Clinical Child Psychology, 30*, 283–302.

Webster-Stratton, C., Reid, M., & Stoolmiller, M. (2008). Preventing conduct problems and improving school readiness: Evaluation of the Incredible Years Teacher and Child Training Programs in high-risk schools. *Journal of Child Psychology and Psychiatry, 49*, 471–488.

Weissberg, R., Durlak, J., Domitrovich, C., & Gullotta, T. (Eds.). (2015). Social and emotional learning: Past, present, and future. In R. P. Weissberg, J. A. Durlak, C. E. Domitrovich, & T. P. Gullotta (Eds.), *Handbook of social emotional learning: Research and practice* (pp. 3–19). New York: Guilford Press.

Wentzel, K. R. (2005). Peer relationships, motivation, and academic performance at school. In A. Elliot & C. Dweck (Eds.), *Handbook of competence and motivation* (pp. 279–296). New York: Guilford Press.

Wentzel, K. R. (2009). Peers and academic functioning at school. In K. H. Rubin, W. M. Bukowski, & B. Laursen (Eds.), *Handbook of peer interactions, relationships, and groups* (pp. 531–547). New York: Guilford Press.

Wentzel, K. R., & Watkins, D. E. (2002). Peer relationships and collaborative learning as contexts for academic enablers. *School Psychology Review, 31*, 366–377.

Wiggins, J. (1973). *Personality and prediction: Principles of personality assessment*. Reading, MA: Addison-Wesley.

Witt, J. C., & Elliott, S. N. (1985). Acceptability of classroom management strategies. In T. Kratochwill (Ed.), *Advances in school psychology* (Vol. 4, pp. 251–288). Hillsdale, NJ: Erlbaum.

Wolf, M. M. (1978). Social validity: The case for subjective measurement or how applied behavior analysis is finding its heart. *Journal of Applied Behavior Analysis, 11*, 203–214.

Yeaton, W. (1988). Treatment effect norms. In J. Witt, S. Elliott, & F. M. Gresham (Eds.), *Handbook of behavior therapy in education* (pp. 171–187). New York: Plenum Press.

Yeaton, W., & Sechrest, L. (1991). Critical dimensions in the choice and maintenance of successful treatments: Strength, integrity, and effectiveness. *Journal of Consulting and Clinical Psychology, 49*, 156–167.

Zins, J., & Elias, M. (2006). Social and emotional learning: In G. Bear & K. Minke (Eds.), *Children's needs: III. Development, prevention, and intervention* (pp. 1–13). Bethesda, MD: National Association of School Psychologists.

Zins, J., Weissberg, R., Wang, M., & Walberg, H. (2004). *Building academic success on social and emotional learning: What does the research say?* New York: Teachers College Press.

Index

Strength of a treatment, 114–115, 133, 159–161
Strengths, 11–12, 11*f*, 40
Strong Kids SEL curriculum, 185–187, 186*t*
Subjective evaluation, 167
Systematic direct observations (SDOs), 49–51, 50*f*, 57

T

Teacher-preferred social–emotional skills, 7, 8*t*, 16, 42. *See also* Social–emotional skills
Teasing, 63–64
Tertiary prevention, 58–60, 75, 175–178. *See also* Intensive SEL interventions; Response to intervention (RTI) approach; Tiered approach to intervention
The Incredible Years Series (TIYS), 65, 76, 199–202, 202*t*
Theory-of-change model, 102–103, 103*f*, 104–105
Tiered approach to intervention. *See also* Intensive SEL interventions; Interventions; Primary prevention; Secondary prevention; Selected SEL Interventions; Tertiary prevention; Universal SEL interventions
decision making regarding, 166–167, 180–181
overview, 58–60, 75, 162–163, 175–178
Tootling intervention, 203–207, 206*f*, 207*f*. *See also* Peer reporting; Praise
Translational research, 23–24
Treatment decisions, 35, 44–49, 46*t*, 48*f*, 166–167, 175, 180–181. *See also* Assessment
Treatment differentiation, 83–84, 162–163
Treatment effect norms, 165
Treatment effectiveness, 115–117, 133, 168, 169. *See also* Effectiveness research

Treatment integrity
data interpretation and, 164–166
intensive SEL interventions and, 115, 133
overview, 82–85, 83*f*, 84*f*, 161–166, 165*f*
selected SEL interventions and, 106, 108
treatment outcomes and, 180
variables that influence, 164, 165*f*
Treatment integrity effect norms, 166
Treatment receipt, 84–85, 163
Treatment validity. *See* Validity
Treatments, 28–31, 35. *See also* Interventions
Type I errors, 27–28
Type II errors, 27–28

U

Uncertainty principle, 26
Universal SEL interventions. *See also* Interventions; Primary prevention
case study, 183–188, 186*t*, 188*t*, 199–202, 202*t*, 203–207, 206*f*, 207*f*
decision making regarding, 166–167, 180–181
evidence-based universal interventions, 60–70, 62*t*
implications for practice, 76–77
overview, 58–60, 75–76, 162–163, 175–178
sample lesson from, 70–75
Utility, 159

V

Validity. *See also* Evidence
assessment and, 158–159
habilitative validity, 118
overview, 22, 25–28, 34, 173–174, 179–180

W

Well-established treatment criterion, 28, 34, 174